1000 MEMORIES OF 1976

PHIL ANDREWS

Copyright © 2021 Phil Andrews

All rights reserved.

ISBN: 9798735246725

INTRODUCTION

Most of us have a year that was special to us. When that year was depends pretty much on how old we were, where we were, what we were doing and whom we were doing it with. That year which meant so much to one person may have been quite ordinary and uneventful to another.

And yet that year, whenever it may have been, so often defines our lives. As such it remains etched in our memories. With any negative events which may have befallen us at the time consigned to the recycle bin of our subconscious, we recall that year and those carefree times with fondness and with yearning.

My year was 1976. At fourteen I had reached a level of maturity which allowed me some cognisance of the world about me, and endowed me with an understanding of most of the things that made the adult world turn, but I was as yet too young to bear any responsibility for any of it. It was the perfect state of being. The right place to be - physically, emotionally and spiritually.

But caveats aside, I do contest that there was something uniquely rapturous and dreamy about 1976 which causes many of those who were lucky enough to have experienced it to remember it with inimitable affection. There has to be a reason why, more than 44 years on, so many recall that wonderful long, hot summer in such meticulous detail.

Over recent years I have tried to understand what it is that makes 1976 the year that stands out for me. Certainly much of it is personal. It was the year that I shared with a particular group of friends in a particular environment around which my whole life had come to be centred. I had other friends, some of them at least equally dear to me, but it was this coming together in one unique moment which seemed at the time to have fulfilled that otherwise undated, and insatiable, longing for the perfect experience.

It was also, for me, something of a last hurrah before I ventured off on a destructive path of my own making, a path which I was to follow for nearly a decade and a half - but that's another story, for another time.

In this short work I have endeavoured to bring together some of the magic of 1976, to create a compendium of facts, happenings and experiences which pay due tribute to what, in the eyes of most of my contributors at least, was a year unlike most others. As well as outlining some of the national and international events which came to define that year, I have dedicated the larger part of this work to the anecdotes and recollections of over a thousand individual contributors who heeded my request for their valued input. As promised I have omitted no contribution offered to me in good faith, no matter how brief or incidental the information given.

I am grateful to the admins of several Facebook groups who permitted me to reach out to their members, and these are listed later in the book. If you're not already a member of those groups, please consider signing up with them and contributing your news and views.

Old times have been and gone, but it is through our memories that they live on. I hope that in my own very small way I have helped, by publishing this short and modest narrative, to keep that indelible spirit of 1976 alive.

1. 1976 IN WORLD EVENTS

Here in the United Kingdom we remember 1976 most of all for the long, parched, dreamy, arid summer which seemed to last forever. It was not the hottest that has ever been in terms of temperatures reached but unlike most heatwaves, which come and go, it lingered. That summer's exceptional dryness led to reservoirs emptying, crops drying out, roads melting, food prices rising, religious rituals invoking God and gods to intervene, the appointment of a dedicated Minister for Drought and an unprecedented incursion of seven-spotted biting ladybirds across southern and eastern parts of the country - nearly 24 billion of them according to the British Entomological and Natural History Society, although whose job it was to count them has never been disclosed.

But while some of us were whiling away our school holidays lying aimlessly in the park on the parched yellow grass, taking care to keep our prized platforms from being sullied by the dry dusty soil, out there it was in so many respects a dangerous world. The Cold War was in full flow, proxy battles being fought across the African continent and beyond on behalf of two nuclear superpowers who vied for ideological and military supremacy. Looking back in retrospect, other powers must have considered it almost surreal that amidst all this Britain put much effort into pursuing a parallel conflict with a remote island nation of some 220,000 souls over fish.

Anarchy in the UK

Neither was our home soil entirely free from danger. Bombs planted by the Provisional IRA exploded in the West End of London, the UK ambassador to the Republic of Ireland was assassinated, hijackings and crude acts of political terrorism were commonplace, political extremism was on the march across the country, and the annual Notting Hill Carnival saw widespread and violent confrontation between local youth and the forces of law and order. In Southall, West London, an 18-year-old Asian boy was cruelly murdered in an unprovoked racist attack.

Responding to the escalation of violence in Northern Ireland two working-class women joined together to form a movement for peace and led tens of thousands of their fellow citizens, Protestant and Catholic, on marches through war-weary streets demanding a cessation of hostilities between the two communities.

Industrial strife too characterised and dominated the British political and economic scene throughout the 1970s. When one considers the silent cries of nostalgic yearning which the decade inspires from those of us who lived and danced our way through it, it is perhaps difficult to credit that historians who lack our emotional attachment record the swinging sixties as having given way to the sombre seventies. Memories of dinners by candlelight inspired not by a desire for romantic ambience but by strikes and power cuts were still fresh in our minds in 1976, and the Winter of Discontent would not be long in coming. In March the Labour Prime Minister Harold Wilson suddenly announced his resignation, with almost immediate effect; he would be replaced by the former Foreign Secretary James Callaghan. One of Callaghan's immediate challenges was having to deal with rampant inflation, which peaked during the year at over 24 per cent, and the need to stabilise the pound led his government to the doors of the International Monetary Fund (IMF) to ask for a £2.3 billion loan. A month after Wilson's retirement Jeremy Thorpe, leader of the UK's third party, the Liberals, also stood down in the midst of a scandal surrounding allegations of conspiracy and incitement to murder.

Innovation and culture

Things at home did look a bit brighter when it came to culture and innovation. The National Exhibition Centre and the Royal National Theatre both opened their doors for the first time, as did the state-of-the-art Brent Cross shopping centre - a whole new customer experience for a nation accustomed to the organic but somewhat less organised environment of the traditional high street. At the same time Wimbledon in South-West London, better known as the home of British lawn tennis, became host to the country's first purpose-built Buddhist temple.

On the land and in the sky British technological progress advanced unabated. The high-speed InterCity 125 high-speed train entered service on British Rail's Western Region, and the Anglo-French supersonic jetliner Concorde made its first scheduled passenger flights into Washington's Dulles International Airport in the face of fierce opposition from a vociferous anti-noise lobby in the US. But sadly also during the year disaster struck over Yugoslavia when a British Airways Trident Three collided in mid-air with a native DC9, killing all 176 passengers and crew aboard both aircraft.

In space NASA's Viking 1 and Viking 2 craft, launched the previous year, entered the orbit of Mars and soft-landed upon the surface, sending back images which were to inform our understanding of the red planet's form and character for years to come. Meanwhile back home the Space Shuttle Enterprise was rolled out for the first time, and would perform atmospheric test flights after being launched from a modified Boeing 747 before venturing forth into outer space some years later.

Operation Entebbe

Around the world 1976 will be remembered for a host of notable events which are still talked about some decades later. The daring Israeli commando raid on Entebbe airport to release over one hundred hostages who had been held by Palestinian militants and two German sympathisers was the inspiration for a flurry of hastily-produced films once it was over. Following the hijacking of an Air France Airbus A300 bound for Paris, which had been diverted to Uganda, the hostages had been held in the terminal building at the airport with the apparent collusion of the country's notorious strongman leader Idi Amin (that was his name, his full title was somewhat longer). After attempts to negotiate had failed the Israeli Air Force flew transport planes into the airport under cover of night and elite forces engaged in a desperate fire fight which left one Israeli commando, three hostages, 45 Ugandan soldiers and all the hostage-takers dead. Shortly afterwards the United Kingdom broke off diplomatic relations with Uganda after it emerged that Dora Bloch, an elderly British-Israeli hostage who had been left behind from the rescue, had been murdered evidently on the orders of the Ugandan government. Elsewhere in Africa four mercenaries captured by the government of Angola, three British and one American, were sentenced to death. Civil war was raging in that country between three groups which had formerly comprised a movement against Portuguese colonialism, and hostilities were joined by such distant and disparate regimes as South Africa and Cuba as the conflict became a proxy battle between the various Cold War powers. And in South Africa itself demonstrations led by schoolchildren broke out in the township of Soweto after an attempt by the government to impose Afrikaans as the language of instruction. The brutal reaction of the police sparked an uprising which led to hundreds of fatalities.

Elsewhere in the world there were also memorable events aplenty. Argentina saw Isobel Peron overthrown and replaced by a military junta headed by Jorge Rafael Videla. As civil war wracked the Lebanon, Syrian forces intervened to oust the Palestinian Liberation Organisation (PLO) and associated militias. In the Far East Vietnam was formally united and the murderous Pol Pot proclaimed a new constitution in Cambodia. And Mao Zedong, founder and leader of the People's Republic of China, passed away aged 82 leading to a brief spell of in-fighting in which the radical Gang of Four, led by Mao's last wife Jiang Qing, was out-manoeuvred by premier Hua Guofeng.

Closer to home, French Prime Minister Jacques Chirac resigned and was replaced by Raymond Barre.

Of course many of the innovations that we take for granted today have their origins in those earlier times. In 1976 the Apple computer company was founded by Steve Jobs, Steve Wozniak and Ronald Wayne, whilst the technology giant Microsoft was officially registered.

US Bicentennial (1776-1976)

Also in 1976, the United States of America was celebrating its bicentennial - 200 years since the Second Continental Congress pronounced its Declaration of Independence in Philadelphia. The official American Revolution Bicentennial was in fact a huge, prolonged and quite beautiful series of celebrations and observances which attracted visitors from all over the world, culminating in a day of joy on 4th July 1976.

The soon-to-be outgoing President Gerald Ford (he would be replaced by Jimmy Carter in the impending New Year) watched over firework displays in cities all across the country, while a fleet of tall sailing ships gathered in New York City before later heading on to Boston. The navies of several nations were represented at an International Naval Review inspected by the President, which concluded with a salute from the British guided missile destroyer HMS London.

There were presentations, parades, exhibitions, street markets and celebrations of every conceivable kind. Many public service vehicles, including an Oversees National Airways DC8 aircraft (registered N1776R), were painted in the red, white and blue of the US flag. Special television and sporting events were hosted to commemorate the great day, and nations across the world sent symbolic gifts to the people of America.

On July 6th Queen Elizabeth II and her husband Philip made a state visit aboard the royal yacht Britannia and presented the Bicentennial Bell on behalf of the people of the United Kingdom. It was a replica of the Liberty Bell, also made at the Whitechapel Bell Foundry, which bore the inscription: "For the People of the United States of America from the People of Britain 4 July 1976 LET FREEDOM RING."

In spite of all the economic difficulties and privations of the period, 1976 encapsulated a spirit of hope and great joy. In the fierce heat of the summer a man famously fried an egg on the pavement near Oxford Circus. Irish radio broadcaster Henry Kelly was later to observe: "1976 was a good year because we were so much younger then."

MAJOR UK AND INTERNATIONAL EVENTS OF 1976

January

- British and Icelandic vessels clash at sea as the Cod War escalates
- A 42-year-old Leeds woman, Emily Jackson, is the second woman to be murdered by Peter Sutcliffe, nicknamed "the Yorkshire Ripper"
- Pol Pot proclaims a new constitution for Democratic Kampuchea
- Morocco and Algeria clash in the Spanish Sahara
- The USA vetoes a United Nations resolution calling for an independent Palestine
- First commercial Concorde flight takes off from London Heathrow airport to Bahrain
- Twelve Provisional IRA bombs explode in London's West End
- The Philadelphia Flyers play a Soviet Red Army ice hockey team before 17,000 spectators, eventually winning 4-1

February

- The National Exhibition Centre in Birmingham is opened by the Queen
- An earthquake in Guatamala and Honduras kills 23,000
- Spanish forces withdraw from the Western Sahara, which declares independence under the name of the Sahrawi Arab Democratic Republic
- Cuba's constitution of 1976 is enacted
- Iceland breaks off diplomatic relations with the United Kingdom over fish

March

- Brent Cross Shopping Centre opens in north London
- Direct rule from the UK parliament is imposed on Northern Ireland
- A cable car crash in Cavalese, Italy, results in 43 deaths
- Harold Wilson resigns as British Prime Minister
- Princess Margaret and Lord Snowdon announce their separation after sixteen years of marriage
- Isabel Peron is deposed in Argentina in a military coup. General Jorge Videla becomes leader
- Special Category Status for political crimes in Northern Ireland is ended by British Secretary of State Merlyn Rees
- Production of the iconic Hillman Imp ends after thirteen years

April

- James Callaghan becomes Prime Minister of the United Kingdom
- Apple computer company is formed in the USA
- An industrial explosion in Finland kills 40
- Portugal's new constitution is enacted
- A bomb placed at the gates of the Soviet embassy in China explodes, killing four people
- The two dollar bill is reintroduced to mark the United States Bicentennial
- Reclusive businessman and aviator Howard Hughes dies, aged 70
- Robbers in Melbourne, Australia make off with A$1.4m in bookmakers' settlements

May

- Harold Wilson's Resignation Honours List controversially includes many wealthy businessmen of his close acquaintance
- A train crash in Schiedam, the Netherlands, kills 24

- Jeremy Thorpe resigns as leader of the Liberal Party
- 20-year-old Marcella Claxton is badly wounded in a Leeds hammer attack
- More than 900 die in an earthquake in the Friuli region of Italy
- Britain and France commence Concorde passenger services into Washington
- Syria intervenes in the Lebanese civil war
- California wins a surprise victory against France in a major wine-tasting content in Paris

June

- Iceland and the UK end the Cod War
- Francis E. Meloy Jr., the US ambassador to Lebanon, is assassinated in Beirut after being kidnapped
- The trial of murderer Donald Neilson, nicknamed "the Black Panther", begins in Oxford
- British heatwave begins, reaching 35.6 degrees in Southampton - a new UK record for June
- The Seychelles become independent from Britain
- Uruguayan President Juan Maria Bordaberry is deposed by the military
- Soweto uprising begins in South Africa
- An Air France A300 Airbus en route to Paris from Athens is hijacked by Palestinian militants and diverted to Entebbe, Uganda, with 246 passengers and 12 crew on board
- Conference of Communist and Workers Parties of Europe convenes in East Berlin
- The CN Tower in Toronto, then the tallest free-standing land structure in the world, is opened to the public

July

- British heatwave peaks with a temperature of 35.9 degrees

recorded in Cheltenham
- The United States of America celebrates 200 years of independence
- Four mercenaries, three British and one American, are executed by firing squad in Angola
- Women are inducted into the United States Naval Academy for the first time
- David Steel becomes the new leader of the Liberal Party
- A bus driver and 26 schoolchildren are buried in a quarry in Chowchilla, California, but manage to dig themselves free after 16 hours. The son of the quarry owner and two accomplices are arrested
- Israeli commandos free 103 hostages at Entebbe airport in Uganda
- The United Kingdom severs diplomatic ties with Uganda following the death of a British hostage
- The UK ambassador to the Republic of Ireland, Christopher Ewart-Biggs, and a civil servant are killed by a landmine in Dublin
- Viking 1 spacecraft makes a successful landing on Mars, taking the first ever close-up colour pictures of the planet's surface
- North and South Vietnam unite to form the Socialist Republic of Vietnam
- Fire destroys part of Southend Pier, the world's longest
- "Son of Sam" David Berkowitz claims his first murder victim in New York City
- Gary Gilmore is arrested for two Utah murders
- Tangshan earthquake in China kills nearly a quarter of a million people
- The Ford Fiesta is launched, although it only goes on sale in continental Europe and does not become available to UK customers until the following year

August

- Severe drought follows in the wake of the UK heatwave. Some parts of South West England have gone 45 days without rain
- John Stonehouse, the former Postmaster General, is sentenced to seven years imprisonment for fraud
- Jacques Chirac resigns as Prime Minister of France
- First recorded Ebola outbreak takes place in Zaire
- Hurricane Belle hits the East Coast of the United States
- First acknowledged outbreak of Legionnaires' disease kills 29 at a US convention
- 10,000 Catholic and Protestant women in Northern Ireland join peace demonstration
- Over 100 police officers and 60 others are injured as violence flares at London's Notting Hill Carnival
- Big Ben suffers internal damage and stops working, for what would become nine months

September

- 25,000 attend peace march in Derry
- Viking 2 lands on Mars
- British Airways Trident Three and Inex-Adria DC9 collide over Yugoslavia killing all 176 passengers and crew on board both planes
- Space shuttle Enterprise is rolled out of its hangar in California
- Soviet air force pilot Viktor Belenko lands his Mig-25 fighter jet at Hokkaido in Japan and requests political asylum
- Chinese leader and chairman of the Communist Party Mao Zedong dies of a heart attack, aged 82
- Ford Cortina IV is launched

October

- InterCity 125 high-speed train is introduced into service

- linking London Paddington, Bristol and South Wales
- Two members of the Ulster Defence Regiment, a unit of the British army, are gaoled for 35 years for their part in the killing of members of the Miami Showband
- A river ferry in Mississippi is hit by a ship, killing 78 passengers and crew
- The Royal National Theatre opens on London's South Bank
- A Cuban airliner explodes with the impact of a bomb placed by right wing anti-Castro terrorists. All 73 people on board are killed
- Students engaged in a protest against Thailand's military leadership are massacred at Thammasat University in Bangkok
- Cearbhall Ó Dálaigh, President of the Republic of Ireland, resigns after receiving a public insult from the Minister for Defence
- Conservative opposition heavyweight Keith Joseph delivers his seminal policy speech entitled "Monetarism is Not Enough"

November

- The British Secretary of State for Education is authorised to ask local authorities to make plans for the rollout of comprehensive education
- Democrat Jimmy Carter defeats incumbent Republican President Gerald Ford to win the US presidency
- New computer company Microsoft is formally registered with the Office of the Secretary of State in New Mexico
- Over 4,000 are killed in an earthquake in eastern Turkey

December

- UK Chancellor Denis Healey successfully negotiates a £2.3bn loan from the International Monetary Fund (IMF)

- War-torn Angola joins the United Nations
- José López Portillo becomes President of Mexico
- Patrick Hillery is elected President of the Republic of Ireland
- Vietnam disbands the VietCong
- Northern Ireland peace women Mairead Corrigan and Betty Williams are awarded the Nobel Peace Prize

2. 1976 IN SPORT

1976 was a year of triumph and some surprises for British sport, as figure skater John Curry cleaned up at every competition that was worth winning while playboy Formula One driver James Hunt finally triumphed in his gruelling, tantalising year-long personal battle with his friend and bitter rival, the dedicated, cool and consummate professional Niki Lauda.

When Curry took the world by storm at the Winter Olympics he had already won the European Championship a month earlier, and would go on to win the British Championship at Richmond as well as the World Championship to make it four out of four. His routine incorporated elements of ballet and modern dance, and his impeccable display in Innsbruck earned him a staggering 105.9 points from a possible total of 108. Only the judges from the Soviet Union and Canada did not have him in first place. Coincidentally, his main rivals in the competition were from the Soviet Union and Canada, who took silver and bronze respectively.

Hunt meanwhile was a relatively new kid on the block, having signed up for McLaren after moving up from Formula Three just a year beforehand. But his renowned daring and skill behind the wheel combined with the stark contrast in personalities between the flamboyant Briton and the icy Austrian Lauda made for the most compelling battle between two gladiators of the race track for many a year.

Throughout the season their relative fortunes ebbed and flowed, reaching new heights of drama when Hunt won the British Grand Prix in front of his home support before being disqualified and the points handed to his rival. But what nobody had anticipated was the horrifying crash in which Lauda was involved on the deadly track at Nürburg in Germany. Dragged from a burning wreckage and rushed to hospital, the Austrian was given little hope of survival and was even read the last rites by a priest. And yet just six weeks later he was behind the wheel once more at Monza for the Italian GP.

The drivers went into the sixteenth and final race in Japan with Lauda still leading Hunt in the competition by three points. But with harsh conditions exacerbating the damage caused to his tear ducts by the accident in Germany he was forced to retire from the race. Hunt came home third, allowing him to leapfrog his competitor in the points table and claim the World Championship.

Drama at Wembley

Back home at Wembley there was drama of a different kind in early May when Southampton, who plied their trade in English football's second tier, humbly presented themselves to the giants of Manchester United for what was widely expected to be something of a ritual sacrifice in the Final of the FA Cup.

Managed by Lawrie McMenemy, the sixth best team in Division Two ran out gingerly onto the pitch, some of them players not heard of by many and others whose best years were probably considered to be behind them. The bookmakers had them on offer at 5/1 to win the fixture and there weren't many takers beyond the blindly faithful from the south coast.

But having absorbed everything United had to throw at them for 83 long minutes, the now sadly late Bobby Stokes hit their northern tormentors with a sucker punch, and then clung on for dear life. The final whistle blew and Southampton, from the Second Division, had won the FA Cup in what was, and remains, one of the biggest upsets in the history of the tournament.

In the 1975/6 season the Football League was won by Liverpool, the club's first major trophy under manager Bob Paisley, with Queen's Park Rangers from West London concluding their campaign just a point behind in second place - QPR's highest ever league finish. The top tier's most prolific marksman was Ted MacDougall of Norwich, with 23 league goals to his name.

The Wooden Spoon

Also in 1976 the UK hosted a lengthy and instructive cricket tour by a useful West Indies team, who also played a fixture in Ireland, whilst rugby union entertained visitors from Argentina and Japan. In our own Five Nations tournament (Italy was yet to join) Wales won the title, a Grand Slam and the Triple Crown. England ended its campaign with zero points and the Wooden Spoon.

In the States, in the special year of the Bicentennial, the tenth Super Bowl was played out in Miami between NFC champions Dallas Cowboys and the AFC winners Pittsburgh Steelers. The most popular two teams in the country, both were previous winners of the competition - the first time such a thing had occurred in its history. Having been losing 10-7, the Steelers rallied to score 14 points on the bounce. Although the Cowboys did subsequently manage to cut the deficit, it wasn't enough and the Steelers triumphed 21-17 at the end of play.

Every year has its memorable sporting events, and 1976 is no exception. And sport, like any aspect of our culture, creates its own "Where were you…?" moments. Most of us of a certain age can remember where we were in 1976, when the sun bore down relentlessly over the patchy fields and the often ageing stadia whose starkness and simplicity lent them their spirit and their very soul. We salute all the sporting heroes of our day, and remember them with sincere gratitude and affection.

SPORTING MEMORIES OF 1976

January

- Evonne Goolagong Cawley and John Newcome win the first major tennis titles of the year at the Australian Open
- A young Marvin Hagler, later to become one of boxing's all-time greats, loses a points decision to Bobby Watts in Philadelphia
- Welsh snooker maestro Ray Reardon beats England's Graham Miles 7-3 to win the 1976 Masters in London
- Darts player Jack North wins the British Open
- Pittsburgh Steelers beat Dallas Cowboys 21-17 at Super Bowl X in Miami
- Former world heavyweight boxing champion George Foreman knocks out Ron Lyle at Caesar's Palace, Las Vegas, for the vacant NABF title after having been floored twice in the 4th

February

- Manchester City beat Newcastle United 2-1 in the football League Cup Final at Wembley
- UCLA beat Ohio State 23-10 in the 62nd Rose Bowl
- Winter Olympics held in Innsbruck, Austria. Briton John Curry takes figure skating gold
- Muhammad Ali knocks out Belgian challenger Jean-Pierre Coopman in Puerto Rico in Round 5

March

- Oxford beat Cambridge by 6.5 lengths in the 122nd Boat Race with a time of 16 minutes and 58 seconds
- John Curry wins European Figure Skating Championship in Gothenburg, Sweden
- 17-year-old Wilfred Benitez becomes youngest ever world

boxing champion by outpointing Colombia's Antonio Cervantes on a split decision for the WBA light-welterweight title
- Wales win Five Nations rugby union tournament

April

- John Burke rides Rag Trade to victory at SP 14/1 in the Grand National at Aintree
- Liverpool beat Club Brugge 4-3 on aggregate to win the UEFA Cup, Europe's second-string international club tournament
- Ray Reardon wins the World Snooker Championship at the Wythenshawe Forum, Manchester, overcoming Northern Ireland's Alex "Hurricane" Higgins 27-16 in the final
- Raymond Floyd triumphs at the US Masters golf tournament in Augusta
- Australian tennis star Evonne Goolagong Cawley claims her second major title of the year, beating Chris Evert in the WTA Tour Championship at the Los Angeles Sports Arena
- Muhammad Ali gets the decision over Jimmy Young in a heavyweight boxing bout in Maryland

May

- Second Division Southampton beat Manchester United 1-0 to lift the FA Cup at Wembley. Rangers win the Scottish Cup with a 3-1 victory over Hearts at Hampden Park
- Montreal Canadians beat Philadelphia Flyers 4-0 to win the NHL Stanley Cup playoffs
- Ángel Cordero Jr. rides Bold Forbes to first place in the Kentucky Derby
- Bayern Munich triumph over St. Etienne in Glasgow with a 1-0 European Cup Final victory
- St. Helens beat Salford 15-2 to win the Rugby League

Premiership
- In his third fight of the year, WBA and WBC heavyweight champion Muhammad Ali again successfully defends his titles, this time against British challenger Richard Dunn in Munich. The fight ends with a TKO in Round 5
- Liverpool win the English Football League although Queen's Park Rangers take them to the wire, claiming the runners-up spot with the club's highest ever league finish. Division Two is won by Sunderland, Division Three Hereford United and Division Four Lincoln City
- Betty Burfeindt wins her only major golf title by pipping Judy Rankin to the post at the LGPA Championship in Pennsylvania

June

- Britain's Sue Barker wins the French Open, defeating Czech rival Renáta Tomanová 6-2, 0-6, 6-2. The men's tournament is won by Italian Adriano Panatta
- First rugby league World Club Challenge ends with a 25-2 victory for Eastern Suburbs (now Sydney Roosters) over St. Helens in Sydney
- Boston Celtics defeat Phoenix Suns 4-2 to win NBA World Championship Series
- England's Bill Lennard beats Welshman Leighton Rees to claim the News of the World darts title at Alexandra Palace, London
- Newcomer Jerry Pate claims the US Men's Open golf tournament, two strokes ahead of his nearest rivals
- Lester Piggott wins the Epsom Derby on the US-born, French-trained stallion Empery
- Leighton Rees wins the darts Indoor League
- Czechoslovakia defeat West Germany 5-3 on penalties after the European Championship Final in Belgrade had ended in a 2-2 stalemate after extra time
- England and a touring West Indian side draw two tests, at

Trent Bridge and Lord's.

July

- Björn Borg (Sweden) and Chris Evert (USA) triumph at Wimbledon
- Golfer Johnny Miller (USA) wins his only British Open at the Royal Birkdale in Southport, finishing nine strokes ahead of Seve Ballesteros and Jack Nicklaus
- Niki Lauda wins the British Grand Prix at Brands Hatch after James Hunt is disqualified
- West Indies beat England at Old Trafford and Headingley
- JoAnn Carner claims the US Open golf tournament following a play-off with Sandra Palmer
- Olympic Games in Montreal, Canada. 33 African teams boycott the event in protest against the participation of New Zealand, whose rugby team had defied protests to compete in apartheid South Africa. Fourteen-year-old Romanian gymnast Nadia Comăneci wows spectators with the first ever perfect 10 in the history of the Games
- 63rd Tour de France cycle race is won by Belgium's Lucien Van Impe

August

- Niki Lauda suffers near-fatal crash at the German Grand Prix in Nürburg
- West Indies beat England in the fifth and final test at The Oval
- England women's cricket team defeat Australia by eight wickets at Lord's, the first time women have been permitted to play on the main square
- League champions Liverpool beat FA Cup winners Southampton 1-0 in Charity Shield at Wembley

September

- Argentinian rugby union tour of England and Wales begins. Japanese team tours Europe
- French thoroughbred Crow, ridden by Yves Saint-Martin, wins the St. Leger at Doncaster
- Chris Evert beats Evonne Cawley Goolagong 6-3, 6-0 to retain her US Open tennis title
- Middlesex win the cricket County Championship
- Jimmy Connors wins his second Open with a 6-4, 3-6, 7-6, 6-4 victory over Björn Borg
- Muhammad Ali defeats Ken Norton over 15 rounds to retain his world heavyweight boxing title

October

- 90-year-old Dimitrion Yordanidis of Greece becomes the oldest man to compete in a marathon
- Cincinnati Reds beat Philadelphia Phillies 3-0 to win MLB National League championship. American League championship is won by New York Yankees with a 3-2 victory over Kansas City Royals
- James Hunt finishes third in Japanese Grand Prix and wins the Formula One World Championship

November

- Aberdeen win the Scottish League Cup final, beating Celtic 2-1
- Jimmy Connors wins Benson & Hedges tennis tournament at Wembley after successfully persuading organisers to reduce the number of games in the final due to his ongoing injuries

December

- Spain's Manuel Orantes beats Wojtek Fibak of Poland 5–7,

6–2, 0–6, 7–6, 6–1 to win ATP Masters Grand Prix tennis title in Houston, Texas
- Franz Beckenbauer wins his second Ballon d'Or, awarded to Europe's best football player

3. 1976 IN CULTURE

1976 has been described as a cultural crossroads - a meeting point of styles, fashions and ideas which in some respects represented a turning point from the values which had predominated throughout the 1960s and into the 1970s. The political upheaval and the polarised radicalism that we witnessed in the United Kingdom could even have been a harbinger for Brexit, and for the deep divides brought about by the measures introduced to try to deal with the Covid-19 pandemic. Certainly they set the stage for the fierce ideological battles of the 1980s, and the social transformation which followed.

Undoubtedly it requires a substantial leap of the imagination to see the origins of modern political and social discourse in loon pants and bondage wear with torn plaid strips and safety pins, but there is probably no year other than 1976 which could equally be defined by two fashions as disparate as disco and punk - and that's before we even contemplate the cocaine-fuelled antics of the Thin White Duke and his stark, monochromatic Prussian imagery. It was, indeed, the place where the old finally stopped, and the new began. Once the New Wave had come there was to be no going back, and never in the history of popular culture has there occurred such a savage culling of all that had gone before and that so many had held so dear.

But the old ways died out with a flourish, not with a whimper. Tank-tops and platforms were nowhere near as essential to the 1976 experience as they had been a few years before, and yet they were still to be seen in abundance. During those few years which had passed between we had sampled Oxford bags, high waistbands, dungarees and denims, but the principle had always been the same. It was glamorous, and between tinsel and toughness there was no contradiction to be found. It was our time and its sudden passing was mourned deeply, and by many.

Blockbusters and classics

Fashion and music are inextricably linked, but other art forms maybe less so. This is why any changes that may have occurred in such media as film, theatre, visual art or television were probably more gradual and less obvious. Sitcom was predictable, sometimes (when judged by today's standards) highly inappropriate, but it enjoyed a large and loyal following. The football terraces, like the streets, were barren and bleak, but we patrolled them like mutants, fending off outsiders as though they were an existential threat to our being. The cinemas were packing them in with some blockbusters - Rocky, A Star is Born, Carrie, The Omen and All the President's Men to name a few - and television saw the launch of such classics as The Fall and Rise of Reginald Perrin, Open All Hours, I Claudius, Bouquet of Barbed Wire, Ripping Yarns, The New Avengers and The Muppet Show.

On the shelves at the newsagent's we had seventies magazines like Look-In and Disco 45 to keep us up to date with all the news and fashions. And cheap long-playing records with such catchy titles as 'Top of the Pops' and '20 Chart Hits', featuring unknown singers trying hard to sound like the original artists with varying degrees of success, provided an interesting option for those who couldn't afford the real thing. On an entirely different cultural plain the Royal Shakespeare Company began a popular production of Macbeth starring Ian McKellen and Judi Dench at the The Other Place in the Bard's native Stratford-upon-Avon, and the Royal National Theatre opened on the South Bank in London.

Art for art's sake

In the world of visual art though there was one outstanding story which made the popular press and which captured the imaginations of those in the industry at the same time. Disheartened by a system in which dealers and critics lined their pockets whilst those at the pointed end - the painters themselves - often struggled to make ends meet, 58-year-old London art restorer Tom Keating had decided to teach the art world a lesson. For some years he had been producing what he described as "Sexton Blakes", rhyming slang for fakes, and had flooded the market with dodgy Gainsboroughs and Renoirs aplenty which had been enthusiastically snapped up by those who thought they could tell the difference. Each time he would leave what he described as "time bombs" - discreet, cheeky little clues which, to an expert, would reveal the purchase to be something other than what it purported to be. In 1976 he finally came clean, and revealed that there were no fewer than 2,000 of his "Sextons" hanging on the walls of philistines throughout the land. He'd been pulling the wool over the eyes of the art world for a quarter of a century.

Keating was eventually charged in 1979, but the case was later dropped due to his advancing ill health.

TOP FILMS OF 1976

- All the President's Men
- King Kong
- Carrie
- The Omen
- The Man Who Fell to Earth
- A Star is Born
- Rocky
- Logan's Run
- Marathon Man
- The Eagle Has Landed
- Taxi Driver
- The Outlaw
- Carry On England
- Adventures of a Taxi Driver
- The Enforcer
- Pink Panther Strikes Again
- Car Wash
- Bugsy Malone
- Freaky Friday

TELEVISION

- Charlie's Angels
- The Bionic Woman
- The Muppet Show
- M*A*S*H
- Kojak
- Quincy M.E.
- I, Claudius
- The New Avengers
- The Duchess of Duke Street
- When the Boat Comes In
- The Six Million Dollar Man

COMEDY

- George & Mildred
- Ripping Yarns
- Happy Days
- The Fall and Rise of Reginald Perrin
- Open All Hours
- Bless This House
- The Goodies

4. 1976 IN MUSIC

For most of us who were teenagers in 1976 our initiation into popular music had arrived under the guise of glam rock, those early '70s artists with tall stacked boots and even taller egos, who vied with one another for supremacy within the genre as defined by which position was reached in the weekly music charts by their wholly ephemeral latest release.

The way had been paved in 1971 by Marc Bolan and T. Rex, the tinselled pixie with the long corkscrew hair and the glitter beneath his eyes. The Electric Warrior bridged the gap between the outgoing hippy era of the late 1960s and the new age of sparkle. The path he laid was soon followed by earthier acts such as Slade, Sweet, Gary Glitter, Suzi Quatro and Wizzard. There was no protest, no politics, nothing introverted, convoluted or even particularly meaningful about the songs they sang. It was simple showpersonship, harmlessly shocking and unashamedly targetted at the adolescent and even pre-adolescent market. The screaming girls (or boys) fantasising about their idols in the front rows of their gigs would be met from the bus by their mothers on the way home. It was from within the midst of all this that David Bowie emerged quite suddenly into megastardom, his androgynous Ziggy Stardust persona flawlessly capturing the spirit of the moment whilst elevating glammery onto a whole new stratum.

Peak Glam could with confidence be said to have been achieved during the years 1972 to 1974. The original acts were joined by a plethora of others - most notably Mud, The Rubettes, Alvin Stardust and Showaddywaddy - and to some extent the earlier fetish with glitter, glitzy earrings and eyeliner had given way to a wider interpretation of the dressing-up theme, with 1950s nostalgia playing a not insignificant part. Whilst to the purists this may have seemed like a worrying deviation, others embraced it in the spirit of harmless fun in which it was intended. Added into the mix was the emergence of more discerning acts as diverse as

Queen and Cockney Rebel, which left one foot planted reticently in glam whilst ploughing their own lyrical and musical furrows which they could be reasonably sure would survive its demise.

Cultural pendulum

But chart music had a different look by 1975. Whilst a few of the more talented glam acts clung on desperately to whatever shard of relevance cruel time had permitted them, their music began to adopt a form which was less showy, less gimmicky and more worthy in its own right. Nevertheless, by this time the cultural pendulum had swung very much in the direction of disco. The tuneful yet basic Motown ditties of old gave way to an altogether more sophisticated sound, typified by the symphonic anthems of Van McCoy, and the gruff melodic showpieces of Barry White and his Love Unlimited Orchestra.

And this sound carried forth into 1976, where it mixed and matched with a whole raft of other musical themes, not least some interesting covers (Steve Harley's enduringly creative interpretation of George Harrison's 'Here Comes the Sun') and welcome re-releases (The Shangri-Las' doleful 'Leader of the Pack'). Abba recorded 'Dancing Queen', possibly the most lively and disco-oriented of all the band's huge catalogue of hits, and as if to emphasise the power of the dance the year also brought us such stone-cold classics as 'Young Hearts Run Free' (Candi Staton), 'You Make Me Feel Like Dancing' (Leo Sayer) and 'I Love to Love' (Tina Charles). To cap it all, the United Kingdom won the Eurovision Song Content in The Hague with Brotherhood of Man's lovable and engaging 'Save Your Kisses for Me'.

There were, too, some great individual numbers which didn't neatly fit with the lively disco vibe but which were nevertheless uniquely '76 in their sound. Gallagher & Lyle's 'Heart On My Sleeve', Chicago's 'If You Leave Me Now' and Dr. Hook's 'A

Little Bit More' spring instantly to mind. John Miles' 'Music' and ELO's 'Livin' Thing;' are also more than worthy of mention.

For many of us 1976 was the year in which we embraced all that was thrown at us, and jumped into the big magical melting pot which brought it all together in a weird and wonderful summer brew. Even those of us who were not so naturally disposed to disco could feel the love, and for the best part of the year the soul boys and girls, the ex-glamsters, the rockers and everyone else seemed to find common cause in what was going down, and in the experience we all were sharing. It was as though the burning sun had seared our differences and had welded us together in common purpose - whether that purpose was musical, cultural or just to enjoy the season.

A different story

But the latter part of the year had an entirely different story to tell. Whilst the Ramones in the United States and the Damned in the United Kingdom are credited as having launched the phenomenon that was to be called punk rock, it was the Sex Pistols who really set the cat among the pigeons with their anarchic and highly publicised antics, culminating in an appearance on the Today show on British prime-time television in which, egged on by an allegedly inebriate presenter, they let rip a sustained torrent of profanity.

From the fashion to the sound to the ethos, punk was everything that disco, and glam before it, were not. It was rebellious and political, eschewing the rock and roll idolatry which glam in particular had taken to absurd (and deliberately exaggerated) extremes. It railed against the music industry and the establishment, mocked the superstars who had gone before and, with as much ceremony as it could muster, consigned the flares and the flowers to the dustbin of pop history. It denied its rock and roll lineage, turned every accepted seventies' norm on its head, and ripped the rug ruthlessly from beneath the feet of those of us who had danced upon it for so long. It was brutal. It was a veritable execution.

Vibrant and new

And so it is that when we think back to 1976 we will each remember it for different reasons. For the punks it was the birth of something vibrant and new, for the tank-toppers it was the swansong of a thing they had held dear. And yet, all these years on, paradoxically we reminisce together. It was a wonderful and eventful year, whichever way we swung.

It was not, in the author's opinion, necessarily the best year for music. That was never really the point. Rather, it was a defining year in so many ways, as well as one that is remembered with fondness and appreciation by so many today.

UK NUMBER ONE SINGLES

29 November 1975	BOHEMIAN RHAPSODY Queen
31 January 1976	MAMMA MIA Abba
14 February 1976	FOREVER AND EVER Slik
21 February 1976	DECEMBER 1963 The Four Seasons
6 March 1976	I LOVE TO LOVE Tina Charles
27 March 1976	SAVE YOUR KISSES FOR ME Brotherhood of Man
8 May 1976	FERNANDO Abba
5 June 1976	NO CHARGE J.J. Barrie
12 June 1976	THE COMBINE HARVESTER The Wurzels
26 June 1976	YOU TO ME ARE EVERYTHING The Real Thing
17 July 1976	EXCERPTS FROM THE ROUSSOS PHENOMENON (EP) Demis Roussos
24 July 1976	DON'T GO BREAKING MY HEART Elton John & Kiki Dee
4 September 1976	DANCING QUEEN Abba
16 October 1976	MISSISSIPPI Pussycat
13 November 1976	IF YOU LEAVE ME NOW Chicago
4 December 1976	UNDER THE MOON OF LOVE Showaddywaddy
25 December 1976	WHEN A CHILD IS BORN Johnny Mathis

UK NUMBER ONE ALBUMS

27 December 1975	A NIGHT AT THE OPERA Queen
10 January 1976	40 GREATEST HITS Perry Como
17 January 1976	A NIGHT AT THE OPERA Queen
31 January 1976	THE BEST OF ROY ORBISON Roy Orbison
7 February 1976	THE VERY BEST OF SLIM WHITMAN Slim Whitman
20 March 1976	BLUE FOR YOU Status Quo
10 April 1976	ROCK FOLLIES Rock Follies

24 April 1976	PRESENCE Led Zeppelin
1 May 1976	ROCK FOLLIES Rock Follies
8 May 1976	GREATEST HITS Abba
10 July 1976	A NIGHT ON THE TOWN Rod Stewart
24 July 1976	20 GOLDEN GREATS The Beach Boys
2 October 1976	THE BEST OF THE STYLISTICS VOLUME II The Stylistics
9 October 1976	STUPIDITY Dr. Feelgood
16 October 1976	GREATEST HITS Abba
30 October 1976	SOUL MOTION Various Artists
13 November 1976	THE SONG REMAINS THE SAME Led Zeppelin
20 November 1976	22 GOLDEN GUITAR GREATS Bert Weedon
27 November 1976	GLEN CAMPBELL'S TWENTY GOLDEN GREATS Glen Campbell

US NUMBER ONE SINGLES

27 December 1975	LET'S DO IT AGAIN The Staple Singers
3 January 1976	SATURDAY NIGHT Bay City Rollers
10 January 1976	CONVOY C.W. McCall
17 January 1976	I WRITE THE SONGS Barry Manilow
24 January 1976	THEME FROM MAHOGANY Diana Ross
31 January 1976	LOVE ROLLERCOASTER Ohio Players
7 February 1976	50 WAYS TO LEAVE YOUR LOVER Paul Simon
28 February 1976	THEME FROM S.W.A.T. Rhythm Heritage
6 March 1976	LOVE MACHINE The Miracles
13 March 1976	DECEMBER 1963 The Four Seasons
3 April 1976	DISCO LADY Johnnie Taylor
1 May 1976	LET YOUR LOVE FLOW The Bellamy Brothers
8 May 1976	WELCOME BACK John Sebastian
15 May 1976	BOOGIE FEVER The Sylvers
22 May 1976	SILLY LOVE SONGS Wings

29 May 1976	LOVE HANGOVER Diana Ross
12 June 1976	SILLY LOVE SONGS Wings
10 July 1976	AFTERNOON DELIGHT Starland Vocal Band
24 July 1976	KISS AND SAY GOODBYE The Manhattans
7 August 1976	DON'T GO BREAKING MY HEART Elton John & Kiki Dee
4 September 1976	YOU SHOULD BE DANCING Bee Gees
11 September 1976	SHAKE YOUR BOOTY KC and the Sunshine Band
18 September 1976	PLAY THAT FUNKY MUSIC Wild Cherry
9 October 1976	A FIFTH OF BEETHOVEN Walter Murphy and the Big Apple Band
16 October 1976	DISCO DUCK Rick Dees and His Cast of Idiots
23 October 1976	IF YOU LEAVE ME NOW Chicago
6 November 1976	ROCK'N ME Steve Miller Band
13 November 1976	TONIGHT'S THE NIGHT Rod Stewart

US NUMBER ONE ALBUMS

13 December 1975	CHICAGO IX: CHICAGO'S GREATEST HITS Chicago
17 January 1976	GRATITUDE Earth, Wind & Fire
7 February 1976	DESIRE Bob Dylan
13 March 1976	THEIR GREATEST HITS (1971-1975) Eagles
10 April 1976	FRAMPTON COMES ALIVE! Peter Frampton
17 April 1976	THEIR GREATEST HITS (1971-1975) Eagles
24 April 1976	WINGS AT THE SPEED OF SOUND Wings
1 May 1976	PRESENCE Led Zeppelin
15 May 1976	BLACK AND BLUE The Rolling Stones

29 May 1976	WINGS AT THE SPEED OF SOUND	Wings
5 June 1976	BLACK AND BLUE	The Rolling Stones
19 June 1976	WINGS AT THE SPEED OF SOUND	Wings
24 July 1976	FRAMPTON COMES ALIVE!	Peter Frampton
31 July 1976	BREEZIN'	George Benson
14 August 1976	FRAMPTON COMES ALIVE!	Peter Frampton
4 September 1976	FLEETWOOD MAC	Fleetwood Mac
11 September 1976	FRAMPTON COMES ALIVE!	Peter Frampton
16 October 1976	SONGS IN THE KEY OF LIFE	Stevie Wonder

MUSIC EVENTS OF 1976

- Former Beatles road manager Mal Evans is shot dead by Los Angeles police
- Peter Frampton releases 'Frampton Comes Alive!' It goes on to become the best-selling album of 1976
- Beatles turn down $30 million to reunite for a one-off concert
- Madame Tussaud's Wax Museum displays likeness of Elton John
- The Who drummer Keith Moon collapses on stage at the Boston Garden. Some months later he collapses again after trashing his Miami hotel room and is hospitalised
- Wings tour of the United States is delayed for three weeks after guitarist Jimmy McCulloch slips in his bathroom at a Paris hotel and breaks his finger
- Rolling Stones guitarist Keith Richards is involved in a car accident and is promptly arrested for possession of cocaine
- Cliff Richard performs in Leningrad, Soviet Union. Rory

Gallagher later joins him amongst the select group of musicians to have played behind the Iron Curtain when he entertains fans in Warsaw, Poland
- Alice Cooper collapses on stage in Los Angeles and is rushed to hospital
- Tina Turner files for divorce from husband Ike
- 50,000 attend free open-air concert by Jefferson Starship in New York's Central Park. In the UK the Rolling Stones perform in front of a crowd of 120,000 at Knebworth House supported by 10cc, Lynyrd Skynyrd and Todd Rundgren. But in September a free Queen gig in London's Hyde Park tops them all with an audience of 150,000
- Peter Frampton wins Rock Personality of the Year award at the Rock Music Awards. Fleetwood Mac scoop Best Album and Best Group
- First international punk festival is held at the 100 Club in London
- Thin Lizzy cancel US tour after guitarist Brian Robertson injures his hand during a bar brawl
- Rock'n'roll legend Jerry Lee Lewis is arrested outside Graceland after turning up armed and intoxicated in the small hours and challenging Elvis Presley to a gunfight
- Sex Pistols and their entourage shock the nation by repeatedly using foul language on Thames Television's prime time Today show
- Reggae star Bob Marley is injured after gunmen break into his home in Kingston, Jamaica and open fire
- A South London cover shoot for the forthcoming Pink Floyd album 'Animals' causes mayhem after a large inflatable pig breaks loose from its tethers and threatens to stray into the Heathrow flightpath
- Bands formed in 1976 include the B52s, Siouxsie and the Banshees, Clash, The Cars, Racey, Rockpile, Joy Division, Bad Manners, Darts, Fat Larry's Band, Mental as Anything, Tom Petty and the Heartbreakers, Sad Café, Boston, The Damned, Foreigner, Madness, The Rezillos, The

Buzzcocks, Generation X, Tom Robinson Band, X-Ray Spex, Woody Woodmansey's U-Boat, Tubeway Army and U2

5. BIRTHS AND DEATHS

We lost some big names in entertainment, history and culture in the year 1976. Possibly the most memorable, in the light of the manner of his passing, was Carry On legend Sid James. James was performing at the Sunderland Empire Theatre when he suffered a heart attack on stage, which co-star Olga Lowe at first believed to be a practical joke. She began to ad lib but he failed to respond, leading her to realise that something was wrong and so she called for help. Meanwhile the audience was in fits of laughter, believing what was happening to be part of the show. He was 62.

Some immense historical figures also passed in 1976, including Chinese revolutionary leader Mao Zedong and the famed British World War Two field marshal Bernard Montgomery. Another notable death was that of the reclusive businessman, aviator and eccentric Howard Hughes. Hughes, who suffered from a severe case of Obsessive Compulsive Disorder (OCD), famously ate the same thing for dinner every day - steak, salad and peas - but only the smaller peas, leaving the larger ones at the side of the plate. As he grew older his eccentricities had become more pronounced. He died of kidney failure aged 70, having been malnourished and in poor physical condition for many years.

Famous 1976 births in the world of showbusiness include Michael McIntyre, Emma Bunton and Benedict Cumberbatch, whilst sport witnessed the arrival of Wladimir Klitschko, Patrick Vieira and Ellen MacArthur.

FAMOUS 1976 BIRTHS

- Emma Bunton – singer and actress
- Ellen MacArthur – yachtswoman
- Anna Friel – actress
- Lisa Riley – actress and TV presenter
- Benedict Cumberbatch – actor
- Chris Hoy – cyclist and racing driver
- Martine McCutcheon – singer and actress
- Abi Titmuss – actress, poker player and former glamour model
- Cat Deeley – TV presenter and model
- Michael McIntyre – comedian
- Reese Witherspoon – actress
- Wladimir Klitschko – boxer
- Jennifer Capriati – tennis player
- Patrick Vieira – footballer
- Patrick Kluivert – footballer
- Ruud van Nistelrooy – footballer
- Nuno Gomes – footballer
- Nwankwo Kanu – footballer
- Roque Jr. - footballer
- Ronaldo – footballer (Brazil)
- Michael Ballack – footballer
- Francesco Totti – footballer
- Andriy Shevchenko – footballer
- Gavin Williamson – politician
- Alicia Silverstone – actress
- Jack Dorsey - co-founder of Twitter

FAMOUS 1976 DEATHS

- Sid James – actor and comedian (aged 62)
- Bernard Montgomery – WWII field marshal (aged 88)
- Agatha Christie – writer (aged 85)

- L.S. Lowry – artist (aged 88)
- Sir Stanley Baker – actor and film producer (aged 48)
- Benjamin Britten – pianist, composer and conductor (aged 63)
- Howlin' Wolf – blues singer and musician (aged 65)
- Paul Robeson – actor, musician and activist (aged 77)
- Paul Kossoff – rock guitarist (aged 25)
- Mao Zedong – Chinese revolutionary leader (aged 82)
- Freddie King – blues guitarist and singer (aged 42)
- Howard Hughes – businessman and aviator (aged 70)

6. YOUR MEMORIES OF 1976

In researching this booklet I was able, thanks to the generosity of the moderators and administrators of a number of Facebook groups, to solicit the memories and recollections of over a thousand people who were there back in the day.

Of course no two people's experiences were exactly the same. We were different ages, from different cultures and from different parishes - sometimes, indeed, different countries. For some, inevitably, the year brings back bad memories rather than good ones. But I promised those who took the trouble to respond to my appeal for testimony that I would include every sensible contribution and it is my duty and obligation to honour that promise.

The Facebook groups which I was kindly granted access to are listed below (in each case I have shortened the URL for convenience). Please pay them a visit, and if you like what they have to offer feel free to apply for membership.

Please note that, other than **The Spirit of 1976**, I have no personal involvement with any of these sites other than simply being a member:

"1970s" by DoYouRemember.com
https://bit.ly/38GtOuS

Adverts and Products from the 60's, 70's, 80's and 90's
https://bit.ly/2WR7byy

Awesome 70's
https://bit.ly/3aL27Ul

It's Yesterday Once More (the nostalgia years)
https://bit.ly/3pyGIlH

Mid Century Coloniawful
https://bit.ly/3hujNoM

The Bygone Decades
https://bit.ly/3hoP784

Vintage Humour
https://bit.ly/2KTLNpv

The Spirit of 1976
https://bit.ly/2PpbikF

For those of us who were in the UK and are of a certain age the year 1976 will be remembered for the long, sweltering summer and for the drought which came in its wake. Some will recall being bitten by the ladybirds which came in vast swarms to the south of the country - **Tracy Dobson** remembers them well, **Lucy Glover** recalls being covered in them. **Adriana Jeffery-Muddle** recounts them massing on Weston-super-Mare Pier - "they bloody hurt when they bit!"

Marc Rue speaks of "fighting off the hordes".

Sue Fox Harper writes: "It was the year of the ladybirds. I was only 21 and had been married a year. I came home from work and there was loads and loads of ladybirds all along my net curtains. I was so distraught I ran next door to my neighbours and they came in and dealt with it, such a lovely couple."

"I went to Dover Castle and they were all over the stone walls," relates **Val Wilkinson**.

Debra Jermy has vivid recollections of it all: "Thousands of ladybirds filled our plastic swimming pool in our parents garden! I was 8 that year. It was unbearably hot."

"They were all over the pavement when I walked to work!" recounts **Shirley Boggett**.

But they could be quite frightening too, as **Sandra Stennett** recalls: "Just had my second child. Took him in his pram for a walk along Hornsea promenade. Saw mounds of ladybirds in piles at the bottom of each post. I was horrified when a massive swarm landed on his pram. There were ladybirds all over him. I had to get them out of his ears and mouth and get away from the sea front to remove the rest. It was like a horror movie."

BORN IN 1976

Many of course were too young to have noticed. Born in that year were **Bev Allsop**, **Cara Manning**, **John Parsons** ("My poor mum had to carry me in the hot summer heat!") and **Anthony Broomhead**.

And **Kelly Mac** too, who records: "My mum gave birth to me on May 6th. She remembers it being super hot even by May. There are lots of baby pics of me in not much more than a nappy."

Dedicated Steve Harley & Cockney Rebel fan **Florencia Menna** was born on 7th December, 1976.

Pauline Barnes was expecting her first child. "I had a threatened miscarriage at 12 weeks so was off work for a few weeks. There was no maternity leave then, you finished work when you were 6 months pregnant. I remember how hot the summer was. Our daughter was born on 22nd August, 10 days overdue. We came home from hospital just when the weather went cooler."

Christine Evans remembers the year well. "Summer of '76 - after 7 years of trying I was having my first baby. My sister-in-law was also pregnant and we spent a lot of days sitting in the shallows of our local outdoor swimming pool."

Also having her first baby was **Maria Farrow**. "1976, will never forget it. Hottest summer ever."

And **Robyn James** recollects: "I was pregnant all that summer. Got as brown as a berry. Son was born in the December…"

Carol Cunningham was also carrying throughout the blazing heat. "I was heavily pregnant during that heatwave and had cold baths on a regular basis (showers were not common then). Following a huge thunderstorm in July, my beautiful baby daughter was born two weeks early - she still fills my heart with joy 44 years on."

Janet Whitelaw had her first son that February. **Joan Earl** was pregnant with her first boy too. He was born on 22nd October. Her brother **Geoff Stalford** remembers that they were all away on holiday on the Isle of Man during that long, hot summer. **Joyce Dole** was 21, very pregnant and "bloody uncomfortable". **Annemarie Miller** gave birth to a son. **Stephen Dadd**'s son was also born that year, sadly he has since passed away aged 36. **Rita Armstrong** gave birth just before midnight in September. **Patrick Patricia Gerald Freeman** were expecting their third baby during much of 1976 and **Frances Hudson** her second, who was born in August. "With that heat I remember walking through Cardiff Castle with the new baby and my oldest son of 2 years."

Carol Honney recalls: "I found out I was pregnant in the May and got married in the August, I remember putting make up on and it running where I was so hot. Honeymooned in Hayling Island and moved into a brand new house in the September."

Great news too for **Angela Daly**: "I had a baby in May! Was first grandchild and had lots of lovely knitted matinee coats for the baby, then we had the hottest summer ever."

The intense heat brought mixed emotions for **Sue Thompson**. "I was pregnant with my firstborn… hated the hot summer and couldn't wait for it to rain and cool down. We lived in a 200 year old cottage, which was always cool… that cottage was my oasis… I loved it."

Brickbats and bouquets in equal measure for the year too for **Joanne Frendo**: "In 1976 I was 19 years old and pregnant with my second child. Very hard times, always broke, one maternity dress that was washed every night. Walked everywhere I had to go, no lifts in the block of flats where I lived and still today live in the same block, though we've got lifts now. Traffic used to be allowed to go down Mainstreet. I was young and I don't remember being so bothered by the summers, though it would have been easier if we were allowed to go to Western Beach - it was off limits to Gibraltarians, but we used to go to the outer perimeters of Varyl Begg Estate and swim and sunbathe there. Great times."

Joyce Tythe also remembers the summer well. "I had my second baby, a lovely little girl, in June 1976. Wow what a scorcher it was… remember burning the soles of my feet on the concrete outside when going barefoot."

1976 was the year in which **Margaret Trotter**'s first son was born - in July. **Linda Wright** was expecting her second son, who was born in August, whilst having not only the scorching weather but also a lively four-year-old to contend with. **Paula Boulton** gave birth to a daughter in September, and **Maxine Vivers** bore a girl in '76 too. **Linda Wright** had a boy and **Sarita Gillett** was pregnant with her first born. **Marion Borthwick**'s son arrived in the May. "All he had on from May till September was a nappy! Really hot and I remember getting over my phobia of insects; I was constantly flicking them away from him in his pram!"

Veronica Hallett remembers: "I had my son in the February and was able to let him lie in just a vest in his pram."

It was similar for **Sue Gray**: "Gave birth to my first baby May 12th. '76 it was a scorcher. I had my son in his pram in the garden at 24 hours old wrapped up with a blanket. My GP called to see us and told me to get all the covers off him, just kept him in the shade. He was wearing a vest and his nappy lol. So hot at night it was stifling, we had to have every window wide open."

Scantily-clad babies seem to have been all the rage. "I had my first child, Michael, on 7th of January, and I moved into my first house of my own that year in Cwmbran," recounts **Christine Charles**. "it was so hard to keep cool that summer, my son spent all of his time in just a nappy. Saved money on clothes though."

Janet Leighs recalls similarly: "I remember my new born girl in her large pram with just a terry towling nappy sitting outside at the back door and my doctor coming as she was screaming and I could not shut her up - he grabbed her and put her under the cold shower and told me off for not noticing she had a raging temperature - loves the cold now."

And **Julie May Mills** adds: "I had my first child who only wore a nappy for about 7 months due to the heat."

Says **Ann Crisp**: "I gave birth to my daughter. Able to put her in the garden with a canopy over the top of her pram, I had to cover up because I got heat rash."

And **Vicky Hampshire** too: "I was expecting all through that long hot summer. I had my 3rd daughter, who has always been a joy to me."

James R. Wright reminisces: "Our son was born at the end of

May. His first few weeks were spent in a pram out in the fresh air. In fact we put him out in the garden in June and brought him into the house when it rained in September!"

A strong contender for one of the most evocative memories must surely go to **Janet Payne**: "I was pregnant with my second child - a daughter, Victoria Maria, born in October '76. I remember the Indian summer, as it was dubbed, as it was so hot I used to work till lunch and pick up my 2-year-old son Johnathan from his nanna, then go home and put him down for his nap and have a nap myself. It was on one of these occasions when being 6 months gone and hotter than hell I stripped naked and fell asleep on my bed, to be woken a couple of hours later by a squeaking noise. I looked over and there was the window cleaner - lol I'm still blushing now."

Angela Grout lived in the West Midlands but stayed for much of the year with a relative in Poole. "I was pregnant and spent so much time in the water."

Margaret Hutchinson remembers it well too: "I had just got pregnant with my daughter being sick all the time, it was boiling hot and swarms of ladybirds."

Mairi Thérèse Thomson's recollections are prompted by a '70s music legend: "February 1976 I gave birth to my first baby, a boy. Beautiful weather, and I went down 2 sizes from before I had him. And Marc Bolan was still alive. Happy days..."

One could be forgiven for thinking that 1976 was one long summer from January to December, but of course that wasn't the case. **Mollie** puts things into some perspective: "I was pregnant that summer, so the heat was a bit of a nightmare. We also had to queue at a stand pipe in the middle of our village as water was very severely rationed, that was the worst thing as I already had 4 children so keeping them and their clothes clean was a bit of a nightmare. Now everyone remembers the heat wave and the drought of the summer but the winter started early - end of October - and by mid November when my baby was born we had a whole month of freezing fog. It was extremely cold, but on the morning of my daughter's birth the sun was shining. Everywhere was covered in a thick white frost which shone like diamonds in the sunshine. My baby was born in Harrogate General Hospital and the day after her birth the freezing fog was back with a vengeance, and stayed until the new year. I now live in the Cotswolds."

Some compelling memories too from **Verna Emery**: "My first baby, a little girl, was born that year 10 days before Christmas. It was snowing when I came home from hospital. That summer was so hot - I felt faint, I remember some days were so hot that the tarmac was melting and sticking to the soles of my shoes. KC and the Sunshine Band were in the charts."

It's not difficult to understand why, when memories of 1976 are called upon, the focus always seems to return to the summer. It was hot, but it was also very long. That was what made it so special, and so memorable. As **Sharon Wilson** recalls: "I remember so well as I was having my first baby. She was born on August 10th, two days after my birthday. I had to stay in the hospital 10 days (which was quite normal in those days) and it was very hard because the weather outside was so beautiful. When I got home it was lovely to push my baby out in her pram until the end of September as it continued to be sunny and warm."

Louise Bennett was 17-years-old and was bringing her first daughter into the world as the sun bore down, and so spent it learning to be a mum. **Sandra Bonner** gave birth to a son who is now 44 years of age. **Denny Chandler** was having her second baby. **Carole Jennings** was pregnant with her first child, who was born in August, and **Laraine Livermore**'s eldest daughter arrived in the September. **Ann Marsh**'s first baby Linda came into the world on 27th February, and **Margaret Spoor Smith** gave birth in December, having been pregnant throughout the gruelling summer. **Nancy Park** had her first child, a daughter, in January.

Recalling mixed tidings, **Ellen Coleman** remembers: "I was 18 and pregnant with my second child. I worked full time in a factory and at night I helped my mum to care for my dad who was dying of cancer. It was really hot and the beautiful summer passed me by in a blur. I had a son on the 13th of July and dad passed away on the 20th. It was a very bitter sweet year for our family."

It wasn't all joy for **Karen Crookshank** either: "Having my first baby. It was a nightmare. West London hospital, Hammersmith. No air con, no fans, 16 hour labour. Being pregnant in that heat was no fun either."

Jennifer Martin had a scare, which fortunately turned out well in the end: "I had my eldest son - 3lb, 4oz! Had to leave him in hospital for 3 weeks and go home, it was awful going to see him in an incubator. But he was allowed home and we had a lovely summer."

Helen Escudier has fond memories of the year. She commented: "My son was born in March and during that hot summer have happy memories of taking him out in his pram with a large canopy to protect him and spending a lot of the days down our beach hut with his two older sisters enjoying the sun sea and sand."

Ella Powell can testify to just how difficult it was to carry a child in the heat. "I was pregnant with my second child, a boy… he was born August 21st. Hard to carry a baby in that heat.. I already had a 17 month old son."

Sometimes taking a holiday could be the best way of moving on from the ordeal, as **Sandra Reynolds** found: "I was pregnant with my first baby, she was born 3rd September. We went to Torquay in late May for a week's holiday and my husband became self employed."

We should not forget that we didn't all have the requisite mod cons in 1976, as **Sharon Whatley** explains: "I was 18 and had my first baby born in May, and bought a derelict house in Adamsdown that we moved to in the August. We had an outside toilet, just a tap and nothing else in the kitchen. And paving slabs on the floor in the living room."

That applied at work too. "Pregnant with my son and working in a hot, stuffy Romford office with no fans nor air conditioning," remembers **Sandy Rawstron**.

Sally Rusk Victory was expecting, and was living in one room above a shop. "My husband played in a band and he was in England. I was very nervous as it was my first child but all went well TG."

Sadly **Lynn Bailey** had some bad news. "Was expecting my first baby in November. Moved into our first home in June. Lost my baby in August, born premature. Only lived for 2 hours. Went back to work in September."

It was a sad time for **Beryl Simpson** too, although thankfully better news came later: "A sad time that July for I was nearly 25 and told to stay in bed for a fortnight during lovely weather. I had actually miscarried anyway so it was a waste of time. I was off work for five weeks. The doctor told me I was classed as an older mother and that one in three pregnancies ended in miscarriage. What would women of that age think now being told they were an older mother? It was true then for I had been married for 4 years and most of my friends had babies years before me. I went on to have three babies in 1978, 1980 and 1984."

Not everybody enjoyed the warm weather either. "Pregnant with my youngest son and sick day and night all the way through so that while everybody else was basking in the lovely weather I could not wait for it to be over," rues **Cynthia Hayes**.

And **Marion Haslam** recalls: "I had my daughter in June that year, couldn't take her out during the day, no blankets, no clothes just a nappy and had to keep her in the coolest room of the house."

Aileen Huff puts it more simply: "Hot hot hot and I gave birth to my first son."

Janet Rochester provides a useful reminder of how we were made to improvise. "Worked in London all through the long, hot summer being pregnant with my first child. Remember growing vegetables in our garden and having to use washing up water to water them, as hosepipe ban and to conserve water."

It was all numbers for **Margaret Noblet**. "Pregnant with my fourth baby. It was so hot, I felt sorry for my other 3 children as was not well enough for a holiday. Number 4 as the children called him was a baby that just would not settle and cried so much his brothers and sisters did not like him till he was about 2. All adults now but they never forgot number 4."

Jan Mansell compares the year favourably with 1977: "Had my daughter in the August and just remember the endless sunny days being a joy, the standpipes being an inconvenience and looking forward to fully enjoying the next summer which was a disappointment!"

Of course, for many there are always practical achievements in life which help to make a year special, as well as personal joys. As **Janice Marvin** recounts: "My first grandchild was born and I passed my driving test after 4 attempts. I was 42 years old. I have never forgotten 1976."

For **Susie McKenzie** it was something of an ordeal. "I was 12 weeks pregnant when the heat wave began. I was bed ridden because I was threatening a miscarriage. I had a bed in the front room for daytime use so I could watch TV. My sister came to wash and set my hair to cheer me up but within 15 minutes it had dropped again in the heat. The worst thing about it? When I was finally allowed out of bed the weather broke!"

Edna Miekle puts it more bluntly: "I was pregnant during this time and it was bloody murder."

Rose Nicholls had a daughter that year and remembers it being so hot. **Angela Nicholson** recollects: "I was pregnant with my first born but was continually ill due to the heat. Went for a walk around Grafham Water and there was no water in there at all, just huge cracks."

As memories go, there are few so precious as when our children come into the world. Possibly all the more so when they are our first. It's sometimes hard to credit that the brood of 1976 are now heading relentlessly towards their fifties. But the testimonies of so many show us that recollections are as clear now as they were in the blazing heat of the moment. The long, dreamy summer and the year that still means so much to so many.

PUDDLE STREAMS AND SUNBURNT SCREAMS

Some of those I asked for contribution towards this work really did rise to the challenge, and I was especially moved by this poem from **Donna Stone**:

"I don't really remember
The heat of '76.
I was running round
In a nappy
Trying to eat bugs and sticks.
As I got older
And mum would reminisce
She'd go on about
The water tanks
Filling buckets to wash our bits.
Kids playing
In puddle streams
Nights filled
With sunburnt screams
Mums applying Nivea creams
Although I don't remember
The heat of '76
I'm sure my chubby legs were red
From running round the streets."

A beautiful tribute to a beautiful age. **Jon England** prefers an interesting adaptation of prose:

"Dorset coastline village (Seatown); Anchor Inn family-run pub serving Rombouts coffee with individual miniature brew-cup atop the branded mug; fish'n'chips delivered in a Morris Minor converted 'hot' van; warm Corona lemonade gurgling all sparkly in your throat as you'd gulped too much in one go; fluorescent-pink Hubbly-Bubbly bubble-gum; a kid-friendly 'Smuggler's Bar' down by the beach with Charlie Rich, The Drifters, Linda Ronstadt and the Carpenters on the juke-box wafting out the doors over the seaside-encrusted heat-wave; Walls vanilla ice-cream 'sandwiches'; candy-smelling new flip-flops (if you were lucky) and the smell of Hawaiian Tropic and Ambre Solaire suntan foam in aerosols drifting off the beach; caravan holidaymakers swarming the shingle banks at 8:30 in the morning until after 9 at night; midge-bothered lines of local fishermen with beach-caster rods chasing the oily mackerel shoals as they chased whitebait clouds in the tepid heaving spring-tide waves offshore; shandy being drunk by nervous teens in bell-bottom jeans and striped polyester tank-tops trying vainly to look 'hard' and 'cool' at the same time and managing neither.

"Tent/camping field jam-packed with canvas tents and almost every car different and immediately identifiable from their design, orange, turquoise, brown, rust-ready red… each one unique with all the add-on trappings (leatherette steering-wheel covers with breather holes and 'laces'), fuzzy-dice hanging from rear-view mirrors, chrome wheel-nuts, nodding back-shelf dog puppets and luggage racks with snake-belt tie-downs; seawater-rinsed bathing costumes pinned to wooden tent-pole strings and 'daps' lined up (Mum's, Dad's, kids) to dry.

"Tractor-tyre inner-tubes uproariously chucked in the sea and dived in, under, through and lazed on top of; ineffectively bucketing endless water to the vegetable garden; catching, prepping and eating mackerel, pollock, skate, conger, lobster and crab freshly landed in our little dinghy from pots, bottom-fishing and trawl-hooking with home-made 'feathered' traces and home-made lead-weight sinkers made in buckets of damp sand in our garage.

"Mum's death-trap floral sun-loungers ("Mind your fingers") in the front garden trying to find a bit of shade under the laburnum and lilac trees with warmed and tired rose-blooms offering up their wilting perfumes.

"Sticky-sweet strawberries, gooseberries and blackberries trickling down chins as we stuffed in as many 'while picking' as possible. Faint odour of cow muck as local farmers tractors trundled around the lanes and flung out on the surrounding fields."

LOVE IS IN THE AIR

For many 1976 will be remembered as a year of blossoming romance, with the scorching sun and long, lazy summer nights a mere backdrop to life-defining events which would remain with them for many years beyond, and in some cases are still with them today. **Wendy Fox** was married on Easter Saturday, April 17th, at the young age of 21. Even so early into the season Wendy recalls that it was so hot. By June of course the heatwave hat set in in earnest, but **Jeni Hands** still managed to choose one of the only rainy days of the summer for her wedding. As did **Janice Hanman**, who tied the knot on August 28th, towards the opposite end of the heatwave. It was "really hot, then when we came out of church the heavens opened up... first rain after the heat wave for us at least in Gloucester."

Stephen Levine also married in August, as did **Marilyn Zanoletti Hayes** (on the 7th), who went to Wembley the following week to watch Southampton play Liverpool in the FA Charity Shield. And if the fireworks that Second Division Saints had managed to provide during their shock defeat of Manchester United in the FA Cup Final back in May deserted them for their clash with the league champions, they were certainly present for **Jock Bain** from North Scotland, who got wed on November 5th and is still happily married today. **David Tinkler** was wed that year too, as was **Sheila Bell** who is still with her husband all these years later.

Anita Bywater took the plunge in May. "It was windy showery weather. The day after it was glorious weather, it didn't rain again until the day we were coming home from holidaying in Dorset. It was the first week of September."

Ann Eddison got married in September, as did **Millie Blackwell**

(on the 11th). Millie and her husband are still together today, with two daughters and five grandchildren to their names. **Gary Perry** did the deed at the very beginning of the heatwave on April 19th. **Julie Edwards** opted instead for the 20th of June, when the sun burned at its brightest. **Anne Tomlin** likewise on July 10th. **Diane Llewellyn**'s memory for detail is still exemplary 44 years on: "I got married at Sr John's Church, Cefn Coed. It was a beautiful day in October 1976 and Abba were in the charts."

Contrary to what some of today's kids seem to believe we did have colour photography in 1976, but the scape scene didn't always put it to best use. "Got married at the end of July. All the photos show yellow grass or lack of grass," recalls **Doff Mole**.

Everything seems to have ended well for **Nick**, but it didn't quite all go to plan: "Got married in May 1976 - VE Day. Was only married a week and I had to have my wedding ring cut from my finger because it had swollen with the heat. Got my own house, learned to drive then two lovely kids."

Vera Yorke headed off for a sunny break after exchanging vows: "I got married on the hottest day in August '76 and we went to the Isle of Man on honeymoon. We had the best weather and hired a car on the island, so went somewhere different every day."

I love **Jackie Andrews**' story of enforced rationing whilst on holiday with her intended: "I was 19. Met my husband and got engaged 6 weeks later. We had a holiday on the Isle of Wight. It was scorching. The bath in the guest house had a line around it to limit the amount of water you could use. Fabulous 2 weeks! We (recently) celebrated our 43rd anniversary."

Patricia Cross was another 19-year-old bride: "I was married in West Ham Church in September 1976, I was 19. I passed my driving test in the previous June and we bought our house in that month as well, laughable now but we were forbidden to sleep over in our new house till we were married. Most newly weds rented but we had saved solidly for two years for a deposit, much to the chagrin of our parents who could not understand why we would saddle ourselves with a mortgage. People mention the great heatwave but I can't recall it at all!"

And **Lesley Harper** too: "I got married on Valentine's Day in 1976 in the Catholic Church in Bushey, Hertfordshire. It was a freezing day… I was 19 and my husband was 24. Still together and have 2 daughters aged 42 and 39, and 2 granddaughters of 8 and 19."

Jenny Cullum has no problems remembering the weather, possibly prompted by recollections of her attendant's unfortunate reaction: "I married my wonderful husband in July 1976. It was a scorching hot day and my young pageboy fainted during the service! I also remember the ice cream melting at the reception. Apart from that it was a lovely day and happily still together."

Meanwhile **Linda Nicholson** has been busy since getting hitched that year: "I got married in 1976… we are still happily married and we have 10 children and 21 grandchildren."

Anne Humphreys Corcoran's household expanded rather rapidly during those long balmy months: "Got married that year. Also got pregnant. Bought our first house as well, as we wanted a garden for the dog and baby."

"I married my first husband in 1976, August bank holidays - the first bit of rain all summer," recalls **Jan Knight**.

Richard Milner has some distinct local memories from down Dorset way: "Married for the 1st time. Lived at Sandbanks. Saw the fires that were from Christchurch to Wareham that summer."

Nick Page met his wife-to-be in 1976 and they went on to marry the following year. He tells it wonderfully: "I met my wife in 1976. I proposed the day after I met her. We went on a picnic to Windsor Great Park and had the most romantic time ever. We bought some things we would need for the day and still have the 'little brown knife' we used that day. My wife keeps it in a cupboard in our kitchen. She won't part with it. We married the following year. Oh how I loved 1976!"

Inevitably some liaisons don't go to plan, and 1976 was no exception. "Worked in St. James and went to the park at lunch time… unbelievably hot! Got married, big mistake!" rues **Paula Messum**.

Likewise **Kath Mitchell**: "I got married in August '76. Sadly it didn't last."

"Many took advantage of the new divorce laws that came in 1975," **Dorothy and Andrew Taylor** remind us, without letting on as to whether they were amongst them.

But **June Harper** was indeed divorced in 1976. And **Catherine Todd** made a lucky break following a dreadful ordeal: "It was the year I escaped from a violent marriage. I found a refuge and escaped with my three babies."

Alison Hitchcock has a sad story to tell: "1976 saw me married to an unfaithful husband, I had a 4-year-old girl and was pregnant again - due 1st June. WOW what a hot year, I helped out at the local playgroup with a friend that was an alcoholic. She was lovely but died later that year."

And young love blossomed all around in the sun, sometimes leading to future relationships and others, well, remaining simply as memories. **Angela Maclean** looks back fondly with a beautiful piece of prose which entirely captures the spirit: "Wow, I loved the summer of 1976. I was 16 years old. Elton John and

Kiki Dee were number 1 with 'Don't Go Breaking My Heart'. The long hot summer, the whole 6 weeks of the school holidays and not a drop of rain. My cousin came home to Aberdeen, Scotland from Canada. We had a ball. All the kids that was in our street stuck out together from morning till night. Picnics by the River Dee. New relationships started, met my first husband that year. It was a year that I have never forgotten."

Gilly Coulton fell in love, although tantalisingly we are left to guess how that one ended up. As indeed was the case with **Carol Heath**'s liaison: "I was 15, 16 that September. First boyfriend. There had been a drought that summer as so hot. Had spent most of my spare time at Mill Hill outside swimming pool. Boyfriend was a biker, so bought my first pair of jeans. Amazing flares that had to be tied up."

Carol Ann Stunell, then 25, was at a missionary training college in Birmingham and got engaged in the summer. **Shirley Coward** also became engaged, but she and her intended found themselves on the horns of a dilemma: "We had to change the date as if Boro got through to the FA Cup Final he was going there."

Elaine Chambers has fond recollections: "I got engaged this year, it was great. I dragged my poor mother round every shop in Stockport looking for an outfit to wear on the Saturday night. It was sweltering, but she never complained."

And **Elaine Kent** too: "I was 18 and got engaged that year, loving the fabulous hot weather and generally feeling like the world was my oyster."

Tina Breadmore recounts: "I was 19 on this day in 1976 and I got married the next day, which was the day the weather broke. The rain stayed away for our wedding but we arrived in Cornwall for our honeymoon to torrential rain. We divorced after 25 years."

Jean Horsley "fell in love with a married man who gave me my life back after a cruel marriage. He showed me love, respect and made me live my life again."

It was young love for **Sarah Louise Fletcher**, but with an unhappy conclusion: "That year I was 15 and having a great time at college... discos in the evenings, sweltering hot... standpipes on the street for water. Dad and I hauled buckets home after queuing for ages, every drop was so precious. I had a boyfriend whom I loved to bits but was forbidden to see him so we snuck around and grabbed what time we could. Parents decided to move us away to the coast.. I was heartbroken as my whole life was torn away from me. A great year but a sad ending."

A lovely little story from **Elizabeth Bryson**: "I was sweet sixteen and met my first husband that year. Went on lots of trips to the beach on his motorbike or car and house parties were a big thing, then at weekends first job after school in a hairdresser's. Not a care in the world and jobs were plentiful."

Another from **Pauline Grant**: "I met my husband in Blackpool. It was red hot, ladybirds everywhere, the sands were full of deckchairs and everyone was happy, smiling and eating ice creams."

And who could not be touched by this recollection from **Franklin Gill**: "Amroth caravan holiday in Wales. Six-week holidays, met a young lad from France and cried all the way home"?

KM of Hawarden met her husband-to-be during the summer of 1976, and they are still together. "We met in Rascals on Love Street in Chester. The sun never stopped shining and life was good!" she says.

But possibly the most touching tale of all comes from **Caroline**

Davidson, who has memories aplenty to share with us. I'll let her take up the story as it reads so well, if tinged with a little sadness: "1976, one of the years that remains in my heart with the fondest, strongest, memories. After always being the shy wallflower, never having had a boyfriend, I met my love in September '75, and in April '76 we got engaged, on my birthday, age 18, against my dad's wishes. My sister had just come out of a rotten abusive marriage, and I know my dad was only thinking of me. He never spoke to Rog, and would even shut the door in his face.

"That changed as soon as we married, exactly a year and a day later. Rog became another much loved son to my dad (jump 22 years ahead, Rog had terminal cancer, and my dad sat with me, by Rog's side, for 48 hours, in hospital, until he died).

"But 1976, one of our years. Yes the hot summer, the drought and water shortages. 2 weeks spent in the Lake District, meeting Rog's family, showing me all his old haunts. going to the Tuesday night discos on the RAF camp where we were both stationed at the time. 'Don't Go Breaking My Heart', 'Dancing Queen', 'Afternoon Delight', 'Young Hearts Run Free', 'Right Back Where We Started From'; the Bee Gees, Queen, Hot Chocolate, Eagles, Lou Rawls, KC and the Sunshine Band. Disco was king, and queen, and we all wanted to get down and boogie!

"Platform soles, baggy trousers, hair cuts like Purdey from The Avengers , blue eyeshadow, pink nail polish. Seeing Carrie at the cinema, and being terrified. Logan's Run, The Omen, Taxi Driver, McCloud, McMillan and Wife, George and Mildred, The Muppet Show, Six Million Dollar Man - on TV BBC1, BBC 2, Yorkshire and Midlands, the 4 channels we chose from.

"And my job, all I could get, working in the Sally Army canteen on camp - but if not for that, I'd never have met Rog. Yep, definitely a year I look back on, and smile."

HEATWAVE HOLIDAYS

Perhaps unsurprisingly, a good number of those memories which have been sent in involve holidays, often of course to sunny resorts beside the sea. It must be remembered that although some did travel abroad for their holidays, in the 1970s most families still decamped to UK resorts, whether to a hotel by the beach or a camping site in the remote countryside. And quite often those sites would have little to offer beyond the very bare basics. Unlike the homes on wheels that are to be found on caravan sites today, resplendent with satellite television and en suite bathrooms, back then a nocturnal call of nature would often result in a long walk from base across a spooky, unlit field into the dark unknown. Although only seven at the time, **Kevin Mark Keeble** describes the scene perfectly: "My family and I went to Clacton on holiday to a caravan park called Valley Farm (still there). There was no running water or toilets in the caravans at that time. We had to collect our water from the stand pipe near by. There was no swimming pool either then on the park. My parents didn't have a car so we either walked to the seaside or caught the bus. Got sunburnt on my back and with the heat it was difficult to sleep. We would all get dressed up in our best clothes in the evening to visit The Ballroom (this is what we called it then) on the park and my parents played bingo. Bingo was all very official and all the facts and figures had to be written down on a big board showing the number of tickets sold and the tax to be paid. There was actual ballroom dancing still happening then with the adults. Great memories."

Also caravanning during that glorious year was **Christine Beevers**. "The music," she recalls. "Some of the best '70s sounds. Remember going to Chapel at Leonard's in Skegness for our summer holidays. Went on the beach and within 10 minutes had to go back to the caravan because the rocks were covered and they (ladybirds) were beginning to land on us. The Real Thing had the best song of that year. Everyone seemed happy and smiley. I was 15 and wore my Bay City Roller trousers with pride at every opportunity."

Amid all the memories of flared trousers which both preceded and survived Rollermania, it's easy to forget this relatively short period in-between when all the girls seemed to be clad in these baggy, three-quarter length, tartan-trimmed curiosities in reverence to these five boys from Edinburgh who had taken the UK charts by storm for a while.

June Anne Burton has memories of her own: "At the end of the summer in 1976 we went on holiday to a caravan in Rhyl. The heat wave broke on the North Wales coast and we were battered by storms for two weeks. The wind was so strong that it blew the sea down through the side roads of the town. We lay in the caravan being rocked to sleep. My in laws came to stay for a couple of nights and we found out that my sister in law had got married in secret."

Also holidaying in North Wales was **Judith Marshall**, who had just finished sitting her CSEs at school, and **Renee McDermott**, who remembers insects "committing suicide" on the windscreen of the car as well as milk turning to cheese overnight in her fridgeless caravan. And **Helen Foster** too: "I was six and lived in Torrington Drive, Halewood, in maisonettes. Neighbour opened the water mains and we all had a ball under the water. Went on holiday to Llandudno in a caravanette. Used to sleep bottom of the OEM at night and play on beach all day.

Tracy Robertson also [*what are the chances that some of these people's paths will actually have crossed back in that summer, without them even realising? - Ed.*]: "Annual holiday to Rhyl in a caravan, - so so hot on the beach, got sunstroke, remember being delirious for 24 hours with it, shivers then too hot. And don't get me started on the ladybugs, that year set off a life-long phobia of the things."

Carol Hamnett left school and spent two weeks in a "typical holiday caravan" in Great Yarmouth. "Pulling ladybirds out of my sister's hair while walking to the beach. Mum and stepdad got married in the September, I was chief bridesmaid. Loved the pubs/discos and the fab music that was around."

Elaine Sherwood was seven years old and her family spent a whole two weeks at a caravan in Skegness, where ladybirds were the least of her worries: "I vividly remember walking along the beach with a toffee apple only for it quickly to be engulfed by wasps and I had to drop it to the ground. I stood back devastated at the fate of said toffee apple."

For those who preferred a regular change of scenery when venturing forth on a caravan holiday there was nothing better one could have than a mobile caravette. **Jennifer Monaghan** hired one and in 1976 Cornwall was the destination of choice: "My son was 1 and my daughter 3. We rented a Ford caravette for a week and drove down to Cornwall. We parked outside a shop and my husband took our daughter with him and I was going to change our sons nappy. I went to get the nappy and turned and my son was gone. I was going crazy and panicked when a couple went by and looked at me and the door. Here was my son hanging outside the door by his hands. He gets fed up with me telling that story."

As well as caravanning, camping was also a popular holiday option for those on a budget - or even for people who just wanted to stay in touch with nature. One only had to unroll a tent and a mat, and divest the rucksack of a few basic tools and utensils, and the hotel was wherever one desired it to be. It is maybe unsurprising that so many opted for the great simplicities of a vacation under canvas. People like **Christine Anders** who, having been wed just the year before, enjoyed her first holiday with her husband free from the watchful gaze of their parents. Their camping trip to Somerset was "gorgeous". **Isobel Stewart** and her family including four children would always take their tents to the seaside in defiance of their modest financial means. "The old car would take us there and back again. We all used to argue with each other when we were trying to put the tent up but once organised it became home for two weeks. We had a great time, happy healthy children, and the sea and sand for fun."

Not yet even ten years old, **Andrew Thompson** enjoyed "probably my best ever school trip to Middleton camp in County Durham. Great outdoor activities, plenty of hiking. Good evening crack playing sports in blazing sun." Though his story has a hint of sadness: "As a child who (was) seriously bullied later my happiest time as a child."

Ilfracombe was the venue of choice for **Mike Gates**, although unfortunately for him the summer sun didn't make the journey with him: "I was working on the railway (track maintenance) - wouldn't get away with it these days but we just wore boots and shorts with a hi-vis vest tied around the waist. We went to Ilfracombe for a holiday. Water was only available at certain times on standpipes on the campsite. We had a thunderstorm the night we arrived and I don't think it stopped raining for the week."

Sue Kinsley incites a retrospective vision of Only Fools and Horses: "Went on my first holiday with my friend her mum and stepdad. We were 12/13... went camping, the car they had was a Reliant Robin and it was packed full. Also pulled a trailer which had the massive tent and camping equipment in - beds, tables, kitchen etc. We headed for the south, ended up in Perrenporth on a campsite close to the sea had to walk to the beach in socks as it burned our feet. Spent every day in and out of the sea, even went mackerel fishing one day on a boat. Funfair day trip to Lands End, thoroughly enjoyed the 2 weeks - caught the camping bug. Came home, was so tanned people thought we had been abroad. Sadly we moved house to another town in the December and we eventually lost touch but that holiday was amazing. I'm now 57."

Sue O'Connell tried camping for the first time in 1976. "I had a three year old and a six year old and moved in the heat which was horrendous as trying to clean a house. We went on days out for a holiday and went to Fraisthorpe where we were over run with the ladybirds."

It was a first for **Pauline Foyle** too, who had a fantastic time with her in-laws camping in the superb weather in Brean.

And **Iris Goode** too, who takes up the story: "That year was our first holiday. We had four children, we set out in a Morris Oxford from Cwmbran to Ruan Minor in Cornwall. It took us seven and half hours to get there. Then with our friends put a ten-man tent up which took a bit of doing. The kids found the swimming pool so they were out of the way, the eldest looking after them. When the tent was up we had a nice cup of tea and got some chips to make chip butties - they never tasted so good. Later on we went to the clubhouse, had two drinks and crisps for the kids, went to bed and slept like logs. Next day we went to St. Michael's mount where we really enjoyed ourselves. All the kids still remember this holiday."

However **Lynne Reynolds** misjudged the weather somewhat. "So, so hot - worked all through it, then went to Scotland camping beginning of September and got blown over in the tent. Had to go in a caravan, weather was horrendous."

It was "a good year to be alive" according to **Lyn Breakwell**, who enjoyed her summer holiday camping in Devon.

Simon Stephenson-Oliver went camping that year with his best friend Mark Humphrey. "I can remember walking by the beach with a Mr. Whippy ice cream in hand that was smothered in green flies! We still ate it nevertheless!"

Donna Heirene remembers her camping holiday in South Wales well, despite having been only nine: "Went on a spur of the moment away day break with my mum's friend and her sister (who was my best friend) to Three Cliffs Bay in South Wales, camping. Going by train with all the camping stuff and minimal food and money. Stayed on a farm, lived on a diet of cup-a-soups and baked potatoes done on the fire. Met up with my mum's friend's relatives who happened to be Mormons, so family orientated, they kept us amused all day and every day. Ghost walks at night, games on the beach. Being an only child and had never left my parents before, this was the best holiday ever. I remember this holiday with the fondest of memories."

Like the author, 1976 brings back memories of her church club for **Angela Roe**: "I remember going to the beach most days with my boyfriend, car windows open, eating ice creams. No air conditioning in the car then. Laying on the warm sand. Also went camping with a Christian youth club in the Lake District. I left my purse in a motorway café on the way there, with my £16 spending money for the week. Unsurprisingly it was not found. The organisers were very kind and gave me £1 spending money a day from their funds. We had a great week of lovely weather, carefree times."

And **Anita Hobson** reminds us of how difficult it could be in those days just to make ends meet, and to have enough left over for a modest but unforgettable break: "I remember 1976 for the long hot summer. I had two young children, one of 7 the other 4. It had been another tough year - we came from Sheffield and my husband was trying to get a degree. I was working two jobs, as a nurse and evenings at the Fiesta nightclub until 2am, then up with the kids every day at 7am. Come summer we went to Cornwall camping - we went for two weeks but stayed three as the weather was so hot. We had a fantastic time. We had a little thing called an A35, it was a little black car plus a trailer on the back."

Simple pleasures - camping and caravanning - which of course so many of us still enjoy today. The stars we gaze up to from our humble field in Wales or the west country are the same ones that are to be seen from beside the beach in Benidorm, and when the sun is bearing down as it was in 1976 the appeal of a staycation cannot be gainsaid.

RECREATING A BEAUTIFUL MEMORY

Of all the testimonies that I received in response to my appeal, one of those which touched me the most came from **Geoff Leech**. His teenage expedition from North Wales to Newquay in Cornwall in the company of his fun-loving mates was one which obviously made a lasting impact and engendered a deep nostalgic yearning. In fact so compelling were their memories that a few years ago, in 2018, the three of them returned to recreate the photo which they had taken back in the day, right down the colours of their clothing. They sat in precisely the same places, in front of the same landmark, to pose for a photo taken from the same angle. You can see the pictures below, in fact I liked them so much I used them for the front cover of the book (hope you don't mind Geoff).

Here is his account of that memorable outing: "We had just finished our A-levels and we had a long hot summer ahead of us before going up to university. Not all of us could drive and we weren't all 18 but, somehow, one of the lads persuaded some chap to let us hire a minibus for a week. We drove from North Wales down to Newquay, mostly overnight. What followed was a week of sheer joy: chasing girls, body surfing, drinking beer (though nobody would sell us any scrumpy) and sunbathing. We lived on scampi and chips in a basket. One day, we travelled down to Land's End. The Gift Shop (there was only one then) was managed by a chap who played Elton John and Kiki Dee's 'Don't Go Breaking My Heart' on repeat over and over again. Three of us had our picture taken at the famous signpost and it remains one of my treasured possessions to this day. Two years ago, and 42 years after our magical holiday, we had a reunion trip and re-created the original photo. Back in 1976 though, there was the feeling that we had come to end of a significant part of our lives and that a whole new future was about to open up before us."

HI-DE-HI

The other popular concept in the 1970s seaside experience was the holiday camp. Chalets in rows or in blocks like an early housing estate, fun at the swimming pool, lots of supervised activities for the kids to do and entertainment in the evenings provided by severally talented jocular types all wearing the same coloured blazers for easy identification. For those who were slightly better off the same resort chains sometimes also provided hotels, but the principle was broadly the same. Guests ate the allocated meal at the allotted time within a large communal hall, often seated in densely-packed rows, and the choice on the menu was take it or leave it.

Where my family and I used to stay most years, in Cliftonville near Margate, Kent, Butlin's had four or five hotels along the same short stretch of road close to the seafront. Our holidays were considered "posh" by some of my friends, yet we shared a bathroom and a toilet with several other families on the landing and rather hoped that the last user would clean the bath out after using it. At least three of the hotels had a television, but just the one. If the hotel we were staying in was showing BBC1 and we wanted to watch ITV we would go to the one which was showing that channel, taking a seat in a sometimes crowded room alongside many others who had the same idea. On Top of the Pops night it would often be standing room only. There were only three channels, so options were rather limited anyway.

Some of those who contributed to this project enjoyed similar breaks. Like **Jennifer Lovegrove**: "We went on our very first summer holiday together as a little family, with our daughters, Jane Marie aged 3 and Paula Louise aged 1. We went to Warners holiday Camp in Hayling Island. SO hot! My husband burnt his arm really badly on the way home to Enfield, he had driven all the way back with his arm resting on the door with the window down. OUCH!"

Gary Barlow also has a tale to tell: "For the annual 2 week holiday my family went to Skegness Butlin's for week one (it's not as good now - no monorail, no cable cars) and Scarborough for week two… my mother was miffed that all the ladybirds seemed to make a beeline for her! Needless to say the weather was above average… in fact, if you ask anyone of a certain age about 1976 the odds are they will think of the heatwave!"

Jerome Dopson was in the South West: "Went on holiday to Pontins, Brean Sands and Cheddar Gorge, Somerset. I always remember a sign not long before the Pontins holiday camp stating 'You are entering a drought area'. Pretty awe inspiring for a 12 year old. Amazing summer."

"I was only 5 in 1976. I remember the glorious summer," writes **Linda Baker**. "My first holiday at a Warners Holiday Camp on the Isle of Wight. Elton John and Kiki Dee always on the radio. Brotherhood of Man winning the Eurovision and singing 'Kisses For Me' in the playground with a few other girls."

Tracey Bryant worked for the same company. "Went to work at Warners holiday camp with my best mate summer of '76, to see if we liked it, her elder sister worked there and arranged our accommodation in return for working. Best summer ever, staff parties, creeping past guest chalets to get to staff quarters, nobody in their own rooms, great fun, great memories - a summer of firsts."

Enviously there were those for whom it was a living. Imagine being on holiday every week, meeting new people, enjoying new company and new banter - and getting paid for it. **Janet Hanmer** was a redcoat at Bognor back in 1976, while 18-year-old **Ann Orford** was at the Pontins resort at Pakenham, Suffolk [*Pakefield? - Ed.*]. "There was so many ladybirds people were going around with paper bags on their heads," she remembers.

One or two contributors may actually have passed by me as I walked along the Kent seafront, or watched TOTP with me in that crowded hotel room. **Kate Barnes** reports: "Went to Cliftonville with my best friend. Lovely holiday, we both came back well tanned to using baby oil. People who had been abroad had had not so good weather."

And **Karl Senior** was in the same part of the world. "We went on holiday to Margate that summer by Golden Rail. I was 10, I remember the sand was so hot you couldn't stand on it."

DESTINATIONS

As we've seen, what are now called "staycations" were the rule rather the exception in 1970s' Britain. Usually, but by no means always, this would have involved a trip to the coast. And a week, rather than a fortnight, was probably the most popular amount of time to spend away from home. But sticks of rock and sandcastles invoke memories every bit as powerful as paella and pina coladas, and this is evidenced by the fact that so many can still look back with fondness upon them more than forty years later.

Liz Gormally went to Wales for a holiday in the summer of '76 after having moved up from the juniors to senior school. So did **Robina Jones**, whose family stayed in Anglesey, other than her elder sister who took her first holiday abroad in Spain and returned, much to her obvious chagrin, with a paler tan. **Glennis Kearns** went to Rhyl for two weeks, only to find that all her plants had withered and died when she returned home. Six-year-old **Ang Warner** meanwhile went to Great Yarmouth in Suffolk with mum and dad and fell asleep in the sun, with painful consequences, as well as being diagnosed with hay fever whilst away. Up in Skegness **Maureen Barnes** had to take a four-mile walk to her resort in Ingoldmells whilst carrying her suitcase, and was "burnt to a crisp" for her sins. And **Kevin James** was in Skeggy too, thoroughly enjoying a fortnight in the family caravan - though they came home to a storm. But for **Sue Farndell** her ten days in Cornwall were spent in thick sea fog, and it was cold despite being July. In the same area of the world, the appropriately-initialled **GG** had a similar experience: "Working in horse racing I remember it was mostly cancelled because the ground was too hard through July and August. Three months of beautifully hot cloudless days then we packed the car for our two families to go on holiday to Cornwall on September 11th and it started raining and didn't stop for two whole weeks."

In fact Cornwall seems to have been one of the favoured boltholes for '76 holidaymakers. **Paul Milner** was fifteen and had a fantastic two weeks there. "Typically Tropical were at No.1 with 'Barbados' [*Hmm, wasn't that '75? - Ed.*]. A great summer that year."

Jay_wee too: "I had just started college and went on my last holiday to Bude with Mum and Dad. I went on the Radio One Roadshow with Noel Edmunds and won Bits and Pieces after a tie break. I got a Radio One t-shirt and an album which I remember had DLT and another DJ doing a take on Convoy 10/4 Rubber Ducky."

Another tourist heading for the delights of Kernow was **David Clarke**: "Went on holiday to a cottage in Cornwall with my parents and younger siblings. I had just completed my second year at university. I remember crab sandwiches in the pub for lunch and that is where I first encountered scrumpy cider. There was also a teach yourself modern Greek book in the cottage and I read that a bit. I took it up later and can now read it with a dictionary and have visited Greece quite a few times. The temperature in Greece sometimes reminds me of the heat of that summer in Cornwall."

Diane Jackson left school in 1976 and set off to Cornwall for two weeks for "the best weather ever and holiday".

And **JR** was another who opted for a Cornish break, when she eventually managed to get there: "I was married, with 3 boys, in '76. I worked as an assistant head cook in a teaching college. The weather was wonderful, but very hot in the kitchen. For our 1st family holiday we went to Looe in Cornwall. Sun, sea sandy beaches, never know what's in front of you. On the road down to Cornwall there was a long line of traffic. Husband getting sick of slow moving cars in front of us, he shouts out of window: 'Hey mate is this the road to Cornwall?' Car in front puts his arm out, saying yes, husband said 'well bloody move over and give us a bit'."

Rich James didn't quite get as far as Cornwall, but who needed to? "In 1976 got my first real job. I remember driving to work at 6.00 am and the office I worked in near Slough had no air conditioning and would reach 90 degrees by 11.00 am. I do remember a wonderful week's holiday with my folks in Devon. I had just bought a P6 Rover and we drove down on the old A30 as my Mum's family came from near Salisbury. Visited relatives in Axminster and then drove down to Kingsbridge. The weather was stunning. Devon with 7 days of solid sunshine and blue skies with sea breezes. The relatives and my folks are all gone now but will never forget that holiday and that wonderful summer."

Ireland was also a popular destination for many. **Eileen J. McCormick** recalls: "I was 25, had a few weeks in county Cork, Eire, with my kids n my parents and two young sisters. Got great memories of that year, as my mum lives near the sea, I got tanned and could not sleep for days as my back was so tanned and painful."

And **Anne Callinan** has some fond recollections of the Emerald Isle too: "I turned 15 in July 1976. Went on holiday to Ireland. Every day was full of sunshine, happiness and laughter. Danced to 'Dancing Queen' by ABBA and 'Don't Go Breaking My Heart' by Elton John and Kiki Dee. The tarmac melted on the roads from the heat and we were invaded by ladybirds! The heat was intense but bearable, it didn't rain for months."

Of course other destinations were popular too. **Karen Usher** holidayed at Minehead in Somerset with her friend. **Peter Jones** enjoyed a great vacation on the Isle of Man.

Liz O'Reilly has vivid memories of her family holiday as a twelve-year-old in Whitby. "There had been a massive invasion of ladybirds due to the heat and they were attracted to anything white - I mean WHOLE buildings were covered in them. I remember my Grandma sitting on a chair on Tate Hill Pier in a white cardigan and we watched as waves of ladybirds flew in over the water, making a beeline for her as they hit land! She was absolutely crawling with them, it was hilarious to me back then, Grandma obviously didn't see the funny side, I didn't know an old person could run that fast!"

Teresa Shearing and her family had their own caravan and they took advantage of the good weather, taking it to Sussex. "I had my lovely boy, he was just past 1. My mother in law died aged 63 and we inherited half a new house, so we sold our little terrace and with the inheritance moved to a village. It was so hot everyday, we had already bought a caravan and we spent 16 days by the sea in Wittering. It was a lovely year to be by the sea."

"We were on a caravan holiday in Pagham, Sussex," recalls **Lorraine Johns**. "I was 6 years old, nearly 7. We got up one morning, opened the caravan door, to find our caravan literally covered with thousands of ladybirds."

Maria Tamilia made the journey from Wales to Andover, but events took an unfortunate turn: "We were on our summer holidays at auntie Ray's and uncle Benny's in Andover (we'd travelled from Pembrokeshire, west Wales). My mum was 6 months pregnant with my youngest sister and we all went to the Lions of Longleat for the day. We were having a fantastic time. My parents thought it would be 'fun' to put me and my younger sister on the donkeys for a ride. I fell off. I broke my arm and also fractured it and ended up in Winchester hospital, flat on my back, with my arm in traction for 4 long, very hot weeks. I will never forget it!"

Joanne Marshall relays an interesting tale from her stay in Suffolk: "Had my first holiday in Great Yarmouth in a flat at the back of the Windmill Theatre and got excited as I'd seen a Womble going through the stage door, lol. Spent the whole week on the beach then when we got back home in Chesterfield had to use the stand pipes to fill up buckets and pans as there was a drought. Spent hours playing outside, brilliant summer."

Susan Simpson was away in Great Yarmouth too. "Ladybirds everywhere, spoilt outside swimming unless you wanted a mouthful. Plastered children in sunscreen. Not me, said ex hubby, and got badly burnt. Served him right."

Her 1976 summer holiday was just one of many lasting memories from that year for young **Susan Kane**. "I was 10 years old that year - I recall holidaying in Crief (near Stirling!). I remember David Wilkie winning Olympic gold for the breast stroke. I bought my first ever album - 'Off the Wall' by Michael Jackson [*Hmm - Ed*]. I also bought my first ever tennis racket and played tennis in a nearby park. There was a local river that had a small section ringed off to swim in. Heat, water - good to remember."

Fifteen-year-olds **Andy Green** and his friend initially booked into a youth hostel in the Lake District. "The weather was so good that we cancelled the hostels and slept rough! Fab times hitching around and swimming in the lakes in our jeans that would dry on us in an hour! Great times!"

They may have bumped into **Sarah Hague** on their travels: "I remember watching the Olympic Games which were in Montreal that summer. We were on holiday in the Lake District and Nadia Comăneci scored perfect 10s. It was a rare week of perfect Lake District sunshine too!"

Donna Mills was only seven, but she remembers staying at California Cliffs near Great Yarmouth. "Stayed in 'Dunsailin', a little cottage opposite the chip shop just up from the beach. Loved it - we stayed often, ladybirds covering the front window sills and wall."

Judith Turner though got more than she bargained for by the sea in Lincolnshire: "I went to Chapel St. Leonards with the family and made the mistake of wearing a very fetching bright yellow suit on a trip to the beach, and got absolutely covered in ladybirds!"

There are happy memories of Blackpool from **Julie Davis**: "Stayed at a hotel in Blackpool, where they served morning, afternoon and supper time tea and biscuits... I remember wanting to stay there forever lol.... the music was great then too."

"I was 20 and me and my boyfriend spent two weeks camping in Hayling Island, one of my best holidays ever," reminisces **Francesca Moore**.

Geoff Marshall went to Devon before returning for his last year of school. Garry Appleby got sunburnt on his canal boat holiday. But there was very little sun up north right at the start of the season, as **Jennifer Pape** recalls: "We holidayed in Yorkshire, May bank holiday, and had snow. Travelled back to London late at night after the one sunny day we had had up there... the start of the long hot summer. We also later travelled from London to Oxford to collect a trailer tent. Lovely cool ride back down the M1 with all the car windows open."

There was snow for **Julie Archer** too: "I was going on holiday on a barge, it snowed on the Monday on Saturday it was our first day by the way. This was in June, it was the first week of the very hot summer - we had a great holiday."

What seems so noticeable about 1976 is that the memories seem overwhelmingly to be good ones, often even in adversity. No regrets about choosing the wrong month, getting sunburnt, being attacked by swarms of insects or trials and tribulations involving less than reliable transport. 1976 overcame all. No wonder they say it was the best year to be alive.

HOLIDAYS ABROAD

Nevertheless, in spite of the exceptional weather at home many were already experiencing the liberating delights of the overseas vacation. **Dorothy Burridge Johnston** saved up all year for what was to be her first foreign holiday, a ten-day stay in Lloret de Mar, Spain. Sadly it rained for most of the holiday. **Linda Roach** also took her first holiday abroad in Spain, and thoroughly enjoyed the sun despite the fact that by that time it was warmer at home. And amazingly, **Liz Wood** also has a similar tale to tell, albeit with a sad postscript: "1976 was the year I went on holiday abroad for the first time with my boyfriend to Minorca. We went in early June and had a wonderful time. When we got back it was hotter here than in Minorca. I had a dark brown tan from June to September (this is the era of basking in the sun, dark tans being the height of fashion). I remember visiting Blackpool and the plague of ladybirds and getting bitten by them. The standpipes in the street for water, parched fields, lawns. People moaning is it hot or is it me! I loved it. Wearing halter neck tops and short skirts and wedge sandals. Those days are long gone I'm afraid now. Halcyon days, 1977 saw me married to my boyfriend and we were married for 38 years until he passed away aged 60."

Spain, always popular in the Anglosphere even in those days, was the destination of choice for **Linda Turnbull** too, and she made an acquaintance that will be the envy of many. "My husband and I went to Spain on our summer vacation and visited the Salvador Dali museum we were lucky enough to meet him on that day, a day I will never forget."

Paul Brendan McGuire enjoyed the freedom of a round-Europe trip on his Honda 750 motorcycle.

There was heat of a different kind for **Christine Steinegger** who went on an epic six-week school minibus trip to Greece and found herself caught up in a local uprising. **Alan Patrick** was there as well: "I remember my Ford Cortina used to overheat in the London traffic. It had a pathetic 2 blade fan which wasn't up to the job. Went to Greece and Crete on holiday and it was as hot in London when we returned as it was in Athens. The government appointed a Minister for Drought, Dennis Howell I think. He said that it would have to rain until Christmas and, as soon as he was appointed, it started raining!"

Eileen Hardie was too. "Went to Crete on the magic bus... stayed in Matala like in the Joni Mitchell song. Had very little money, slept in caves under the stars and on beaches, hung out for 3 weeks singing on the beach all day and drinking cheap retsina and ouzo. Hitched back with hardly any money left... it took a week. It was cool."

It was sunny Spain for **Jackie Corcoran**. "I was 13 - went on holiday to Benidorm with my best friend Claire and our mums. Funniest week ever. Wore red espadrilles and denim boiler suit and Hamilton Bohannon's 'Disco Stomp' was playing everywhere. Magical and exciting times!"

Anne Davies went abroad for her camping holiday. "1976 was the first year we towed a caravan to the west coast of France, on the Arcachon Basin. Whilst there we joined in the local Oyster Festival... great fun. Two bask bands played in competition and we were encouraged to follow one. Our band played a very catchy tune with a silly little flap your arms type dance, which we all threw ourselves into.... it was a real laugh. On our return to GB, that week on Top of the Pops our tune was played.... yes it was the 'Birdie Song'. Our kids were so excited and we will always remember the fun of that Oyster Festival in France!"

Of course even then there were those who managed to get away to more exotic locations. **Jeni Hall**, for instance. "I graduated from the Oxford Polytechnic with an HND in Hotel and Catering Administration. Worked as a chef during that hot Summer! Went on holiday to Jamaica for 5 weeks in October. Disillusioned by the job market in the UK, I left to work in Sweden. I was 21."

And **Roy Wright**, letting his hair down after a period of gruelling active service. "I was 19 and in the Army, we started off that year with a tour in N. Ireland however my mates and I made up for it after with a holiday in the Caribbean and did we party! We ended up staying a further week. Happy days."

Ali Dee Clarke got to visit the States in that special year for Americans. "I still remember that glorious hot summer well. Just out and about with family and friends. Went to Chatsworth House in Derbyshire one weekend. It was so hot, nearly everyone was cooling their feet in the stream that runs through there. I also went to stay with some relatives near San Francisco for just under a month. It was magical. Fantastic music too. I loved 1976."

Perhaps one of the most descriptive recollections of all, bizarrely, comes from a young lady who was just ten at the time. This is **Allison Findlay**'s story of a holiday that will surely live with her forever: "I was 10 years old and it was a summer of firsts for me. We went on a months long holiday to Toronto. We flew from Heathrow and while waiting to board the plane, I got to see Concorde for the first time. There was a man in the line who was picked up by security for trying to smuggle his racing pigeon on board under his coat. When we took off, we were served Filet Mignon with real plates, knives and forks. A world of difference from airline meals now. I got to see inside the cockpit. In Toronto I got to swim in Lake Ontario and lay on the ground to look up at the massive CN tower which had just been completed. I got my first Barbie, saw Niagara Falls and watched a trucker pour maple syrup over his mile high stack of pancakes and sausages. All in all, heady stuff for a 10 year old."

SNAPSHOTS OF LIFE

Here a few accounts of everyday life in 1976 which will hopefully give something of a flavour of the carefree spirit which prevailed:

"Thirteen in the summer of 1976 and moving into adolescence, most people remember the heat and the water shortages but we still had water fights in the street using bottles or hose pipes. I had started to take an interest in music which at the time was very ABBA and Showaddywaddy but I had started seeing punk in indie record shops in Manchester, though not so much the UK but more of the stuff coming in from the States like the Ramones. Also northern soul and heavy rock had a big impact on me.

"We were freezing everything we could to make lollipops, money was tight and the political scene was changing with strikes and the rise of the National Front. We were not that long after the 3 day week and power cuts of 1973 and that had impacted on me so much that I was determined to make my mark on the world.

"Cycled to Blackpool that summer from Wythenshawe in Manchester with just a map and saddle bag with some clothes. Went with a mate and stayed at my auntie's. Can't imagine letting my daughter do that when she was that age.

"Also found girls and started riding motorbikes on the fields that year. Convinced my mum to buy me a moped for my 14th birthday in November. Rode it on the fields. Still enough of the kid in me that year and went collecting bonfire wood but went to the builders' yards rather than house to house and they delivered trailers full of used wood to our house. My mum went mad. That was also the year I got caught giving the girls across the road gin from my mum and dad's bar. My sisters still laugh at me now.

"Flares and platform shoes and started styling my hair that year as well.

"And finally that was the year where I started buying and selling bicycles and working in a car spares shop which set the direction for my working life. By the end of 1976 I was playing with cars. My friend and I got caught driving a Vauxhall Victor 101 by the police. My friend told his mum and got in a lot of trouble. I didn't tell mine."

Geoff Davies

"That was the seemingly endless summer recalled with the hearing of Elton John and Kiki Dee at no.1. 'Summer Breeze/Harvest For the World' by the Isley Brothers also in the charts. I can remember for the first time ever sleeping in the back garden on a camp bed with just my jim jams and one light blanket.

"The water shortage that followed and the alleged rain-dancers brought in by the government to alleviate the drought. Sure enough and days later, remember running an errand for my Mum in Harrow when the skies just opened up. My cousin and I were absolutely drenched but revelling in the much needed rain. People actually coming out of their houses delighted at this much-needed and nearly forgotten weather.

"Monty Modlyn on the Today programme with an expert demonstrating how we could all benefit from using a mere pint of water per day for washing purposes. How the memories come flooding back. Pardon the pun."

Steve Fisher, Harrow

"1976 was my first year of marriage. I learnt how to iron shirts properly and put one crease down trousers. Just laid turf when drought began. Made tubing from bath's down-pipe to the lawn, to water it.

"A surprise holiday, for first anniversary, staying in a pub at Coverack. Water was restricted, people queued at the pump with jugs. Met many local people who shared their water supply. The whole village, including ourselves, walked across the fields to the neighbouring village, for a hog roast, drinks and dancing. Later in the week, Coverack held their own festival. The two villages held a tournament. It was in fancy dress, and held in the harbour. Teams swam across the bay, pillow fights on a slippery pole, etc. A good time had by all despite the excessive heat.

"For our anniversary, we went to the local restaurant, Barbara's. A wonderful meal of Tornado Rossini and fresh fruit salad. As a surprise, our host baked us a cake.

"Every morning, when we looked out of our bedroom window, we watched the seals in the bay. On the day we left, the heavens opened and it rained for the whole journey home. Now 44 years later, we are still married, have three grown children and return to Cornwall frequently.

"The other memory that sticks in my mind for that year - my husband had never planted potatoes before. When I got home, it looked like a cemetery, with huge mounds of earth at the bottom of the garden. He didn't realise you were supposed to build it up as the plant grew. Come Autumn, we were the only people (local) who had a good harvest of potatoes. Who would believe it?"

Lynda Joyce Tucker

TOO HOT TO WORK?

An industrious people doesn't allow a little thing like an unprecedented heatwave to come between it and its endeavours. Many of our contributors wrote in to give us a helpful overall picture of working life in Britain in 1976.

Possibly one of the worst places that anybody could ever wish to work during the intense heat of that summer would be in an iron foundry, but **Geoff Arnold** did just that throughout. "No rules about being too hot, 7.30 till 17.00 - and overtime."

Sharron Green was picking tomatoes, under glass! **Ricki Handford** and his workmates at his factory in Leamington Spa took things into their own hands and walk out around midday because it was too hot to carry on. **Michelle Cahill** was sent home from her work in London too. As she points out, there was no air conditioning in those days.

And **Kevin Chapman** has a related, not to mention amusing story: "I remember that was the year that I started work in a factory, it was so hot a mate and I decided to bunk off for a while to get in some sunbathing. There was a meadow at the back of the factory with very long grass so no one could see you. After a while, I looked at my watch and to my horror found that we were missing lunch break. We got up to go when we heard a voice asking what the time was. When we looked around dozens of heads were popping up everywhere, I am not sure who was left working the machines but everyone had a good tan. Happy days."

Steve Miller went one further and quit his job entirely. "I was 18/19 and I quit my job to spend the entire summer at Danson Park Lido in Bexleyheath, Kent. So many girls, the best time of my life."

Bill Dumbleton had been working for the London Fire Brigade for two years but this was the first time he'd seen fires breaking out everywhere due to the weather. Even the brigade's own vehicles were overheating and breaking down in numbers, so much so that the armed forces and their Green Goddesses were deployed to make up the numbers. **Paul Clarke** too reports having had to go from fire to fire almost without cessation due to the intense sun. And **Ray Collier** was clocking up the overtime tending to fires for up to eighteen hours a day.

Chris was in the same line of business: "Spent that summer with the fire brigade. It was a very busy and hectic time with crews often working double shifts to maintain a modicum of fire cover. We had open plains, forests and many farms in our area in the south and we got used to having visiting appliances based in the fire station providing cover as all ours were out near enough 24/7. During that period we got a call to attend a chip pan fire in a house on a council housing estate a few miles from the station. The only appliance we had available to attend was a pump unit from London, of course in LFB markings. When the crew turned up at the address, the elderly lady whose house it was took one look at the appliance and stood with her arms folded blocking the gate. Her comment was: 'You're not local from the town fire station, you're not coming in'. Three of the crew lifted her up and moved her out of the way to loud protests while the rest of the crew went inside to extinguish the small fire. Some people!"

Fellow fireman **John Megan Edwards** found himself on the horns of a maybe predictable dilemma: "I was a firefighter out every watch on grass, heathland and moorland fires. When we went to a 'normal' fire had to try to conserve water."

An ice-cream factory might seem a much better place to working in the circumstances. Let's hear from **Jan Topping**: "Had my first full time job working at Walls ice cream factory. We couldn't keep up with the demands of the hot weather, as you could imagine I was waiting to go and train as a nurse and did this job throughout the summer. We worked half an hour on packing then half an hour on filling, then half an hour off on break. We used to go outside and sit on the lawn - we could eat as much ice cream as we wanted and those bloody ladybirds - everywhere was covered and I remember the stand pipes going to get water. It was the first year I never had a holiday, was saving all my money for when I was training. We used to go to Tiffany's night club on a Saturday night, we had a great time. Also we'd go to the local pub with the boys and have a game of darts or just sit in the beer garden."

The construction game can't have been much fun either, as **John Parry** confirms. "I was working on a building site and lost 3 stone in weight - God, could do with some help now. I remember the pubs running out of beer, boy was it a hot one or what? Never to see the likes of that again I feel. all that said and done we never ran out of water where I lived."

Paul Brooks was also in the building trade: "Building a housing estate in Brandon. Suntanned and needed drivers' licence before being able to sign on the dole in the winter after finishing the job."

John Watson was doing it too, but he had an extra role to play: "Me and two other labourers turned up on a new site. One Monday, in April 1976, we were going to be building (surfacing) a very large storage area. The ganger pointed to a road roller (steamroller) and asked if any of us could drive it. The other two showed no interest, so I said give me half an hour's practice. I climbed in. There was no ignition key. I had to literally walk around the site looking for something that would fit. A large nail, bent and flattened, got the job done. So there was me playing around in this big slow thing thinking aye aye, I've got a cushy job here. I spent all of that hot summer inside that thing. The exhaust pipe came up through the floor and out of the roof, so it was like having the heating on, and in a greenhouse on those sweltering days. I must've lost quite a bit of weight, but I never checked. Anyway, no proper health and safety, and no tickets, or training required. I've never driven one since."

"Worked as a chambermaid in the mornings, spent every afternoon on the beach and every evening in Margate pubs," **Julie Bell** remembers fondly.

Farm work was also something of a challenge in the sweltering heat, as **Chris Nicholson** found out. "I passed my driving test. Worked on the farm during the hottest hardest hay time and harvest I can remember, The ground was that dry and hard even the plough wouldn't work."

It wasn't fun for everyone on the farm, however. **Sara Jonas**' then husband was a farmer and she remembers the crops being dry. And sadly it got worse: "He had a very bad accident because he was on the too of a trailer full of hay. Because it was so dry, the load slipped and he came down with it, causing injury to the back of his head. He was blue lighted to hospital and was in intensive care."

I can't think of a more lucrative line of business to have been in that year than **Peter Boseley**'s : "Summer of '76 1 was building swimming pools - the most we had done, 20 pools in one year. No holiday that year, tan was ok though."

Encouraged by her parents to seek gainful employment and not hang around at home doing nothing, **Mandy Brown** left school on Friday 25th June 1976 and was at work on Monday. **Kim Roberts** did the same, but missed the fun in the sun and wished she's stayed on at school. Another who didn't hang around was **Tim Shaw**. "Living in Devon, did my O-Levels and got a job working in the kitchen of a steak house. Got my first moped and remember the lines of traffic as the M5 hadn't been finished. One of the greatest summers."

Heather Irvine determined from the start that she was going to be a high flyer: "It was the year I started as an air hostess! Thought all my birthdays had come at once.... it was such fun!"

Also starting out on a new career path was **Judith Marshall**. "Came home from holiday and on 5th July started work for a firm of Sale Hill & Davenport, solicitors. I left in 1987 to have my first daughter. Worked there on and off for the next few years covering holidays, illness etc. Went back permanent part-time in 1998, continuing working for the same solicitor when we merged with another firm in 2003 and stayed there until 2019."

And **William McBride**: "I'd left school and just started my apprenticeship as a baker. We still had a tourist industry on the Isle of Man then and was enjoying long summer days on the beach and promenade, some of the best days of my life."

Tina Henley was also just starting out. "I started work in Woolworth's, Oxford Street. When I got my first pay packet I went straight into Ravel shoe shop and bought the shoes I had wanted for ages, my first decent pair I actually had, and I was so pleased with myself that I bought them myself, as almost most of my shoes were cheap ones my mum bought from Curtess shoe shop. I spent nearly all my wages on them shoes, but I thought they were worth it, and still do."

David Jones left school and joined the GPO. "Uniform was horrendous in that glorious summer. Fantastic year."

And **Garry Steel** was on the post too: "I was 22 and working as a postman, and had to be up at 4.30am. It was so hot at night, for about 4 weeks I slept every night on the garden swing. Woke every morning just as it was getting light feeling very fresh, unlike my fellow workers!"

Kevin James worked underground at Darfield Main in what must have been unusually uncomfortable conditions. **John Debbage** took up his first job after leaving college. "No summer holiday as I had just started. It was a plant that baked electrical components. I was in an office at the side but it was stifling, fortunately there was an open air pool nearby. I went before work, lunchtime, and after work. The water surface was covered in ladybirds."

Another who recalls the insect invasion was **Alan Hurst**. "I was working in Laing's offshore rig yard in Hartlepool as a welder and remember all the handrails on the scaffolding being covered with the ladybirds. We didn't dare use them in case we hurt them."

Mick Short can remember that summer clearly. "I was working on a motorway driving a bulldozer with no cab I can distinctly remember taking the wife and kids to the seaside one evening and I was the brownest man on the beach or shall I say the most sunburnt."

One of the more consequences of the drought of course was that reservoirs and rivers actually started to dry up. The fish of Kent had cause to be particularly grateful to **Michael Powsey**: "During the hot summer of 1976 I was working with the Environment Agency, my team's task was to rescue fish from the rivers that were drying up and take the fish to local lakes. Area was Kent. Main river affected was the Darent."

John Lambton had something of a baptism of fire in his new vocation. "First year in the police at Notting Hill Carnival, dustbin lids at the ready."

One inevitable consequence of the heat was that it was bound to expose any shortcomings in personal hygiene. **Helen Pariser Hubbers** opened a clothes boutique that year and remembers many of her lady customers not wearing deodorant. **Margaret Morgan** left school, took a fortnight's holiday and then began work with S.R. Gent, then one of the biggest suppliers to Marks & Spencer. **Rosemary Johnson** was living in a commune in Aylesbury, and began work at the local employment office which required her first to attend a six-week training course in Reading. **Margaret Bull** meanwhile began to train as a teacher.

1976 was a year of many new adventures for **Debs Wright**: "Long hot summer! Left college, went to work for British Airways at Victoria Terminal the following week. Ran away from home to get married in November. Hung out with punks and all sorts. King's Road and World's End, my stomping ground. Great times!"

They were exciting times too for **Jeff Dingsdale**. "Started a new chapter in my life - new town. Started work in a steelworks at seventeen, being left at home rest of the family on holiday. Remember the alarm clock melting in the heat. Going to watch Manchester City play home and away, money in my pocket for new clothes, listening to my cassette player and buying records by Rod Stewart and Marc Bolan."

Sharing could be daring in the heatwave and drought, as **Susan Norris** recounts: "My first summer as a married woman, worked ridiculous hours as a PA, burnt my shoulders going to the sandwich shop and came every evening and we shared a bath, an inch and a half deep, even eating our dinner in there."

Russ Allen was working at the funfair and ended up with sunstroke. **Kay Streatfield** was a house mother at "a boarding school for naughty boys" and spent her summer holidays working at the Guildford Lido. **Norma Wood** had a pub and remembers the water coming in stand pipes. **Kathleen Pethers** moved from High Wycombe to Corby in 1976 as her husband had a job teaching at Kingswood Comprehensive.

Andrew Watton was on the move too. "Changed jobs in February which involved moving from Worcestershire to Bristol. Many memories including the end of my first relationship and sharing a vicarage with a curate and an engineer from the BBC in Whiteladies Road (famous for wildlife programmes)."

One would have thought the Middle East would have been riskier in the sun than back home in Blighty, but not according to **Stuart Davies**: "I was in Saudi Arabia working as a diver on contract to Aramco. Came home on leave and got burnt - different heat."

It's the music that brings back the memory for **Peter Westenberg**: "Just finished school and went to work at an agricultural college in Plumpton, Sussex. It was a hot summer and the radio was playing the new hit from ABBA called 'Money, Money, Money'."

And then there's this beautiful, heartfelt, happy-ever-after testimony from **Carl Ambridge**: "I was working at my first job, in an office of all things, because if you knew me you'd know I'm not the office type. I opened an account at a new bank and fell in love with a cute red haired teller. I was flirting with her every time I was in there and working up the nerve to ask her out. So on a Saturday night while out at a bar with my buddies, guess who was sitting two seats away. This year was our forty first anniversary. Don't let anyone tell you there's no such thing as love at first sight."

John Hull fell in love through work too, and there's a photo to prove it (right). "I had just finished my Engineering apprenticeship, at Chance Brothers, then made redundant in '76. Then a few months later, in September, married my girlfriend Karen, whom I met at Chance's."

And **Jim Philipsz** happened upon the girl of his dreams as well, although we don't know how that one ended: "Left school for the 2nd time in July at 16 years; wasted some time with chores, pubs, girls, chillin' with friends and enjoying the music of the day, especially Bellamy Bros' 'Let Your Love Flow', which I love and have asked to have played at my funeral. Started work on 20th September for UK Civil Service from which I have some good and bad memories including falling in love at 17 with my floor messenger Doris who had beautiful long red hair."

Brian McAfee overcame all obstacles to secure his job in '76: "I went to a job interview ten miles away when my car got a puncture. Luckily enough there was a taxi rank nearby and I asked it to take me, but found that I didn't have enough money for the fare so I asked him to drop me off when the money ran out. I was a smoker in those days and when I arrived I found I had left my cigarettes in the car. At the interview I had decided the day was a write-off and my concentration was on a packet of cigarettes in front of my interviewer, which he eventually offered me one. I then had to walk home and retrieve my car. I got the job."

Meanwhile **Irene Langley** reports: "I was at Montreal as a mothers' help had an awesome time. The Montreal Olympics was on, it was brilliant. Made good friends."

The hospitality industry has always strong the author as a great one in which to work, and never would this have been more so than during that glorious summer. **Brenda Cross** started work at the select Savoy Hotel in London, which she describes as "a fantastic experience." **Peter Farmer Giles Sludden** was employed at the Grand Hotel in Llandudno, and got married on 10th September - "the day the rains came". **Jean Clifton** started driving lessons in '76 and worked in a hotel as a chambermaid, a job which **Susan Shields** also did: "I had just finished my GCE O-levels and I had a summer job, working as a chambermaid at a seaside hotel in North Wales. It was a gloriously hot summer and I had a fantastic time before returning to school to start my A-level studies."

But not everyone has fond memories of working in the heat of 1976. **JS** takes a different view of things: "I remember '76 as the worst kind of weather. I do not like it too hot and that was too hot. I was working on the old racecourse track in Lower Kersal so was subjected to the heat every day. Getting up every morning looking wistfully to the sky for dark clouds.. only seeing blue. Not a summer I enjoyed at all."

CARRY ON MATRON

Okay, the film was made in 1972. But it would seem from our contributions that in '76 hospitals and health centres were still a place that a whole lot of people wanted to work. Here are just a few people who were plying their trade in medicine during that year:

Gill Lane began her nursing career in 1976 as a seventeen-year-old. She was at an orthopaedic hospital in Rhydlafar, Cardiff. **Gillian Stella Bufton**, then 22, graduated as a Registered Nurse at the then Guest Hospital in Dudley. **Virginia Farrell** was in her second year of nursing training at Southampton University Hospital. She qualified as an SRN the following year. Also in her second year was **Carol Evans**, who was in St. Albans. "I was on nights along with several of my student colleagues and as it was too hot to sleep inside during the day, we decided that at least we could sunbathe on the grass outside. As far as I can remember we didn't have sun cream, resulting in very tired sunburnt student nurses on nights that night."

Elaine Marshall remembers: "I was a newly married 21-year-old working as a student nurse. We upped and moved to Somerset, away from friends and family in Sunderland, Tyne and Wear. We moved for a cleaner, better lifestyle to start out life journey together. Never regretted it."

Kath Thompson was undergoing "nurse training at Frenchay Hospital in Bristol. On nights all through the hot summer. 4 nights on, 3 nights off for 12 weeks. Made lifelong friends."

And **Sue Whyte** has an equally interesting story to tell: "I was two years into working as a social work assistant at Bolton General Hospital. Sat outside in the sun every lunchtime with the phone put through the office window to answer as our manager was a lazy cow. Applied to Manchester University to do my social work qualification and started there the following year. Happy days. Stayed a social worker until my early retirement after 37 years."

Robin Lawrenson was undertaking ambulance training but ended up requiring the services of his colleagues. He takes up the story: "I was on my ambulance training course in Cheshire, May 1976. After we beat the local police at football, I started showing off on my motorbike - and went through a leaded window wearing only shorts. So, full-leg plaster from May-September, and wooden crutches, throughout the hottest summer I had ever known. Oh, the itching. They got me a stool in the local pub - a 2 mile hobble - even though I was a bit underage. I even chatted up a girl there. Triumph over adversity!"

It was very hot working inside all the time, recalls **Kevin Creasey**, who had just left school and was working as a domestic at Cuckfield Hospital. Things were probably worse still for **Theresa Quinlan-Britton**, who had to commute every day to University College Hospital on the underground.

Lorraine Elliott was new to the job, and what an initiation. "Newly qualified nurse working in the operating theatres of a London hospital, top floor with floor to ceiling windows which ran the entire length of one wall. What with the big high density lights we had to work under (no halogen then) and the huge windows we were dropping like flies, I don't think I have ever been so hot in my entire life... and our feet were so swollen by the end of our shift we couldn't get our shoes on."

And **Val Fieth** was working in nursing too. "1976 one year into Welwyn Garden City. Two daughters, 2 and 5 - at school and nursery. Staff Nurse at QEII hospital. First NHS hospital 1948? Now destroyed and houses built."

Kathleen Dean enjoyed the heat, even if her make-up was a casualty. "Second year student nurse on pediatrics. Hot sticky days and hot sticky nights. Prefab nurses home. So hot that when you put make up on we had to rush out of the home before it melted. A great year."

According to **Lyn Craddock**, there were no special favours for the medical profession where the drought was concerned. "We were threatened with stand pipes if we didn't reduce water consumption. I was a nurse struggling in a hot hospital."

Then as now, our nurses, doctors and others in the medical profession were a credit to their profession and to our country, and we owe them a huge debt of gratitude for keeping us all safe and healthy.

SERVICE IN THE SUN

There are of course others too whose unyielding service to the nation we take for granted. Many of our contributors joined or were already active in the armed forces in 1976, and some of those fine people shared their memories with us:

Chris Ayley has a fascinating if little-known fact to share with us, from his own experience working with a highly specialised unit. "Doing my military training in the Intelligence Corps. Funnily enough during the hot summer it was a chargeable offence to not take your salt pills every day. People were fainting on the drill square."

Thomas Strutt was involved in the Cod War, up in Iceland, for the second time. Also at sea was **Kevin Brett**, who witnessed the demise of a Ton-class minesweeper which had been on its way to an official visit in Hamburg: "Sadly, my abiding memory of 1976 was witnessing the collision and sinking of HMS Fittleton, September 20th, while serving on HMS Mermaid."

Meanwhile on shore, **Peter Sellars** was serving with the Royal Engineers in Hameln, West Germany. And **Wendy Chapman Aû**'s family were in Germany too: "In 1976 I was 7 years old and living in Verden, Germany. My dad was serving in the British Army. I remember the seemingly endless summer school holidays, long sunny days when me and my friends would be out all day on our bicycles, only returning home for lunch, a cold drink or sometimes ice-pops and choc ices."

Also in the army was **Jan Mitchell**, whose duties led her to miss the British summer: "I was in the army and was selected to be one of three women to join 117 soldiers on the first exchange trip to Australia and New Zealand for four months. I went to New Zealand only to discover it was their winter! I couldn't believe it, first time I knew of a British heatwave and I wasn't there."

At seventeen **Chris Pennington** joined the Army. "The summer was hot with hosepipe bans," he recalls.

The end of **Bex Reddy**'s father's military career meant a move away from the Cavalry Barracks in my own stamping ground of Hounslow to Hindley, near Wigan, where he became a bus driver. "Me, I was 2 at this point... but I do remember escaping Pie Town for Croydon, South London in '78."

The other section of the British armed services of course is the air force. **Sue Fairweather-Amor** recounts: "I remember it well. I was in the WRAF, stationed at St Athan. Part of 1976 I was on nights, so during the day we use to sunbathe outside the block where we lived. Loved it."

But **Michael Wilson**, who was a Minute Man Missile tech, was processing out of the RAF at just that time.

Kevin Fellows went to live in Germany, and got himself a job with the US military at Taylor Barracks, Mannheim, making lots of friends amongst the GIs. In the 1980s he returned there as a British soldier.

SOME MORE WONDERFUL TALES

Sometimes individual accounts are so richly detailed and evocative that they need no preamble. Here are a few that I particularly liked:

"I was 24, just out of a 3 year relationship. Had friends in Canada so decided to pack my bags and bum off. I went for twelve months to work as a children's nanny. Although my friends lived in Toronto I went west to Winnipeg and had a great year although very homesick and met lots of friends. I met my best friend that year.

"Although I married when I came home and had a family, my friend stayed single. She is still my best friend and all my kids and grandchildren call her auntie. She loves this because she Has no family.

"Was introduced to ice hockey, which I loved, and if I could help it I never missed a game. Canada had a fantastic summer also so didn't miss out there. Came home 1977, met my husband 1978, married in 1979 so I suppose if asked I would have to say they were 4 good years to me. But nothing compares to having my family - three children, four grandchildren - they are our world."

Eileen Bates

"This was the year that I bought my first sailing cruiser, a Vivacity 20 named Ciau Bella. On the Saturday I entered a yacht race from New Quay on the west coast of Wales down the coast to Cardigan, where the town was hosting the 600th anniversary of the National Eisteddfod. We started off at 10.30 with a slight south westerly breeze and got up to about 4 knots. The Eclipse yachts were gradually putting ground between us, or should I say water, whereas the other slower classes were way behind.

"About an hour later the wind dropped completely and left us in the doldrums. The sea was like a mill pond. After an hour of this it was time to get the sandwiches out and kettle on, or it could have been cans, although whilst out on the Old Briny I never touched alcohol. I had a lot of respect for Davy Jones.

"All of a sudden in the middle of Cardigan Bay there was this almighty splash followed by another, causing the boat to rock. Not knowing what it was, and being a bit frightened, I decided to put the outboard on and make for the estuary leading into Cardigan itself.

"Then the splash makers showed themselves and escorted me across the bay - a school of about twenty or so dolphins weaved in and out in front of the boat and on either side. I was a bit frightened at first as they were nearly the same length of the boat, but eventually got used to their presence and company. They stayed with me up to the bar into the estuary. An experience that will stay with me for as long as I live."

Dilwyn Phillips

"One year out of my apprenticeship as an electrical fitter in Portsmouth Dockyard, I applied for a job at the electrical company of Plessey. Looking back now unbelievably for the interview I wore a cream brushed velvet jacket with wide lapels, French loons and cowboy boots. I got the job and remained at that site through many takeovers until the Covid crisis just last year, when I took voluntary redundancy as I'm only one year from retirement.

"The reason I left the Dockyard was like so many others. We contributed to a Widows and Orphans Pension Fund. This meant if you were to stay in the Dockyard and died your dependents had a little security, however if you left in the first year as a fully-fledged tradesperson all your contributions were refunded. This amounted to £400 which equated to ten weeks' wages. Most handed their job in, collected the money and restarted the following week, I however went away from refitting naval vessels and started a career in the aerospace business.

"My favourite music in 1976 would have been Supertramp, Led Zeppelin, Black Sabbath, the Rolling Stones, Pink Floyd, Caravan and Camel but I guess that says more about me than the music of the time. The local pub was a regular thing and house parties afterwards many weekends. I was twenty-one years of age and had never been abroad yet two years later went every single year."

Tony Sullivan

"1976. We were one year married in the July and had moved into our first home. We lived in a little village called Caol near Fort William. Found out we were pregnant with our first son. The excitement and wonder of what our child would look like. Fitting out our home and preparing one room for a baby.

"We celebrated our wedding anniversary at the wedding of our bridesmaid, down in the borders at Galashiels. It was a glorious July. The sun seemed to shine forever. No one knew we were pregnant as I wanted to wait. It was our secret for a few months, or so I thought. Into the third month, my mum asked if I had anything to tell her. She said their were two of me looking out of my eyes. It was time to tell everyone. Won't ever forget that summer of '76."

Lorna Drummond

"I was 10 and while it was great fun for me, for my dairy farming parents in Dorset it was harder: the tarmac on the road melted, which stuck to the cows' hooves (and my sandals!) and Dad then had to clean it off the cows, making extra work at milking time. At the same time the constant thunderstorms led to power cuts and Dad had to switch on a generator powered by his Ford tractor, in order to milk the cows, but it worked the milking machine much slower than the electric did and the milking took him twice as long.

"The ladybirds - so many ladybirds - I can remember seeing thousands of them, 5 or 6 deep in the flower beds. And there were the concerns about water shortages - we were being bombarded by adverts everywhere to be frugal with water... we were even being advised to 'Save water, bath with a friend'! Imagine saying that today! My younger sister became quite poorly with heatstroke, and everything seemed to be slower - life was languid [I am the admin of Bygone Dorset, a history and nostalgia group]."

Carole Dorran

[Carole's Facebook group can be found at https://www.facebook.com/groups/BygoneDorset – Ed.].

"My Dad was a teacher so we had nice long holidays. In August 1976 we went to visit friends in the Netherlands for 3 weeks. I will never forget the journey home. As we started to leave Dover Port, we couldn't believe how brown the countryside was. After the lush green of Holland (helped by canal irrigation), to come back to an almost unrecognisable looking Kent was nothing short of astonishing. And of course back then, no online news of the drought and no English newspapers, so we were taken completely by surprise."

Mike Lyon

"A memorable year for me. Beginning of year divorced one year with 5 year old son, feeling sorry for myself and working part time in a launderette that I enjoyed. Got flu bad in March, diagnosed with Pneumonia and ill for 3 weeks. A lovely hot summer, went on holiday in a caravan to Weymouth then came back to be told the launderette was closing and I was out of work. Got a job delivering leaflets, joined introduction agency and can remember pre-online days. Met up with a couple of dates but didn't tell, then third time lucky we met end of September - it was like electric between us, and married the following February. We had a daughter in 1978 and we now have 5 grandchildren between our son and daughter. My husband adopted my son from first marriage, still together now age 78 and 79."

Margaret Smitherman

"I was 13 and into the latest music. Had my first record player that played 45s. Platform shoes where I often went over on my ankles - the pain. Not into boys, into poaching with my dad, rabbits and pheasants. Camping at Creighton sands, climbing on rocks on the beach. I was one of a big family always into typing -

learned to type on a big old Bakelite typewriter. Had it all of a week until my brother chucked it out the window, smashing it to pieces.

"Dad worked down the pit so it was my job to shovel the coal allocation away every 3 months. Dad was a keen gardener and sold veg door to door. Only 2 dolls ever I had was a Pippa and a Tiny Tears. Used to go collecting horse muck in an old pram on Sundays for Dad's garden - got sixpence which was a lot of money then.

"Used to go to the lido, walked for miles, worked hard to earn every penny… no TV but a radiogram (posh), where dad played 33s - Frank Sinatra and the Rat Pack as well as Max Bygraves and Val Doonican. Got a TV in '77, we were envied on the street. Dad looked after all around us, helped feed many families over the years as well as down the mine for 37 years.

"We picketed on the frontline during the strike. Sundays were for family after our chores… card and board games in the afternoon or a 10-mile walk at least. 8 siblings in a tiny house all disliking each other, lots of fights but Dad let us sort it between us and if we didn't all 8 of us got a whack on the backside. We loved them days though."

Yvonne Vassall

"I was at senior school and taking my O-levels that long hot summer! I didn't do very well in them as I blamed the school for making me sit by the window, in a jacket and tie (which we were not allowed to take off). The window couldn't be opened and I cooked! Because we were taking exams, we were allowed to not be in school apart from exam days! So when not taking exams I used to be up at 5.00am, cycle 4 miles to a local farm and do strawberry picking till midday (too hot after that!). But I used to eat as many as I picked! Today I don't like strawberries that much!

"After strawberry picking I cycled back home and went in the river all afternoon! Such happy memories. Later on that year I used to go mushroom picking in a local field, early in the morning so I could pick enough for breakfast. We also used to visit my Uncle on a farm and pick horse mushrooms - they were the size of a dinner plate and 1 would fill a frying pan! Great for a breakfast, we picked so many that my Mum froze some (we had several potato sacks full of them) and had mushrooms all winter long!"

Gordon Hargest

"I was 18 and my girlfriend/fiancée was 16 on June the 26th 1976. It was a Saturday and we got the train to Withernsea from Leeds city station. When we got there the roads, cars and pavements were teaming with billions of ladybirds. Was like being abroad, that summer was way up in the 80s and 90s. We basically spent most of our time living on the beach and eating mussels and winkles. We were so in love and it was so romantic, we swore we would stay together forever and we came back to Leeds in the September of that wonderful year and rented a house for £4.00 a week. Then the owner wanted it back so we applied to the council and got a 2-bedroomed back-to-back on East End Park. I was working as a decorator and she was a home bird, but then it became a problem, she wouldn't go out at all and I would go out with my mates. The long shot is I came home one night to find her with someone else. I was heartbroken and went home to my Mam's. I still look back sometimes and think...what if?"

Paul Walsh

"I worked shifts in a large factory in Witton, Birmingham. I remember the heatwave really well. The factory backed on to the Fazely canal. One evening shift it was noticed that the tinder dry canal bank had started to burn, because of the closeness of the factory we had to do something about it. We contacted the fire brigade (I remember they were having to use the green goddess engines to help with the pressure they were under). They said that there was no way they could get to us, so quite a few of the shift went out to beat out the fire. It took us a while but we managed it. I must admit the overalls that night had to be peeled off."

Arthur Rodway

GROWIN' UP

For many of us thinking back to the mid-seventies invokes memories of our childhood, or of our adolescent years. It's easy to forget that those whose stories call upon these experiences are now in their forties, fifties and early sixties, and yet still they are often related with such clarity as well as with a hankering fondness.

Early childhood memories are of course entirely different in character from those of our teenage years, whichever period they happen to belong to. At that age we are unquestioning of the authority of our parents, upon whom we depend for guidance and protection. Later on, by contrast, we are impatient to assert our independence, believing as we do that we have stumbled upon a revealed truth in life which had never suggested itself to anybody of our parents' generation.

We'll consider the testimony of our '70s teenagers in due course. In the meantime let's take a look at some of those earlier anecdotes and consider how they tally with our own recollections. Beginning with **Steve Clucas**: "I was 11 and was a sea scout. We held a donkey derby in Swindon at the polo ground. I came second in two races, guest of honour was Sally Thomsett of Man

About the House. Amazing year."

And **Davido Di Lorenzo** struck lucky too: "I remember walking across Carshalton Park, aged 8, avoiding stepping on the cracks in the scorched earth. On my way I saw two 50 pence pieces side by side glinting up from the ground. I picked them up excitedly, five times my weekly pocket money, and thought how I would never have seen them in the usual green grass."

The unusual heat from the scorching summer of 1976 brought results for **Jane**'s big brother as well. "I was 11. Just about to start senior school. My brother was doing his O-levels and I recall that the pass marks were lowered due to the heat. I remember the heat, cool baths and sleepless nights but at the same time it seemed like fun. I was living in Medway, Kent at the time."

I guess Down Under they were used to the heat anyway. **Mandy Congerton** was there: "10 years old, lived in Christie's Beach. Used to ride our bikes, jump off the Port Noarlunga Jetty, slide down sand hills on cardboard. Fishing. Always busy having adventures. Only stopped to nip home to eat, then off again. Heaps of fun."

John Blake's account of his adventures is especially lucid: "I was 12 in May of that long hot summer. The days consisted of playing tracking (a long version of hide and seek over an extended area) on Woodgate Valley in Birmingham, a brand new council estate we had just moved onto. It could be played on foot but we were mainly on our bikes, Raleigh Choppers with lollipop sticks shoved into the spokes that made a sound like a motorbike, pretending we were in the Hell's Angels. Our arms got sunburned holding on to the handlebars. We would try and spot the latest P-reg cars on the estate, mainly Escorts, Minis and Cortinas - a Capri if we were lucky. Long games of Subbuteo in each other's garages whilst listening to badly-recorded Top of the

Pops on our cassette players - The Sweet, Alvin Stardust, etc. Watching The Sweeney and Kojak, and The Six Million Dollar Man on TV. Finding a discarded Playboy or Mayfair mag over the woods was always a treat to us pubescent lads. Them were the days!"

Some were too young to have remembered very much. **Lee Potts** was one year old, as were **Dellie Bean** and **Helen Barker**. **Amanda Evans** fondly recalls sucking on 'Tip Top' ice pops in the infants' school playground. Karen Carter plays for hours on the brown grass of her local park, unfortunately stepping on some glass in the paddling pool [*remember them? - Ed*.]. She was five years old at the time. Six-year-old **Diane Binns** played out in her bikini and wellies.

Lever Yvonne though recalls a great deal, despite having only been three years old: "I vaguely remember a very hot long summer. Loads of ladybirds. Building sandcastles with my bucket and spade with a wee fish in the spade. Jaws. 'Don't Go Breaking My Heart' - Kiki Dee and Elton John. My dad driving a wee green Beetle and unfortunately my granda passing away."

John Sherwin has plenty of young memories too. "I was coming up to five years old in summer 1976. I started primary school in the September and the weather was glorious! Our school playing field was as hard as concrete with long, deep cracks running across it. To anybody my age, whose first summer in their living memory was that year, it sets the bar impossibly high for the rest of your life! No summer will ever, ever compare with that one."

And **Sharon Lance** recalls: "In 1976 I had my 4th birthday but before that my brother was born in the January. I don't remember much about the heat but my mum told me about the water shortages. My mum's favourite band at the time was Abba... I still enjoy listening to them now."

Unsurprisingly those who were slightly older engaged in more elaborate pastimes. "I remember 1976 very well," **Tracey Dutton-Hacker** explains. "I was 11 years old during that long hot summer. I remember the kids popping bubbles of tar with sticks that formed on the road. The nearest water standpipe was right outside my gate so it was very handy during the prolonged hosepipe bans and water shortages that often occurred. I was to start high school in September of this year which was both exciting and daunting."

Erika Fidler was eleven too. "I had left junior school and was going to high school in the September. Water fights in the street with all the neighbours with hoses. Went to Whitby for our holidays and got covered in ladybirds."

And **Angela Genner Rhodes**. "I was 11 and scared to death of big school coming in September. All my junior school friends were going to a different school so I would be out on my own. It was my last summer of innocence, endless sunshine days spent outside playing turning into long cold winter of my teenage years."

We all loved a disco in 1976, and whilst the days were for school, the nights of course were quite a different matter entirely. "I was 12. On a Friday night it was disco night at the boys' club. There was a mixture of music like rock n roll, '60s music, northern soul and punk to music of the day. Different dress, teddy boys and girls, mods, skinheads and punks - we all got on, and finished with 'Hi Ho Silver Lining' with all arms linked," recounts **Elaine Green**.

Anne Yates was nine and lived in Wolverhampton. "We had a field behind our house and it was so hot the field set on fire and came towards our house. It was frightening and something I will always remember."

And seeing things catching light was not unusual during that dry summer, as **Beverley Westbury** concurs: "A fire started over the fields by us (natural area, long grass called Coombs Wood). Firemen came and put it out then stayed spraying us kids and generally playing around with us, never forget how happy we all were."

Kay had just started secondary school, and her culinary experiences were not untypical of that age: "Grange Hill started that year, used to rush home to see it! I lived in a small village in the North East called High Grange. Spent our summer going on walks with salad cream sandwiches and making dens!"

Dean Blundell was not too young for a spot of innocent vandalism: "I was 8 and remember the tar on the roads being that hot you could pick holes in it with a nail. Also it was the year we went on a family holiday to Sandy Bay in Exmouth. The sand was so hot you couldn't walk on it barefooted."

And I'm presuming (and certainly rather hoping) that **Phil Benyon** was young too: "Think that was the summer I discovered that ants randomly spontaneously combust. Noticed this whilst observing with a magnifying glass."

There was a big occasion to prepare for for young **Janice Barrett**. "I was about 9, my sister was due to get married. Had a wonderful time looking for my bridesmaid dress, shoes and hat. Loved the hot summer playing British bulldog, hopscotch, skipping and just messing around with my friends on the Tollgate estate in Kilburn. I remember badgering my mum to see if she had an empty washing up liquid bottle so that I could fill it with water and have water fights with the rest of the kids. I loved playing 2 balls up against the walls of the flats. I'd give anything to go back to those days in one way but at the same time if I did I wouldn't have my husband, kids or grandchildren."

Southport swimming pool was the destination of choice for **Kath Aly**. "Went in my neighbour's van, and their three children and me used to go every day. Towel and costume only need. Can taste the salt now. I was 9."

Amanda Taylor was nine that summer. "Every day of the summer holidays played outside. Visited my Dad's cousin's farm and saw the cows being milked, and saw all the little calves. Also had a ride on a tractor."

In Huntingdon Primary School, Nottingham, school desks were taken outside into the open air due to the stifling heat, **Lesley Prince Watts** tells us. **Adrian Fowler** was six and remembers playing out in Basingstoke's dried out canal in a summer that "seemed like it would last forever." **Helen Harrison**, then five, recalls being a passenger on her father's pushbike as he cycled along by the river, no helmets of course! **Dave Pimlott** got a Formula One pedal car for Christmas, and **David Stewart** started secondary school. Nine-year-old **Julie Rogers** and her sisters wore lemon dresses as bridesmaids at a wedding, in the hope that they would stand out against the grass in the photos - only they didn't. **Tammy Jane** felt safe and sound cycling or roller skating around her neighbourhood, despite only being eight.

Richard Wayne Sutherland was five and a half, and sends us a photograph (right) of him looking angelic and suitably fashionable during that year. For **Shannon Bennett** 1976 brought some daunting experiences: "I was six... we moved to a better area, we lived next to an awesome park but homeless took over. Went to see the new house, missed my step, landed on my chin. Blood everywhere. Parents almost got divorced over drinking, dad threw a plate of spaghetti at mom. She refused to clean it up. We tip toed over noodles for weeks."

Lisa Roe was a girl after my own heart, a late-night Radio Lux enthusiast. "I was twelve and got my first very own transistor radio which I used day and night. I had just discovered Radio Luxembourg. Long hot dusty summer... loved it."

And **Fiona Martin** revisits a scene the likes of which many of us will have been familiar: "My mum's neighbour and friend set up her sprinkler outside and all the kids in the street came to jump through it. I was 10... it was an epic summer of outside play and adventures."

Marina Walker has a lot of memories to share. "Oh gosh, my memories of 1976 conjure up so many memories. I was 10 years old and the tarmac in the playground was strangely soft, together with a foot high of heat shimmer, something I'd never seen before and we tried to touch it. On the UK news taxi drivers were frying eggs on their car bonnets. My friends and I couldn't understand why we struggled whilst running or bike riding, we hadn't before? Flying ants swarmed our streets.... people were dying on our beaches one of which I witnessed, it was horrendous as we were all permitted to watch events unfold (I'll never forget the screams)........ Good and bad to be remembered forever!"

Amanda Burnett reports from Hampshire: "I was eight years old and in Aldershot (home of the British Army). We lived on the camp so there were lots of children. Remember the heat and all the kids just being out in just their underwear, oh and the ladybirds... they were everywhere!"

Being affected by the sun didn't spoil the '76 experience for **Mike Hazelden**, who spent some time at one of the author's other favourite holiday spots. "I was 12. We had the best holiday I ever had on the Isle of Wight.. The hot summer was amazing, sharks were close to the shore and my thoughts were still very much about Jaws so I wouldn't go in the water. My dad had a

VX490 car with overdrive on the gearstick. I remember him playing Queen's 'Sheer Heart Attack' album as we cruised around the Isle of Wight and I suffered from sunstroke, my one and only time ever. What a great year."

Drought and water rationing are a common theme in accounts from contributors. **Jackie Hayes** remembers: "In 1976 I was 12, I remember the water shortage and having to go with containers (anything you'd got) to bring water to your home, the tar on the roads melting and people frying eggs on the concrete! But the one thing about it I remember the most, was the first time it rained, everyone came out their houses to just stand in the rain!"

Susan Musgrove remembers it too: "I was 7, and born in Bristol. I remember the water shortage due to the hot summer. Having to save the bath water to water the plants and not being allowed to flush the loo to save water. And when it did eventually rain everyone in the street cheered."

"I was 12, I just remember me and my brother having the best fun camping out in the garden every night, the excitement when the standpipes turned up in our street for us to get water. We weren't bothered about hosepipe bans and not being able to wash the car or water the garden as that was up to adults to worry about! Us and our friends grew up in the country and we were all pretty feral to be honest as it was different times so we didn't have a bath every day anyway so that wasn't a problem, apart from school and a few chores we pretty much fended for ourselves tramping round the fields and riverbeds and avoiding the grown-ups," **Gemma Watkins** recalls.

Nick Carter was twelve too. "Spent most days in the school holidays floating on old doors and logs made into rafts on a local lagoon by the River Calder in Yorkshire. I had my older twin brother and sister and a few mates there, and our baby sister Rachel who was 3 had to come while mum was at work. As we relaxed on the water my brother noticed Rachel wasn't on the bank and began to paddle back towards the shallows and he dived in and pulled our sister out. We made her promise not to tell anyone she nearly drowned and my mum didn't find out till my sister's funeral in January this year, as they used the story in the eulogy of her life."

Liz Price recounts it all. "I was 11, it was so hot. Us kids used to fry eggs on the pavement [*I hope none of these folks actually ate these eggs - Ed*]. Water would be turned off certain times of the day, so we would fill up kettle, bowls of water. A gang of us would go on picnics and play."

Another egg-fryer was **Andrew Doctor**. "We lived near Edinburgh, I was 10 and our family went to Great Yarmouth in the first two weeks of July with our tourer caravan to Cherry Tree Farm caravan site... scorching, you could fry an egg on the pavement."

And hydration was a concern for ten-year-old **Julie Swallow Elliott**. "I remember Dad driving us to Pitsford reservoir. It had all dried up and had large cracks in it. I remember feeling worried as I thought we were never going to get any water to drink."

Nick Reiss though was able to sate his cravings with sugar. "I was at primary school and about 8. I remember going to Colchester to visit my older sister. We went to the seaside from there - Walton On The Naze I think. My memories of these beach visits are a melange of images of adults drinking Pomagne, us kids with cherryade, sand-filled sandwiches, regular wasp invasions, jellyfish-filled seas and swimming with uncountable amounts of ladybirds floating with us."

Ladybirds were an issue for **Debbie Poole** too. "We went to Weston-super-Mare from Tamworth for a day trip on a coach and I can remember the windows of the bus being blacked out nearly by the ladybirds. I was 8 at the time, it was like a horror movie to me then!"

For **Gaynor Holt**, a fond reminisce: "Arrrh the summer of '76, picking the tarmac on the pavement with a stick, going to the park with a pack of sandwiches and a bottle of Tizer and staying there all day (no parents, just your brother, sister and other neighbourhood kids, endless hot days and no school). Wish I was 6 again."

Julie Minott muses warmly: "It was the summer before I started secondary school. What an amazing time I had with friends. Out all day and long warm evenings. Special memories of a wonderful time I will never forget."

And **Peter Williams** speaks of "heat, road mirages, the smell of an asphalt playground, urban pre-teen existence. And the radio was always on!"

Patti Pay was eleven that year. "I remember collecting ladybirds one day to see how many I could get, great fun. I remember watching all the butterflies. Being taken to Broadstairs with my parents and playing in the sea that was warm. Best ever summer."

Cooking oil was probably not the wisest substitute for suntan lotion, but experimentation is an essential part of growing up. **Rebecca Okell Bougourd** takes up the story: "I was 12 in '76 and I remember sunbathing in the garden all summer whilst listening to Radio 1. We weren't allowed to use our Mum's Ambre Solaire (factor 4) so we drenched ourselves in cooking oil! We also put lemon juice in our hair so my brother and I were bleached blonde, little brown berries."

The heat inspired some bizarre fads too it would seem, as **Donna Howells** explains: "I was 8 years old and remember the latest craze was collecting the melted yellow paint from double yellow lines. My ball of paint was the size of a football. I was very proud of it. I remember a school trip to Dan yr Ogof caves. It would have been late July towards the end of the school year. My mother dressed me in a cool cotton blouse and skirt and I froze because caves, well they are underground and heatwaves do not penetrate through tonnes of rock! My baby brother was born in 1976. So I spent a lot of time learning to overcome pangs of sibling jealousy!"

John Holland has some quite vivid memories of the whole year. "I remember the year started with January gales. We moved house in April and our new house was near a wood and you could see the trees that had fallen. I started a new school and it was sunny every day that term. We had a teacher called Miss Lovely (actual name) she used to take the class to walk on the beach and would buy us all ice creams. Summer was great as a few new neighbours moved in and suddenly I had two new friends my own age as we got to know the new area. Oh and the rain finally came on Bank Holiday Monday and flooded a camp site near where I lived."

Dean Merchant was ten at the time. "I remember it was that hot camped out all six weeks holiday and every corner where we lived had all our mates' names inscribed in tarmac. It was that hot the tarmac actually melted, we loved it."

Children in East London enjoyed some games I must admit I'd never heard of, as **Janice Dumont Nicholson** reports: "I was 10, from east London, Bethnal Green. Remember my dad every Sunday - a trip to Southend in the 6 weeks holidays. Having great friends around the flats just all playing together, run outs, tin tam tommy, two balls up the wall, cannon and many more. Such happy days."

Robert Farrow, meanwhile, invokes some iconic cultural classics from those bygone days. "I was 6 in 1976. Around Spring I caught a bad dose of chickenpox, I was covered head to toe in calamine lotion! If that wasn't bad enough, our Radio Rentals TV blew up! Myself, parents and six siblings went without a telly for about a week. Amongst others, we missed the last ever episode of Man About the House and Great Britain winning the Eurovision Song Contest with Brotherhood of Man's 'Save Your Kisses For Me' (we listened to it via BBC's coverage on the radio). I eventually recovered from the pox, with plenty of Lucozade (in the orange crinkly paper) and copies of Whizzer and Chips comics!"

All in all 1976 was a great time to be young - indeed, according to a study by the New Economics Foundation, the happiest year of them all. But for pre-teens, as we've seen, it had a magic all of its own. Now we're going to take a look at the year as seen by some who were slightly older.

BEING A TEENAGER IN '76

I turned fifteen in the autumn of 1976. It might be interesting to see how those of that same age group remember that year, and how their recollections of events may concur with or diverge from those of the younger ones. For some on the south coast of course, there was one big occasion which will understandably stand out above all others, as **Stephen Eckersley** proudly points out: "The summer of '76 is indelibly seared into the memory of this, then 16 year old football mad boy, leaving school. The weather was glorious and the summer long but above all Southampton won the FA Cup against all the odds for the only time, and I was there to experience it. For any Southampton supporters, the events of that weekend at the beginning of May are as unforgettable as anything that can be imagined. Pure ecstasy relived over and over again!"

Inevitably the giant killing probably had less resonance a few miles along the coast, where the soccer is blue. **Lorraine Clegg** was in Portsmouth: "I was 15 and went with the family to the

Navy Days at Portsmouth dockyard. It was so hot, we were queueing to go down for a look in a submarine, they could only take one family at a time, we were the next family to go down, when for the first time in my life I fainted. The sailors got an ambulance for me and as they loaded me into the back, my dad said rather loudly, just take her I'm not giving up my place. I spent the rest of the day in the Navy hospital on my own while everyone else went down into the submarine!"

And it was all happening at sea too for **David Edward Hart**: "Down the beach every day in the school holidays with my mates running around in cut off jeans - really tanned, my mate Nigel's shorts were knackered so his mum cut him a new pair, only about an inch or so shorter than his last pair so he had two white rings around his legs. Jumping off Boscombe Pier and being shouted at by the council blokes. Bobbing around on lorry inner tubes - could get two of us on them... great times!"

Liz James has fond memories of the school exchange trip. "In the summer of 1976 I was 17 and I took part in an exchange programme between our local authority (LB of Barnet) and its twin town, Siegen, in Germany. The German contingent came over for the first 2 weeks and then we went back with them to Germany. We had loads of activities with the group and got to meet a lot of people from other schools in our district. One of the highlights for me in London was a river cruise down the Thames. In Germany, we also did a lot of planned activities, including visits to Cologne and Frankfurt. We visited the Opel car factory on one trip. And we did a lot of clubbing and drinking. It was an absolutely magical summer, one I'll never forget."

Ann Cooper remembers her school play: "Was at college in Hereford. We were performing a play around the schools and in Hereford Cathedral. The glue holding the props together melted in the continuous heat. At the end of the play, I had to lie on the floor for about 20 minutes until it was my turn to speak. In the cathedral, I fell asleep! The old floor slabs were so cold!"

1976 was quite a hectic year for **Jayne Hunt**. "Just left school, went to college, the first in my family to go to college. Learnt shorthand and typing, ended up being friends with a girl in the same class at school, who I hadn't been friends with. Fell in love, had a great time, got my first job, had lots of laughs, and some tears, had a baby got married. Too much to put down now, still going strong, and making adventures."

For some, **Pamela Reilly** included, that adolescent spirit will live forever. "The summer I left school anything could happen, my life was in front of me, an adult at last. Take me back to that time - long hot summer, great music and even the clothes. Still haven't worked out this adulting thing."

Sometimes the heat couldn't be taken for granted, as **Helen Price** relates: "The year I sat my O-levels. Extremely hot outside, so went into school (St. Marys Convent, Middlesbrough) dressed in warm weather clothes, only to sit in the main hall for exams. All of the long curtains were closed and the hall was so cold. I recall taking my English Lit exam almost shivering."

We've already heard from one person who tried to substitute oil for suntan lotion. **Melanie Gosling** was another: "I was 16 in September 1976. I recall my sister and brother-in-law were home from Singapore where they lived at the time with my young nephew and niece. We had a family get together with my elder brother, sister-in-law and his two children. I also remember trying to get a tan by covering myself in baby oil. The outcome wasn't good!"

Patricia Gardener (then Duncan) of Portishead, Bristol suffered a drawback. "I was 18 and was learning to drive. 2nd August was my test day, I sat out in the sunshine looking at my highway code on my lunch break. I had a pre-test lesson at 2pm, test at 3pm. Lesson was OK but as I sat in the waiting room to be called for the test I started to feel odd. Shrugged it off, did the test, started to feel headachy and needed a drink. I totally messed up and I failed. Later on I had full blown sunstroke from sitting out in the sun! I did pass later on in October when things cooled down. We have a page called Portishead Past on FB - very popular [*see https://www.facebook.com/groups/223014959023325 – Ed.*].

Susanna Frances remembers the fires. "I was 13 and I remember the really long hot dry summer, the hedgerow fires and my mother driving past them in the middle of the country lanes. We could feel the heat through the walls of the cars. and grown-ups doing grown-uppy things in all the terrible heat, and wondering why?"

And **Jeremy Parry** was actually fighting them. "May 19 1976 I was at boarding school in Sussex on the edge of Ashdown Forest. I was 13, it was my mate's 13th birthday and we were fighting a fire on Ashdown Forest."

Marc Rue got his first motorcycle on the road once his sixteenth birthday arrived in November. **G.H.** of Bristol went on a school trip to London, aged fourteen, and when she got home it finally started raining. **Jane Myers** started at Bradford University, studying French and Spanish. **Carolyn Crowe** was at senior school and **Janet Reckord** was just starting high school. **Tina Tickle** was a student, engaged to be married, loving the hot weather and without a care in the world. **Shirley Dafney** ran away from home.

Angelica Fountouris remembers: "Was that the year of heat wave. I was 13... Bay City Rollers' era - yuck. I went to high church on Sundays, then had all the family ironing to do for the week, Usually sat on a board with my friends kicking our heels, popping chewing gum, or playing kerbs, kick the tin, hide n seek, until ironing, bath, time, hair wash for school the next day."

Nick Fleming was "having my hips pinned, a long hot and painful summer. I was 14. On a brighter note City won the League Cup [*that's Manchester City - Ed.*]."

"It was just a beautiful long hot summer," says **Annie Brazier**. "I was 16, the ladybirds covering my mother's washing and being told to go careful because they bite. The tarmac melting... going to the beach and being unable to stand on the sand barefoot it was so hot... it was so hot that you couldn't sleep at night. At 16 I enjoyed that long hot summer... we played football in the Victoria Park, went on every ride at the fun fair."

Kim Gill was leaving school. "I think there is only one thing to remember about 1976 and that is the summer. I left school and in-between exams I spent every single day at an outdoor swimming pool and dropped into my Nana's for tea on the way home."

Some familiar musical memories for **Jacqueline Bertho**. "Took my O-levels in June '76. Spent July sunbathing in parents' garden. Listening to Radio 1, mornings especially great with "the Radio 1 Road Show". 'Don't Go Breaking My Heart' by Elton John and Kiki Dee played every hour. Eurovision Song Contest winner 'Save Your Kisses For Me'."

"Myself and two best friends were out and about in the town and the seafront wearing our platform shoes, twinsets and high waisted baggy trousers. We were 16 and the world was our oyster (and so were the boys on holiday)," reports **Julie Ann Burgess**.

Claire Elisabeth Conroy was "a teenager with a plant mad grandfather, couldn't understand why the hosepipe ban caused him so much interest!"

A detailed reminisce from **Julie Mason**: "I was 14. I remember revising for exams sat in the garden in the heat, then wishing I could watch the tennis on the TV. During the school holiday I remember having to stack small bales of hay in our front field on our farm along with my brothers and sisters and getting burnt from the sun. Also remember stacking the bales in the barn and finding that my brother had put a grass snake in my coat pocket. He knew I hated them. So hot at the top of that barn and then being terrified of jumping down off the top of the rick, as this was the only way down."

Tina Roberts missed our glorious summer, although she wasn't really in need of it where she was. "I was 16 and living in Kimberley, South Africa. We left the UK in 1975. I missed the long hot summer of '76 in England but was more than happy with the permanent heat and sunshine in SA."

Happy memories abound for **Sally Childs**: "The long hot summer. I was 15. Skipping school to sit in a field and didn't have a care in the world. Mum and Dad still alive, I'd love to go back just for one day."

Jo Stevens looks back with affection from afar: "I was 15 and on a language course in France. I was an Army brat and we lived in Düsseldorf, W. Germany at the time. I then went back to Germany and we all went 'home' (England was always home… I've lived in Tasmania now for 32 years and I still call it home!) to visit family. I could not believe how dry and hot it was… have these conditions been beaten? One of the funniest things I remember is trying to explain to the French family that I was staying with in Les Sables d'Olonne that I was going to travel across the Channel on an aeroglisseur. I had dutifully found the French equivalent. They had no idea what I was talking about so I drew them a picture.… ah they said… an 'oovercraft'!"

Like so many in that glam-steeped era, **Evie Beattie** had a childhood crush: "I was 14 that summer and remember a few things distinctively - the paint on our doors and windows bubbling up in the heat, no water and I had a huge crush on Dave Bartram from Showaddywaddy."

Keith Dagnall kept up with the times. "I remember the infestation of ladybirds, was it just local to the Wirral? I'd left school and had options. Who'd have thought it, I was sixteen, I had four offers of apprenticeship, a beautiful girlfriend, and the hottest summer on record. Signing on for what benefits I was due was no hardship. I could give my mum some 'keep' and pay my own way. I sold my Raleigh Chopper bike that summer, and bought Chelsea boots with drainpipe jeans."

Mike Hooper experienced a brief period of unemployment too: "I was19, I quit my job with 3 weeks' notice and told my new employer I had to give 5. 2 weeks off in the sun and claimed dole for the fortnight (naughty I know but it was the only 2 weeks I was unemployed since I was 16, 63 now)."

Jill Fairweather regrettably had an accident which marred her summer somewhat. "I was 13. I was asked to look after my friends horse called Shandy while they were away. I thought it would be a good idea to ride her bareback... wrong idea! She galloped away with me, me being totally inexperienced with horse riding, couldn't stop her and fell off breaking my arm. I spent the WHOLE of the wonderful heatwave and 6 weeks school holidays in a plaster cast. I vividly remember when the cast was removed my arm was bright white while the rest of me very tanned."

Pauline O'Brien didn't enjoy a lot more success when it came to equestrian pursuits: "In 1976 I was 14. I spent the school holidays horse riding at a local farm. How hard the ground felt when I fell off - I wasn't very good at the horse riding lark! Weirdly, also that there was a dead badger on the road to the farm. It got rather smelly as the time went by."

Debbie Jane Gillard agrees that 1976 was the best year of our lives [*where have I heard that line before? - Ed.*]. "I was 17. Living in Orpington having moved from Sydenham back in 1969. Best year of my life. Wearing proper hot pants... you know the bib and brace type and very short. Hopping on the back of the boys' Chopper bikes. Playing tennis, rounders, acrobatics aplenty and secretly fancying boys from the neighbourhood. Family gatherings every Sunday and salmon and cucumber sarnies for tea. Attended SELTEC College Lewisham Catering and having a light ale with the professors at lunch. Waking up in the bath after a night of partying in London bedsit. Taking my little brother to see Star Wars and me being bored to bits. Lots of stuff... youth club, platforms etc."

"Left school, had a week in Heacham, walked to Hunstanton every day, my brother and sister in law came one day and we were sitting on Heacham beach till late at night," recalls **Janet Moody**.

Julie Simpson recounts: "I was 14 in the middle of that summer. Spent a lot of it on the rowing boats on Queen's Park Lake. Had my first kiss that summer but didn't like it. Had most of our school lessons on the lawn, I don't think the teachers wanted to be inside."

Great memories too for **Sue Geach**: "I was 14 and at boarding school. I remember swimming before breakfast and also after prep, we all would sit under the shady trees near the cricket pavilion. When I had a leave weekend I would spend all my time with my pony and ride for hours and have many adventures."

Ellen Cuthbert was about to leave school. "Had a boyfriend, now my husband. Went to discos, parties, had fun. Had a Saturday job."

Ian Rogers found himself distracted somewhat from his studies. "Studying for my O-levels and for most subjects it was the first time I had actually understood them. Then the heat took over and I spent most of the time in the garden and ended up building a race bicycle from scratch. Needless to say my O-level grades were not great."

The weather was even superb for a while in Manchester [!!], as **Jill Bell** testifies. "1976 was the year I left school. I did all my revision in the back garden, in the red hot sun. My mam bought a large umbrella so I could sit out and revise. I was lucky enough to leave school in the June and not start work until September, when the kids went back to school. I started work as a civil servant 44 years ago and I'm still there. The summer was amazing, I used to go to beach with my friends. Living in South Shields it was only a bus ride away. We went to visit my cousins in Manchester and went by National coach. Going across the moors you could see fires smouldering in the dry grass. In Manchester we couldn't breathe as the air was so still, not like Shields were there was always a slight sea breeze. Long hot summer days. We were in Manchester when the weather finally broke and remember running outside and dancing in the rain."

Some great recollections from **Judith Jones**, who was banished from the land: "I was 16. The year I took my GCEs. It was so hot, most of my revising was done on the beach, watching older guys playing football on the sand in their cut off jeans. We used to lie on tinfoil and use Hawaiian Tropic factor 2, so everyone had fab tans. I had a boyfriend that drove round in a VW camper van. He had long hair and leftist leanings, and my Dad disapproved so much that I was sent to my Uncle's in Canada. I went to the Olympics while I was there. An amazing year. Fantastic music, wonderful memories - and I passed my O-levels despite scant revision. I have written a song about it which I'm currently recording. Would you like a link when it's finished? [*Yes, please do send it to us - Ed.*]

And finally, an uplifting tale by **Jane Rose-Greenberg** of triumph from adversity. "End of first year at Uni living in halls of subsistence (residence); I was rushed to hospital suspected appendix. Whole hall waved me off (very embarrassing). Anyway, recovered well and joined in the last two weeks of sunbathing; catching train into central London, enjoying some air from open windows, catching the 00:59 train back and sitting outside until dawn broke. Delighting in the final year friends passing their degrees. After end of term took a holiday job, luckily in cool store. Then a quick holiday to the South Coast and back to Uni for my part one term and new friends."

OLDER IN '76

I also received a number of fascinating stories and anecdotes from respondents who were a bit older in 1976, or who at least had responsibilities and maybe more adult concerns to attend to. For **Caroline Avery**, it was the beginning of an exciting new business venture: "I had a baby in '73 and went to a gym. In '76 I started to do keep fit at local clubs. Well I got over 100 people coming to my classes, loved every minute of it so started to work for myself. During the day I started going to retirement homes, they loved it as well. Went to college, loved it, best thing I ever did. I worked till I was 70."

Pat Adams was bringing up a one-year-old baby boy. And like **Shirley Kerr**, **Kathryn Bird** was trying for a baby all year and became pregnant the following year. "I was so brown the doctor asked if I'd been abroad, no I said - just Chapel St. Leonard's."

Having had her first child in 1975, **Anne Blackledge** (née Wilson) found herself spending 1976 running around after a small toddler in the ferocious heat. **Cynthia Jackson** remembers being sunburnt in Borth, Mid-Wales, and her son making the pain worse by touching her raw skin. **Melinda Maarouf** was learning how to be a wife and making a home, while **Beryl Lucas** was trying to feed three children. **Jim Speirs** was living in Cape Town, South Africa with his wife and three young children during the Soweto uprising and remembers it well. **David Wot Langley**, on the other hand, was 21 at the time enjoying adventures of an alcoholic nature and doesn't remember much about the year at all.

Also 21 was **Michael Sheriston**, who was preparing to join the management team at the Strathdon Hotel in Nottingham. He remembers pike biting canoeists at the National Water Sports Centre "because the water was so low and the food chain had been broken." Sadly though Michael lost his grandfather that year.

Naomi Jane Carter had a one-year-old son which, along with the heat, led to sleepless nights. **Jackie Rowe** was a young married mum living in a two-room flat. **Angela Russell** was bringing up two young girls and recalls all three of them running out into the rain when it finally came. "The smell of the earth was wonderful."

Mark Thomas was on strike from the GEC. **Helen Taggart** speaks of "a summer to remember", playing with her daughters aged 5 and 3, who were brown in the heat. And **Elaine Stephansky** had daughters of 3 and 6, with whom she had water pistol fights on the beach. **Rita Anderson** was 32, had three sons and was enjoying life. And **Elaine Ellery** recalls attending a street party with her son (see picture).

I like this from **Mary Hughes**: "I had a wild daughter who would never walk if she could run. We went to a stony beach one day, and I thought she wouldn't be able to run on those big stones, but she did! She was about three years old."

As the owner of his own leaflet distribution business the author has some sympathy with **Pamela Foster**. "I remember it was a scorching hot summer, my son was 5 and I was doing a part time job delivering leaflets. We had to keep stopping to have a drink, in the half term and took my son out with me. I gave him a few leaflets to post and he put them all through the first letterbox! We walked away quickly!"

Celia Weir reports from Scotland: "1976 was the year before I got married and I remember one Sunday morning in the horrible heat, walking to the bottom end of Kilmarnock with my soon to be hubby, to watch the demolition of the 2 cooling towers which were a welcome sight on returning to Killie. The first tower went down as expected but the second twisted slightly and we ended up covered in dust."

A distressing experience for **Angie Vanner** too: "Was 23, had 2 boys aged 5 and 2. Spent days at the open air swimming pool in Chingford, or in the garden. My youngest son had a tortoise which got jammed in-between the rocks in the rockery and cooked - it was awful."

A pool in the garden was quite an asset in 1976. **Carolyn Mills** had one: "I had a pool put in the garden in March and by the summer my two sons had SO many friends (fair weather friends?)."

If you didn't have a swimming pool, a paddler sometimes did the trick. "I remember the long, hot summer of 1976 very well. My daughter was already at junior school, and my 4 year old son started infants in the September. I remember spending most of our time in the garden, my son lived in his swimming trunks and the paddling pool. Loved it." remembers **Reena Ruffell**.

Hilary Goodman found the heat troubling. "So hot, hubbie in Bahrain. PVC furniture almost melted. No water rationing. Children playing out all day without sunscreen! Too hot to eat, sleep. Windows south facing, help."

Yvonne Gwendoline Bodily struggled a little too, but it was a good year for her all the same. "It was my second year of my second marriage. The weather was very hot and I fell pregnant with my fourth child. We spent a lot of time travelling about on a motorbike visiting places like Bournemouth but it was the hottest I had ever known it. I became pregnant with my fourth son, it was so hot and the grass everywhere had turned brown. I felt uncomfortable with the heat but I was happy because earlier that year my husband adopted my other three sons."

And having to work in the heat was no fun for **Sheila Vickers**. "I had two young sons aged 5 and 3. I remember helping out at the school fair. I was on the toy stall in the playground, it was sweltering with no shade."

The ladybirds spoiled what had been a fun experience for **Edith Ward**. "My husband and two very young children along with myself went to the beach in Leigh on Sea Essex. We were having a very nice time and then this cloud of ladybirds came across the water and descended on us all, it was dreadful."

Thomas Richard Martin must have been raking it in. "I lived in a tiny bedsit, with only a 2ft square window for air. So that summer I was working three jobs. My main job was a night shift at a rubber factory, I got home at just after 6am and went straight out to spend the morning laying tarmac. I'd get home about 12:30 and go to sleep for a few hours when I started work at the local pub until just before 10, when I started my night shift."

Pauline Linfoot has an interesting story to tell. "I was 25 and glad I had my 3rd baby the year before. It must have been awful that year for anyone who was pregnant. We went to Roundhay Park in Leeds with the kids. There was the fair and all sorts on like Planet of the Apes. One who was dressed as a general jumped over into the crowd and frightened the kids. It was a good day even though I ended up with blisters on my shoulders with it being so hot."

George brings us the following account from Shropshire: "I was 22 and living in a little flat in Telford with my girlfriend. One thing that sticks in my mind is that one of the neighbours moved his hi-fi speakers out onto his balcony and played the Rolling Stones record 'Emotional Rescue', over and over for weeks on end. I had an MGB soft top at the time and it felt like we lived in the tropics."

And from **Trish**: "My childhood friend had emigrated to South Africa with her family. In 1976 she came back for a visit and brought her husband and family over too. Although we wrote to each other regularly we hadn't seen each other since we were 14 in 1958. The first thing she said to me was 'how on earth do you stick this heat?' (she explained that in SA the heat was different, not so humid). We had a wonderful time for a few days."

It seems they had barbies back in '76 too, although I never got invited to any. "We had a butcher's shop, and my husband brought meat home that he struggled to sell with the heat, for example stewing meat. Everybody wanted BBQ food naturally which of course he supplied, but please feel sorry for my two kids, having to eat hot pies and stews, sitting there with sweat pouring out of them lol. No they didn't come to any harm, still makes me smile remembering that," recalls **Sheila Hill**.

And there's this nice reminisce from **CM**: "It was the first summer after I had got married in Nov '75, which had had been a good summer too, and was living in Liskeard in Cornwall. We used to get in from work and head straight to the coast, about 8 miles away, to swim in the evenings, and weekends would be spent at the beach too. When the weather finally broke (just after a Minister for Drought had been appointed) I remember standing outside in the rain enjoying getting drenched to the skin."

There was a valuable lesson to be learned for **Joyce Natzler**: "In the hot summer of '76, I had two pen friends from Austria staying with me and my husband and two children aged 3 and 18 months. I was taken ill and one of my Austrian friends saw an ambulance across the road and asked them to see me! I was taken to hospital and stayed in for over a week with kidney stones! Which taught me a lesson to drink more water! In those days it was better for the children not to visit me and those 9 days were so long that my little girls seemed so different when I got home! My mum told me that my eldest daughter was looking everywhere for me. I have been very lucky not to have any kidney stones again! So keep drinking water."

There was sadness but later also joy for **Ingrid Ransome**. "I remember 1976 only too well. I was 29, married with one child and living on the beautiful Gower Peninsular, Swansea. My best friend's husband (2 young kids) was killed in an industrial accident in the May and I had a miscarriage in the July. The hot summer was hard work. I went on to have my second child in January 1978."

And **Jackie Safran** found a novel way of keeping cool. "I was just back from 2 years with the FCO in Chile. I was sharing a flat with another girl from the FCO who had just come back from Cairo. We were living in Knightsbridge, just across from Harrods, over a dairy. We were glad the building was old and damp cos we could lean against the walls and cool down. Who expected London to be hotter than the countries we had recently left?"

MOVING ON

Folks back then didn't move around between districts quite so much as they do today, but the responses we received still suggests there were a good number who did. Who would have wanted to have been a removal man during all that stifling heat?

Sandy Bridges "went to see a bungalow in September and it was in the actual day when it poured down with rain for the first time in months. We looked out through the window at the back garden because it was tipping down, and we bought the bungalow. We moved in on 18th December. The lounge was orange wallpaper, the hall was bright green wallpaper, the bedroom was mauve and a mauve carpet! Bright colours in those days!"

Also on the move was **Anne Johnson**. "In June of that year I moved into my house. It was the only one completed in what was to become a cul-de-sac on a new estate. For 4 weeks I lived alone in what was an area of marshy grassland with builders' tracks, piles of bricks, hares, hedgehogs and the occasional fox appearing through the tall grass. There were many wild flowers including wild roses, the Northern Marsh orchid and also many skylarks' nests. I still have the wild roses in my garden. During that first winter, the land returned to marshland and it became dangerous to walk in the garden. I took a 5ft beanpole one day and, with perfect ease, pushed its entire length into the ground with one finger. All is built up now and has become a large area linking up with two others."

In was fun in the sun for the family of **Winifred Watt**, despite being so far north. "We had just moved to the north of Scotland from Devon and lived in a coastal town. My 3 daughters just couldn't believe they could come home from school, get into swimsuits, and run down into the water day after day."

Sheila James Mitchell moved away from the sun. "Very hot and dry. We moved from London to Northern Ireland at the end of August and we saw green grass for the first time in months as it still rained in NI!"

And **Janet Johnson** has happy memories: "My partner and myself bought the lovely house I live in. He has since passed away but we were so happy in it together with our children."

Marie McGreachan does too: "It was the year I moved in to my house. What a summer, the paint and emulsion dried in no time, kids played outside all summer school holidays, and ice poles - omg freezer was full. Also washing dry in one hour - sheets, curtains, kids' jackets. Washed everything in the house."

Sandy Marchant also still lives in the home she moved into in 1976. "Moved into the house I still live in now, September time. No back lawn, just a dust bowl. Hosepipe ban came in and we were so lucky it did not apply to us, but a few hundred yards down the road had to use it."

After having been married in October 1975, **Nigel Barrett-Cross** and his wife moved into their new home. "The new mortgage on our first home dictated that the exterior shall be redecorated so, with some help from my dad, we spent the summer of 1976 painting the walls of our house. Finished days before the deadline."

Glennis Kearns remembers: "I had just moved into my first house with a garden and I was very enthusiastic about it. My young children enjoyed their first paddling pool in the garden. Then of course we got the hosepipe ban. However it was a beautiful summer and we still moaned it was too hot."

Eileen Brown had just moved into a new home and spent the summer of 1976 decorating. And **Janet McMenemy** was pleased not to have to go out to work in the heat of the summer, having moved into a three-bedroom house with her three-year-old daughter and two-year-old son. **Sandra Akerman** and her new husband made the move from London to the beautiful Suffolk village of Rickinghall. Unpacking after a move was hot work for **Jean Griffin**, having three daughters under three. **Ann Macdonald** left England for Australia with her two young children and is still there today. And **Marion Smales** and her family bought a nice house in Tollesbury, on the Essex coast, after having escaped from life in a London tower block.

Carolyn Staples made the move to beautiful Dorset. "In 1976 we moved from Rochester in Kent to Poole, Dorset. What a wonderful time we had exploring all the beautiful beaches, discovering the villages and their history. By the end of the summer we were all healthy, happy and so pleased we had moved there. We all live in Ipswich now but all loved our 10 years we spent in Poole. Almost forgot the winter of '76, saw snow on Bournemouth beach. The locals said we brought it with us."

"I STILL LOOK BACK ON IT AS THE GOOD OLD DAYS"

Some of the submissions we received painted a more holistic picture of life in 1976. It would be helpful to take a look at a few:

"Had just bought our first house, but inflation was moving so fast our builder went bankrupt halfway through. Got a government grant, but it didn't really cover it. Had a long hot summer trying to cope with a house with no water and a one year old.

"Here in Northern Ireland it was the height of the troubles. Supermarkets were a novelty and socially most people turned to drinking at home instead of going out to pubs. A bottle of vodka cost £3 - the equivalent of about £40 now! Everything was more expensive. I remember having to borrow a neighbour's iron until mine arrived from my catalogue. Most people used catalogues to buy things from.

"The majority of us women did part time work. We had lots of coffee mornings, Tupperware and Pippa Dee parties. We all walked everywhere with our prams as very few had the luxury of two cars. We'd only four channels on the TV which ended at midnight and early morning TV was open university. All the children played outside as there were no computers and TV didn't start till 4 for them. I still look back on it as the good old days."

Lorna Alexander

"My son was born November 1975. We had our first house, a terrace in Sheffield that cost us £4,000. The hot summer, I remember washing terry nappies and putting them on the line, they were dry in about 10 minutes. I remember glorious sunsets and huge moons, there was a moon that was unusual and hit the news headlines. I can't remember why but it was something to do with Venus. My husband went out with other locals to fight the fires on the moors around Sheffield. There were rows of people guided by the fire brigade with sacking beating the flames out. It seemed like the summer was never going to end."

Avril Froggatt

"1976, what a hot year. We had to save the washing up water to put on the plants in the garden and vegetable plot. My mum put a brick in the toilet system to save water on every flush. We weren't allowed baths or showers, just had to wash down.

"Our dog was put down because she was old and had a growth on her breast. The vet said she wouldn't survive the surgery due to the heat. Medicine has moved on since then.

"10cc with the classic song 'I'm Not in Love' being played at parties, and on the radio. I remember lying on my bed in my bedroom looking at the sky, feeling so hot and uncomfortable. Then black clouds appeared on the horizon, and finally the weather broke, and down came the rain with a lightning storm. What a year…"

Lezley Barbara Bold

LET THE MUSIC PLAY...

...was in the author's view one of the most beautiful songs of that year. But whether or not Barry White did it for you, nobody can deny that music played a seminal role in providing the culture and the vibe which defined those times. Some of your memories reflected that truth.

Some of us who were young in '76 actually thought of the Rolling Stones as oldies, even though they were still in their thirties. But **Jim Partington** headed south to see them live. "I'm from Oldham and I went to London for the first time to see a girlfriend and to see the Rolling Stones at Earls Court, which cost me £3 for my ticket! I remember they opened the show with 'Honky Tonk Women' and the sound system was bloody awful. During the next few days, we wandered around London taking in the sights in the scorching hot weather. Unforgettable!"

Sue Bradley seems to have had one of the better seats. "My husband went to see The Rolling Stones at Earls Court, ticket was £5."

And **Les Chester** saw them at Knebworth, and still has the ticket to prove it (right). **Keith Miller** performed a number of gigs north of the border: "I was 15 in 1976 and was playing in a band working in Central Scotland based in Lanarkshire... lots of memories of Working Men's Clubs and Miners' Welfare Clubs etc. Also many fond memories of gigs at the Glasgow Apollo."

1976 was an epic musical journey for **Chris Duxberry**: "I was getting ready for secondary school, trying to get my mum to sew tartan on for the Bay City Rollers. Went to first concert - Queen - then Showaddywaddy in the summer. Then by the Xmas of '76 my first Mohawk hair cut. '77 - The Clash."

Tony McQueen also found punk (presumably?). "Was 10 at the time, and the summer was spent mainly in Alexander Palace or Park Road outdoor pool, not a care in the world, then I turned the radio on and this loud strange aggressive music come out of the speakers, my life changed for ever."

"A great year for gigs," remembers **Mark Cunningham**. "In '76 I saw the Stones, The Who, Wings, Queen, The Clash, Pistols, Lynyrd Skynryd and more. A stunning year!"

"'I'm Mandy, Fly Me' – 10cc, 'A Little Bit More' - Dr Hook, 'Mississippi' – Pussycat. Happy memories of the summer in the garden. Waiting to start secondary school in September. I think it was the last summer of playing out. The next year and years after that we just walked about or sat on each other's doorstep," remembers **Julie-Anne Queenie Wilkinson**.

1976 also invokes thoughts of 10cc for **Jo Holmes**. "Listening to 10cc - number 1 in the charts. Countryside fires on the news. Pick your own strawberries day out."

Schoolday memories too for **Angela Bellamy**: "Finished school after doing my O-levels. Wonderful hot summer. Reading pop festival on August bank holiday where it poured with rain all weekend. My final fling before starting my nurse training on 6th September."

Life was great for **Ann-Marie Osborne**: "I remember 1976 so well. Had a good job in the Daily Mirror - secretary to the publisher of the Sunday People - and a great friendship group. Got my flat and went to live with my boyfriend who I had been with since 1970. I was just 15 then and I believe it was the year we all went to see the band Lynyrd Skynyrd at the Hammersmith

Odeon. It was a really hot summer and most weekends we went to the beach - Eastbourne, Folkestone, Clacton-on-Sea. A carefree time of music fun and freedom."

Caroline Fry recalls listening to a beautiful song in a beautiful resort on the south coast. "The year I got engaged. The Real Thing was number 1 with 'You To Me Are Everything'! We saw them live at the Village Bowl, Bournemouth. The long hot summer, one of my favourite years!"

Some great musical memories for **Malik Tahir** from Australia: "I was in Adelaide University, South Australia. Went to the Slade concert Memorial Drive and also a few Blues concerts - Willy Dixon and The Blues All Stars, Sonny Terry and Brownie McGee."

Sandy Brooks recollects: "Remember that hot year went to an outdoor concert. One of the bands playing was Mungo Jerry playing their hit song 'In the Summertime'. Fitted in well with that year."

And how better to end this section than with a memory of a free festival, from **Michael E Wynn**? "Had just left school and went to my very first rock festival - Stonehenge free festival. I believe it was the first time it had a barbed wire perimeter fence round the stones so you couldn't get close to them. At the solstice sunrise, the druids and attendant photographers did their thing in virtual silence in the middle. Inside the perimeter and evenly spaced round the outside were a ring of policemen who were clearly part of the ritual. They stood, hands clasped behind their backs gently rocking on their heels. Just outside the wire there was a stage playing music, painted and robed people dancing, and the usual festival scene. A vivid memory was seeing a very tanned and tattooed middle aged man sitting cross legged in the middle of a transparent geodesic dome reading the Guardian. I was also surprised at how many folks where completely naked. Hawkwind where fantastic [*Why am I being left with these enduring visions* of Stacia? - Ed.].".

SPORTING MEMORIES

Whether one was playing or watching, there was must to remember about sporting life in 1976. **Norman Howson** was a competitive cyclist. 1976 was "my best year in competitive cycle racing. Best position, 8th in a 12 hour time trial, 240miles. 20mph!"

Danny Rylance was happy that St. Helens won the Rugby League Challenge Cup Final against Widnes. "Saints were massive underdogs because of their ageing players and were skitted, and nicknamed Dads' Army."

"In 1976 I was 13 years old," writes **Tracy Gulliver**, "and it was the first year I ever watched Wimbledon because I knew the Queen was going to be there during her Silver Jubilee [*Hmm, think that was 1977 - Ed.*]. I was gripped watching my first ever tennis match and watching Virginia Wade holding up the winning trophy was the icing on the cake and I've been watching it ever since! Another great memory for me is cheesecloth tops!"

Chris Leeman and some friends walked the entire length of the Pennine Way, all 272 miles of it. "After 4 days 4 of us ended up in hospital with heat stroke."

And of course there was that big upset at Wembley in May. "1976… hot sunshine… Southampton Football Club won the F.A. Cup, my favourite team. I was in London at this time too! Not so long after we were expecting twins! Brilliant year all round," says **Janet Whittington**.

FOR SOME IT WAS NOT SO GOOD…

Even the most memorable years don't turn out well for everybody. As crowds top up on their tans on sweltering beaches, eating ice cream and listening the classics sounds of the day, sadly there will be those elsewhere who are enduring sadness, hardship and personal tragedy. Some respondents were kind enough to share their personal experiences with us, and our love and respect go out to all of them.

Jennifer Jane Renee suffered heartbreak when her mother was taken from her far too soon. "A very challenging year for me. My mum became ill at the beginning of that year and died of a brain tumour aged 54. I am from Manchester but was living in Newcastle with my boyfriend at that time. Over the course of that long hot summer, I split with my boyfriend, had a couple of affairs, left my job, got back together with my boyfriend, moved to Essex, got a job in London and parted again from my boyfriend. A strange year that coloured the rest of my life."

And **Julia Thomas Arning** had to endure something similar. "It was the year of changes to be sure. I left school, my mum was diagnosed with breast cancer. She fought like a tiger but the battles ended 3 years later, and they emigrated to USA."

Then 25 years old, **Josie Pennington** sadly said goodbye to her father, aged 62, on July 7th. **Mags Arnold** had lost her beloved dad, also 62, on Christmas Eve just before the year began. And tragically **Marion Kenny**'s five-year-old son passed away with cancer in May, while **Caryl Heley** lost her son in a road accident.

Jayne Beswarrick had a motorbike accident and was in hospital on a rubber mattress on traction for the whole summer. **T. Jonathan Lewis** was seven and spent Christmas in hospital with a burst appendix.

Jill Smith says 1976 was one of the worst years of her life. She was nineteen at the time. And **Steffy Moon** agrees. She moved house and started high school, and it wasn't a good time for her. **Ann Bolton** was in the old Lowestoft hospital having a hysterectomy then recuperating so missed a lot of the beautiful weather.

Illness struck too for **Debbie Stringer**, who nevertheless put on a brave face. "I caught meningitis which was not common then. Spent a lot of it in hospital but when I came out I enjoyed what I could. Sad thing was I missed my last week at school, still I was very lucky and won't forget that year."

Clarice Boland experienced real difficulty too. "As a wife and mother I was struggling to look after my children because my husband was continually unfaithful. I had young children and he left us without food or money to buy any."

And **Ann Grayson**: "In 1976 my husband had his first heart valve replacement. The next year it leaked, so a new valve was put in in 1977. A year later the new valve was rejected so in 1978 a pigs valve was put in which lasted until 1994 when his last heart valve was fitted."

Sean Willis recalls: "My brother was run over during that summer and I spent a lot of time going to visit him. It was awful that it was hot outside and he was stuck in a hospital bed with his leg elevated and a pin through it. We were both 12 years old (not twins, step-brothers) and I know we would have had a great summer together if this had not occurred. Walking away from visiting always saddened me but I am sure he was suffering far worse than I was."

1976 also brings back sad memories for **Shane McCarrick**: "I was just a kid. My dog, a Dalmatian named Snoopy, got run over and killed by an electric milk float. Ever since I've had a Mr. Bean moment anytime I see an electric vehicle. Recent times have not been good."

But possibly the most chilling read comes courtesy of **Keith Bedson**, to whom I am grateful for taking the time, and retaining the emotional strength, to relate the following account of what must have been a sad and frightening childhood. "I finished school at about 3.30 pm on the Friday, all excited for a decent summer holiday break. As I walked into the back garden I must have kicked a small stone which hit my old man's rockery and damaged a plant. Now, my dad, being a complete psycho, accused me of trying to destroy his garden. I was given a good hiding and sent to bed with no tea. One of my brothers. Mickey, sneaked me up a jam butty but got caught. That meant both of us in our bedrooms until Sunday, again with no food. My mum cooked Sunday dinner and went to work at midday. As we had eaten we had to wash up, dry and put away the dishes between 3 of us. my brother Ian dropped something but it didn't break. The old man went ballistic and gave all 3 of us a good hiding, smashing Ian's record player and radio with his fists. Now, me and Ian shared a bedroom and he wouldn't let me use his record player or radio, so as dad smashed the player I laughed. What a stupid thing to do. the last thing I remember is a radio flying towards me, and next I woke up with a very sore head. We had to spend the whole summer holiday in our beds. The horrible old b*stard even took away our trousers so we couldn't go out anywhere. now imagine that hot summer laid in bed all day with no radio, TV or record player, or no books, magazines or newspaper to read. All your mates playing in the street, having fun. not allowed to talk to each other as it disturbed the old man's TV time. Only allowed to get up for 1 meal a day and to use the toilet. How much of an animal was he? That is my memory of the lovely hot summer of 1976. Hard to believe I know, but every word of this is true."

SOME MORE MEMORIES

The response to my appeal for recollections from the year that was 1976 was amazing, and there was obviously much overlap between everybody's individual experiences. Nevertheless no two stories are ever the same, because no two lives are the same. Here are some more memories from that year from Facebook users...

Susan Hewitt recalls Cornwall in the heat of the summer. "I was living in a seaside town in Cornwall and I can remember the pervading smell of ozone as all the seafront businesses shops and cafes used seawater to wash their floors and pavements to save tap water. And the seagulls nesting on roofs, it was so hot the nests were drying out and cracking and the baby birds were falling out."

For **Angela Haigh** the abiding recollection is "chumping for wood in power cuts walking down a main road in pitch black. Year we hired a colour TV and I spilt a drink on our new room carpet lol."

Aloysius Walker can recall "playing pitch and putt in Shaldon, Devon, which is on the side of a hill, having so much trouble because the ball wouldn't stop rolling as the grass was parched."

Sylvia Painter was in North Wales when the weather finally broke. "We were on the beach at Llanddulas on July 2nd when we heard thunder in the distance inland... we decided to go back to our house in Denbigh at the bottom of the hill on Rhyl Road. By the time we got back 30 minutes later it had started pouring with rain then huge hailstones came down. All the windows were wide open so dashed in to close them... within 15 minutes the water started backing up on the main road and was up to our window sill when a fire engine came through and caused a bow wave and we could see there was 2 feet of water at least. Gullies were all blocked with dust from the 6 week heatwave! Our neighbours' houses were all flooded... we were lucky!"

Nick had a similar experience down in the South East: "The summer of 1976 we went to a car rally in Mote Park, Maidstone, Kent. It started as a nice dry day with a picnic then the drought broke and we all got soaked to the skin."

Still more egg frying, this time from **Debbie Jane Savage**: "I remember it being really hot and trying to fry an egg I had took from my mum's fridge on the path outside and it started to work. Just a clip around the ear stopped it cooking. Loved making dens up in the local woods with friends - we kept cool in the woods. It was all fun back then. Oh and I had a big crush on the new boy band Our Kid, with their song 'You Might Just See Me Cry' - lol, loved the lead singer [*his name was Kevin Rowan – Ed.*]".

Strangely some of the most evocative memories from the seventies involve television adverts, which even if simple by today's standards were often pleasingly creative. **Phil Cuthbertson** recalls: "Oh Lori, the Alessi Brothers, Brutus jeans and the advert to go with it - 'I put my blue jeans on, I put my all blue jeans on'. Wrangler check shirts that I would iron myself cos the creases had to be perfect, along with the crease in my jeans! Happy days."

And these were carefree days for **Gary Blake** too: "My friends and I had a great summer riding our motor cycles around the south coast. On one trip our girlfriends had removed their jackets and were just wearing bikini tops. We were pulled over by the police and the girls were told to cover up as they were causing a distraction to other road users!"

In the north of England, **Avtar Gill** remembers the local authority urging prayers for rain: "I recall the local council in Leeds asking places of worship to pray for rain and the Sikh Temple (Leeds) performed an all night recital of hymns praying for rain. I don't recall the outcome, however."

Nick Franklin's neighbour struck (literally) upon a novel way of getting around the hosepipe ban. "Helping my dad build a kitchen extension. We knew we were getting close to water pipes when digging the footings. Our neighbour was helping as it was a joint project for both kitchens. As he was digging I said to him to be careful of the water pipe. On his next chop with his spade he went straight through the mains water pipe. I remember my dad being livid and for the next 3 days we had a swimming pool rather than kitchen footing."

Jean Alfonso was in the enviable position of experiencing both the scorching British summer and the bicentennial celebration in the USA (about which more later). "I will share my memories of the hot hot summer of 1976. I now live in the USA. That year I went back to England to spend time with family and friends. Remember seeing cows dead in the field from the heat. I flew back on July 4th, and as we flew over the statue of liberty in New York there was a marvellous firework display. America was celebrating bicentennial year."

Dave Hails remembers lolly sticks and wrappers lying around in the streets, as well as ring pulls from drinks cans which of course were completely detachable in those days. **Stephen Dadd** was doing a slate roof which - wait for it - you could fry eggs on! A wonderful lido in Millhouses Park, Sheffield hosted **Kitty Maloney** and her three-year-old son over many days, and **Kevin Huggett** played for days at the swimming pool in Purley Way (right).

Chris Hayward recalls a work colleague returning from holiday and telling him that she had poured butter down the drain that had been melted by the sun. **Steve Allwood** recalls walking home in the heatwave, **Anna Falcon** walking through melting tarmac.

Lin Whitehouse's family lived in Verdun, with an amazing swimming pool. **Brigid O'Sullivan** remembers that the water was cut off by the works on the M4. **Gail Ingrey** played cricket in the heat with her had in their back garden. **Patricia Pearl Seaman** danced in the rain after having waited weeks for it to arrive. **Jim Young** enjoyed a fantastic summer after buying his first new motorbike in May. **Garry Appleby** resprayed his Ford Anglia, and smashed up his RD250. **Veronica May** returned to England on a very hot day in June to see her family after living in Australia for six years, and noticed how brown the grass was. **Rose Rennard** also had a surprise visit from Australia - her eldest sister Josie. It was the last time she saw her. **Pamela Ducca** meanwhile was living in Canada. **Essaid Motamid** was closer to home in Bath - and knew a Phil Andrews [*wasn't me – Ed.*]! **Mark Elsworth** was doing his A-levels in the "incredible heat". **Sophie Houston** passed her eleven-plus while enjoying the sunshine. **Hazel Wilkinson** learned to ride a horse on what is now the Beverley bypass. For **Tony Heron** 1976 was simply "the greatest year ever", and **Steve James** was having what he describes as "the best times, unlike now.". **Michael Baker** wants to know what became of streaking - **Christine Hunt** remembers them too!

"Sometimes before we had kids we would bring our sleeping bags and spend the night. Plus we camped together, so everyone could just go into their own camper. Great memories!" says **Karen Burdett Level**.

A slightly chilling memory from **Mark Stuart**: "I was in little Loch Broom on the west coast of Scotland, I happened to be on one of the most beautiful beaches in the world and observed something that at my age then meant nothing but now after remembering that and reading up found what I saw disturbing. I watched a group of people in hazmat suites going onto Gruinard Island near Ullapool that our UK government bought for an English pound in 1942 to test out the affects of anthrax. Best holiday I can remember if I ignore that."

And dodgy chemicals were not only to be found on remote islands, as **Glenda Dibbs** can bear witness to: "Water in the school swimming pool hadn't been changed, just more chlorine was being added. My son picked up athlete's foot and it spread. He had it everywhere you can think of... lost 3 layers of skin on his hands... they were so sore that he couldn't even do buttons or zips up... even had it in his ears. Still has skin problems through that infection."

And the heat itself caused blisters too, as **Tracy Davies** explains: "The hot summer... me and my brothers all had blister burns on our shoulders. I slapped one of my brothers on his blister and it burst, but convinced my mam that it was my other brother, he got slapped all over for it. Only owned up to that a couple of years ago."

It's funny the things that some people remember. For **Lisa Bailey** it was "sweltering hot, scorched grass, halter neck tops, red ants and white dog poo [*whatever became of it? - Ed.*]".

Sonia Yarnton challenged the weather to do its worst. "I wore my swimming costume and a thin skirt to go food shopping and was amazed to see many more women doing the same! The first time it rained, we just sat out in it shouting 'bring it on'!"

Gwyneth Ann Owen has memories of the Great Wen: "The only time we went to London we went because my brother was getting married near Trafalgar Square. Very hot, we spent most of the week in the parks. It was also our first visit to the theatre in Drury Lane - Billy Liar with Roy Castle."

And **Pat Lefevre** remembers "one forlorn little tree in the kiddie park dying of thirst... so she carried her washing up water down in the lift and walked it to the park to water it every morning... it survived."

Jeanie Knight "stood behind my mother, buckets in hand, in the queue, waiting for the water turnpike. I can even remember the dress she was wearing, because I was looking at it I guess. Sky blue mini dress with yellow and white daisies on it."

Meanwhile **Brenda Gould** "got baptised and we had to have permission to use the baptismal pool. Next day it rained for weeks."

Confession time for **Tony Reeves**: "We had a large group of friends, every weekend we would go to someone's house and drink, dance, sing, have a good time, then to our disgrace drive home drunk."

Sharon Oldham recalls the drought: "I remember the water being turned off at intervals and standpipes being located on the street. My father filled pots, pans, buckets, washing up bowls etc with water. Kind of defeated the object looking back."

And **Hazel Dower** "was sun bathing in my back garden and the next door neighbour came out. She was a right chatterbox so I made out I was asleep then I did fall asleep and got a very burnt back, ending up in A&E."

Angela Haynes tells us: "My husband was at college, group of lads caught by local paper photographer cooling off in the fountain at lunch which made the front page."

"I was thirteen. Living in South Wales. We went strawberry picking in Hereford, just over the border in England. Put the strawberries into the back of the car. We had packed a picnic. Found a shaded place by a river, unpacked the food and the pack of butter we had brought with us had melted. I remember my mother making me a kind of hat out of a neck scarf to try to shade my head. When we got back to the car the strawberries had turned to mush. This was my little sister's birthday treat," remembers **Rhian Hicks Adlam**.

Elaine Purvis remembers it as a year of music and movies, and a timely visit to the States. "I was 15 years old. That year we went on holiday from Scotland to stay with relatives in California, USA. The music was fab - England Dan & John Ford Coley's hit 'I'd Really Love to See You Tonight' and Wings' 'Silly Love Songs' was too. I bought 'The Eagles' Greatest Hits' and my mum let me buy a bottle of Nina Ricci L'air du Temps perfume. It was bicentennial year and we went to Disneyland around 4th July. We were allowed to stay up late to see The Beach Boys play live at Disneyland. I went to the cinema to see The Omen and Ode to Billy Joe."

Meanwhile **Carolyn Duimstra** went in the opposite direction. "I was 15 and arrived in New Zealand. We had lived in Africa for the previous 11 years."

Margaret Abruzzo grew quite attached to our spotted invaders. "I moved out to Italy, lived out there. Came home to see family every summer holidays and Xmas and I remember the ladybirds, it was amazing! I love them now that I live back in England and have an allotment, I really welcome them!"

June Thomas recounts: "I remember the summer of 1976, too hot for me, I remember the day the rain came, it really was a blessing. I remember the smell of everything being washed by the rain."

And for **Jan Watson** it was some characteristic '70s-style government advice which resonated. "Save water, bath with a friend! I vividly remember dad emptying the washing up bowl onto the garden and the cracked earth everywhere."

Gail Hoban also recalls: "Remember water bowsers on the corner of our road, fetching a bucket every morning.. Garden baked, throwing bath water and washing-up water on the lawn to try and keep it alive. Washing bone dry in half an hour on the line, and something I'd never seen before - cracked earth. So hot couldn't sleep at night, that's my memories of '76."

All in all, I think **Tony Wright** speaks for us all: "Left school at Xmas '75. Started work in January. As the year went on, punk started to appear. The weather just got better. Weekends were spent down the local park, loads of beer. Had to stay out the way, as we were too young to be drinking legally. Brilliant summer nights, someone always had the tape deck. So lots of Bowie, Roxy, Slade, and more were listened to. Could go on and on. Oh for a time machine. See a lot of old friends who are not here now. And never come back to this goddam year."

So let's conclude this fascinating compendium with some stirring memories from **AJ** in the Channel Isles: "The first thing that always springs to mind when that glorious summer of 1976 in Jersey is mentioned is the smell of the drains as you walked through the town and how dirty the pavements were. Each household only had the mains water supply turned on for 2 hours a day which turned out to be a huge mistake as people filled their bath just before the water was turned off, then when the water came on, pulled the plug out to run a hot bath. To save water we were advised to put a brick in the toilet cistern and I'm sure some of those bricks are still there to this day. There was a notice in some of the pub and public toilets that said 'If it's a wee leave it be, anything bigger pull the trigger'. The soft sand on the beach was too hot to walk on barefoot. We went swimming when the evening tide was coming in over the sand because it made the sea so warm. I was working in a bank and the men were permitted to wear shorts with their shirts instead of suits and discard their ties."

HERE COMES THE SUN

Whilst everyone who was there in '76 remembers the spirit and the vibe, and whilst everyone has their own personal story to tell, it is evident that the one overriding recollection that most people have is of the searing heat which stayed with us for so long and brought in its wake shortage and drought. They say the memory plays tricks, and this is undoubtedly reflected in the unmitigated affection with which these challenging times are remembered in spite of the hardships. But it is clear nevertheless that there was something very special about that year which inspires such wistful longing and a profound sense of having belonged to a moment the memory of which burns in the soul.

There was a song released in the summer which was timely in the extreme and rather sums it all up. 'Here Comes The Sun' was an old Beatles number, penned by George Harrison in 1969, but when it was covered by Steve Harley & Cockney Rebel in 1976 it felt like the signature tune of a unique and glorious experience that was already being shared by so many. For some of us amid a year of mixed musical messages it kind of rose effortlessly to the fore, and encapsulated it all to sublime perfection.

7. MEMORIES OF THE US BICENTENNIAL

Meanwhile stateside there was something of a party going on. The 4th of July is Independence Day, but 4th July 1976 was the 200th anniversary of the Declaration of Independence of the United States of America. Or, as it was otherwise known, the United States Bicentennial.

In fact celebrations of this momentous occasion began as far back as 1st April 1975, when the American Freedom Train launched in Wilmington, Delaware and embarked upon a mammoth 21-month, 25,000-mile journey around the 48 contiguous states of the US (that is excluding Alaska and Hawaii, for obvious reasons). The Battles of Lexington and Concord in Massachusetts, which began the military campaign which culminated in the US achieving its independence, were commemorated shortly afterwards in a major address by the then President Gerald Ford.

Once 1976 had arrived and America had gotten its hands into the meat of the celebration proper, there was to be no stopping the festivities. In true American style no expense nor effort was spared. Fireworks, naval displays including a flotilla of tall-masted sailing ships comprising a truly international fleet, and a state visit by the Queen of the United Kingdom on the Royal Yacht Britannia with a symbolic presentation of the Bicentennial Bell on behalf of the British people were just a few of the central attractions. Equally important though were the celebrations which took place in the cities and towns, and in individual households, the length and breadth of the country.

In this section we've tried to capture the spirit of the Bicentennial from the perspective of the ordinary American. Let's take a look at what our US contributors had to say…

THE NAVAL DISPLAY

J.M. remembers the flotilla. "My husband sailed with the tall ship flotilla that made the rounds of a number of American cities for the Bicentennial, and wound up in our home city of Boston for the Fourth."

Jerry Gogliormella recalls the beautiful spirit of it all: "I was 20 years old and what I remember most about '76 was all the buzz about Operation Sail, the tall boats. I spent most of that summer painting fire hydrants the colors of the American flag. How they closed down the Belt Parkway so families could watch the big event. And an overall good feeling about our country and it's history."

Rina Kagel still has the photographs: "Graduated high school, went to the roof of the twin towers in NYC, spent July 4th watching OpSail from the Towers a few days later. We have photos of OpSail!"

There are some similar memories for **Lori Dunlap Fahey**. "1976 I was 14 and I remember OpSail in the New York harbor. I was in the harbor with my dad in our 38ft sail, we sailed to the harbor and I remembered all the tall ships and made us look like a small dinghy. Great memories of that trip."

Some actually served upon the ocean wave, including **Philip Harville II**. "Just getting out of the navy after being on at the time the biggest aircraft carrier the navy had, in Vietnam for evacuations having recently turned 19."

And **Gay Porter** also. "I was in the Navy working on tugboats in Norfolk, VA. I was in the first group of females to work on Navy tugs. Quite an experience, worked on them for 3 years."

Bruce Wildfeuer "was serving on board the USS Nitro... spent the summer of '76 cruising to different countries in the

Mediterranean. Like a good sailor I got drunk and puked in 7 different countries!"

Jesse Powers was going through Navy boot camp at Great Lakes, Illinois. **Donald Honeycutt** by contrast finished his enlistment in the US Navy. "Headed home in my 1973 Nova SS hatchback."

Memories in perfect detail from a young **Patricia Mintell**: "I went camping with my family all over New England and learned a lot about the history of America, and we went to see the tall ships come into Rhode Island. It was a foggy morning and out of the mist came the masts of those tall ships! I was 11 years old and I never forgot it! Then we went to see the train that had the Liberty Bell and King Tut! It was a very awesome summer and the memories are precious."

TOO YOUNG TO REMEMBER?

Of course many of us old folks tend to assume everyone was around and doing something wild during that year, which it's easy to forget was, at the time of writing, 45 years ago. Not so of course, for many it was but the first tentative paddle into the shallows before setting sail upon the meandering river of life...

Alexia Thomson Hanley was a baby in '76, but relates that her parents were heading for a divorce in that year. The same heartbreak sadly befell **Rob Strenth**, who was eight. It's easy to forget that '76 didn't work for everyone. "My parents were getting divorced. After years of waiting for the Bicentennial it was a bust. I didn't feel like watching any fireworks. My mom and I moved out of our house at the end of July and I had to give away my beloved St. Bernard. It was a terrible summer."

Laura Roche Arbogast was born in 1976, but everyone in her family has since collected Bicentennial quarters for her. **Jay Levy** was a 1976 baby too, while **Astrid Quay** just about made it for the big year by arriving in December. Alas **Chelsey Pfiffner** missed the deadline, emerging forth the following month. **Willow Katz** and **Catherine Damphousse** were one. **Pamela Marvin Lim Niedermeyer** was in kindergarten. **Shannon Racculia-McConnell** was two, as were **Kenny O'Connor, Cindy Capraro** and **Nicole Bremner**. Also two years old was **Kristen Faust**, although she does remember wearing a colonial costume for the celebrations. **Jeanette Silva Layton**, two as well, recollects that she was with her mother when she became an American citizen. **Lisa Nassy-Harrison** was six years old and looking forward to starting grade 2, whilst at the same age both **Christine Taylor** and **Victoria J. Huber** have memories of the Olympics on the TV. Five-year-old **Kerry Reed** was at a 4th of July parade and the only concern she can recall having was that her brother had lost his shoe. **Carmen Merrero** was eight and **Elaine Barr** was nine, as was **Patricia Milke** who recalls going to the beach to play with her Barbies. **Kathy Coonley** was three and growing up in San Francisco, and thinks she was probably into Donny and Marie.

Lisa Alexander Baltierra had similar tastes: "I was 3 years old and obsessed with Holly Hobbie, Raggedy Ann, and Donny and Marie. And Hee Haw. In December 1976 I got a new baby sister."

Jamie Mari was a '76 baby. "I was busy being born! June 10, 1976. It was also my uncle's 18th birthday AND his graduation from high school. My grandma was torn on which one to attend and she did her best to be at both (I also graduated on my 18th birthday, in 1994. And my youngest son shares my and my uncle's June 10 birthday!)."

Kristie Pennock seems blessed with the benefit of handed-down information. "I understand I was puking a lot - regular formula didn't agree with me, and I got switched to soy [*We never had that in the UK for years after - Ed.*]. I also apparently spoke very early, and my first word was 'book' I was living it up back in the day!"

Rosemary Moon was born to a young mother (right). "I do know that I had some hot Raggedy Anne and Andy gear in my nursery that she shouldn't have been able to afford," she jests.

Chris GE comments: "I was 6 months old in July '76. Great year and I am proud to be a bicentennial baby! Both of my parents were graduates of Woburn (MA) High School class of '76 too! One of the largest classes (baby boomers)."

And **Heidi Evans** also has the benefit of some respective information. "I was a baby barely starting to toddle, so my memories are pretty vague and may actually be a little later but I do remember all the grown-ups *talking* about the bicentennial and being allowed to hold my first sparkler."

D. Jordan Berson was two but has a good memory. "I was two years old but remember it... My parents were working as counselors at a summer day camp in New Jersey, and they brought me along for the day on a few occasions. I recall being forced to take a nap I did not want to take in the back of a new Dodge Aspen station wagon (one of the camp vehicles). I remember being quite unhappy being left alone in the car like that."

Kelli Núñez has good musical recall for one who was so young at the time. "I was 5 years old, preparing to begin kindergarten. Watching lots of TV and playing with my dolls. One album that really stands out in my memory from that summer is Johnnie Taylor's 'Eargasm', which included to big hit 'Disco Lady.' My mom had the album. My uncle had the 8 track. Was played constantly."

HIGH SCHOOL MEMORIES

High school seems to be a life experience that has pride of place at the heart of US culture. Certainly here in the UK we see a great deal of it on our television screens. So what was it like to have been at high school during 1976 and the Bicentennial?

Kathy Arvia had just finished her freshman year. "Went to Door County for the Bicentennial. Hated going there. My brothers were old enough to be left home but not me. Although that might have been the summer my bff came with us. We were good at sneaking 6 packs."

Janet Carrillo has a fascinating story to relate: "Just finished my junior year in high school, found out I was pregnant. Got married on July 3rd. He was a private in the army - we were not rich, had a little apartment. Poor guy, I didn't know how to cook, clean, do laundry. So I refer to him as my guinea pig. We were blessed to have a healthy daughter on Christmas Day. But the one good thing I did was get my GED months before I had her. Graduated months before all my friends."

It was junior year too for **Camille Trentacoste**. "Every year, the senior and junior classes put on competing plays, called The Spring Show. We were the only junior class that ever won because we were wholly cynical; the title of our play was This Is Your Life, Uncle Sam. Total patriotic bicentennial schmaltz and everybody went for it."

Jolene Cross was a freshman. "I was 14 years old and a freshman in high school. Me and three of my friends decided to skip school and go swimming at a mill dam. I went over the dam and thought I was going to drown, something clicked in my head and I quit fighting and I got out of it, but when I got home my mom asked me what happened cuz I was all scratched up and I told her I fell off the baseball bleachers at school!"

Janine Randall laid on a patriotic play as well. "I was in Jr. High and my brother was in High School. The High School did a patriotic play about the history of America. I played a passenger on a ship bringing immigrants to America. My brother played Groucho Marx. Otherwise, a special 4th of July parade, ending in fireworks that night."

Susan Patton Salisbury took part in a patriotic prom. "I was 16 years old living in rural east Kentucky, where I still live. Everything and every product seemed to be festooned in red, white and blue. Our high school prom was a patriotic theme with 10-12 foot posters depicting the likes of Uncle Sam and the Statue of Liberty lining the gym forger walls. Red, white and blue flowers and streamers, Stars and Stripes hung from the rafters. I wore a Gunne Sax (my absolute favorite brand in that era) lacy, high necked dress in pale peach. I took home two of those huge posters after the prom to keep. Our school library had students collect and set up a display of 7-Up cans that, if all put together like a puzzle, had an image of Uncle Sam. Pepsi came out with a commemorative Bicentennial bottle, I still have one. Log Cabin syrup issued glass bottles with 1776-1976 on the bottle. My cousin was born July 4 of 1976. His birth certificate was decorated with flags and patriotic images. Since my memories are so fond of that time, I have bought anything with that year on it as I enjoy my hobby of thrifting. Before I even realized it, I had a good sized collection of 1776-1976 items, which I now display every year during the month of July."

"That was a very memorable year for me," recalls **Carla Tedford**. "I had a little hippy boyfriend (gorgeous blue eyes) and we wandered all over Orange County, CA and had a great time… keg parties, southern California beaches, hiking, his parents had a great block party for July 4th. And, I graduated high school.

Some musical high school memories from **Amy Fortin-Davidson**, as well as sadly some real tragedy: "1976 was a big year in my life. I graduated from High School so it was my last summer at home. I joined the local militia unit as summer employment where I did landscaping work at the local cemetery. It was the summer my parents were involved in a car accident while on vacation. The injuries my mother suffered contributed to her death. 7 years later. I left for college that fall at her insistence. I remember listening to Peter Frampton, Bruce Springsteen, and Alice Cooper while hanging out with my friends at the local park. It was a small mining town on NW Quebec so there wasn't much for an Anglophone to do."

It was graduation year for **Diane DeLaney Kane**. "Graduated from high school in 1976, we were able to have our school colors tassel and a red white and blue one. I didn't turn 18 until after the election in November so I wasn't able to vote. President Ford lost to President Carter."

Like **Suzanne Smith Ware Barger, Sheryl Bacon** was heading for junior high: "I was fresh out of elementary school (K-6 in CA) and very excited to be going into 'junior' high. A highlight of 6th grade was getting to go to Disneyland as a school field trip. Because it was the Bicentennial Disney had a bunch of special programming to celebrate. I remember trying out to be a cheerleader (didn't make it) and spending most of my days either in the pool or at the beach. Mom would give us money for the bus and snacks and we'd walk to the bus stop and take the OCTD (Orange County Rapid Transit District) buses to Huntington Beach... at 12 years old! I don't recall going on any summer vacations that year. That may also have been the summer that I read Gone With The Wind."

Teresa Hawkins graduated from high school in June. "It was the bicentennial so everything was red white and blue. One of my friends had a car with a prized 8-track in it and we cruised all over town listening to Thin Lizzy's 'Jailbreak', 'Frampton Comes Alive', and REO Speedwagon," she recalls.

1976 brings back fond musical memories for **Jan WM** too. "Class of '76 high school graduation, SuperJam at Busch Stadium. Fleetwood Mac, Ted Nugent and many more. Starting college, parties, beaches and fun."

Sherry Corbin "graduated from high school in June. Am sure I worked during summer to go to junior college. Great growing up in a small town."

And **Cheryl Kincaid Snider** recounts: "I graduated high school. Worked at a Mr. Steak, and went to college. Met my future husband but I didn't know it at the time

Also graduating was **Robin Humphreys**, who got married too - for a time at least: "I graduated high school in 1976 - the Bicentennial year. Got married on June 12th, which didn't last very long. Got my first job at Westinghouse on Reform, Al. In October of that year a lot happened for me... a good year for me."

So did **Georgeline Jean-Charles** - graduate that is, not get married. "Yes wonderful year, graduated HIS in June 1976. 1,000 graduates, long graduation. Our song, to reach the impossible dream."

Tracey Martin Spencer remembers: "I graduated high school that year. Was already working full time at Ocean Spray Cranberries in Hanson Massachusetts as I was allowed to leave school in January before graduation, as I had earned enough credits. I remember our caps and gowns were white with stars and stripes on the shoulders. Bicentennial Year was a big deal."

And **Stephanie Stokes Meyer**: "I graduated SH and started my first big adult job at an insurance company in downtown Indy... Used my older sister's ID to get into the bars with all my work friends… so much fun!"

It was someone else's big moment that **Lisa Coates Leeming** was toasting. "Celebrating my brother's high school graduation and the bicentennial opening of Fort Stanwix in Rome, New York."

Meantime **Margaret Carole** was just starting out on that phase of her educational journey. "I started high school, got my driver's permit. I remember watching the huge fireworks display in New Orleans on the river. 'Slow Ride' by Foghat was everywhere! At least five times a night at the roller skating rink!"

Still a high school junior was **Norm Fourier**, but he had other talents too. "Had a job working at a gas station, but that was when a bell would ring when you pulled up to let me know so I could jump up, pump your gas, clean your windows, check your oil, and check your tires for the proper air pressure. All for free. You didn't even need to get out of your car. Riding my motorcycle, and meeting new people wherever I went (great times!)."

John Lautner was just entering his junior year. "The Bicentennial and the election were very big that summer. The political parties had their conventions that summer, and that event was on all three networks. Being in the Detroit area we got

Canadian Television (BCC) and had a couple of UHF stations that had other programming. Our hair was all way long, we guys all had this huge helmet of hair, that was the style. Funky plaid print clothes, very unreal fabrics. Pot. Pot was everywhere."

Memories of patriotic fervour predominate for **Leanne Fritzell Coleman**. "It was the summer between my junior and senior year of high school. We were, as every summer down the Jersey Shore, at Sea Isle City, in Cape May. My friend Debbie and I were in the car with my parents at 2pm, on 7/4/1976 [*that's the 4th of July the way our American friends do it - Ed.*] when the traffic came to a complete stop. Then... church bells! Fire whistles! Car horns! Everyone screaming and clapping and shouting USA! USA! USA! It was amazing."

Big musical memories for **'Records' Randy**: "I graduated from high school as a member of the Bicentennial Class of 1976. On the fourth of July I attended the Bicentennial Jam, which was an outdoor concert held at the local speedway. Twenty-thousand of us suffered in the extreme heat to hear Head East, Rick Derringer, Frank Marino and Mahogany Rush, Ted Nugent and Foghat. Although Foghat was the headliner, Nugent literally blew them away. Apparently, no one realized that Nugent had blown out an entire side of the sound system with his encore of 'Stranglehold'. Foghat came out thinking they were blasting 'Fool for the City,' but only one side of speakers emitted sound. Fans immediately began to file out, they'd come to see Nugent anyway."

Beth Wagner Perez "was seventeen, graduated February 1976 and bided my time until I turned eighteen in the fall. Got a full-time office job and my own apartment. I also met my future husband. We are still together... forever."

Beth Wallace "graduated High School... Bicentennial year. Was great, everything had '76 on it. Got my first Zippo lighter, has '76 on it. Nobody will ever forget 1976, oh got drunk a lot."

The "world turned upside down" for **Rhonda Kimmel** in 1976. "I graduated from high school and spent the summer lifeguarding, teaching swimming and selling Avon. I was a first generation college grad in 1980 but everything started in 76! 1976 changed my life."

Yet another HS graduate was **Lori Day-Hamilton**, who has a beautiful if poignant tale to convey. "High school students painted the mural at Pardo Dam honoring the nation's bicentennial. It was fun driving by it for decades recalling all of the fond memories. Sadly it has faded and like old memories, the beautiful art is chipping away."

Mary Allen was a "Bicentennial high school graduate in south central Iowa. We enjoyed a group of school mates that spent time that spring meeting at one of the two city lakes. One had a great spillway with a green slime that enabled us to 'foot ski' down. Such great memories! That spring and summer was all about awesome friendships. Bicentennial at its best!"

Jan Foecke was declared Ms. Bicentennial at her high school. **Nita Parker** graduated from hers in May. The Elvin Bishop song, 'Fooled Around and Fell in Love' was one of her favourites from that time, while fellow graduate **Steve Piontkowski** played recreation baseball as a catcher and listened to Aerosmith, Neil Young and Bowie. After her graduation **Patti Potillo** finished cosmetology college in 1976. **Catherine** of Lancaster, PA quickly tired of being introduced as a graduate of the "bicentennial class of McCaskey". For **Kevin O'Callaghan** it was to be the last year at HS, while **Brenda Czerwonka, Liz Tompkins, Cindy Scott McAllister, Cheryl Hightower Farmer, Denise Riviere McCarthy, Brenda Schoonhoven Mitchell** and **Janet L. Chronister Casuscelli** were 1976 graduates too. **Tammy Olson**'s high school actually used the slogan "Spirit of '76". **Barbara Flynn** recalls: "I was 18 years old. Just graduated from high school in June of '76 and Jimmy Carter was running for President."

Michelle Algernon Poutre underwent a defining experience and emerged the better for it. "In 1976 I graduated from 8th grade middle school. Toward the end of that same summer, I got into a fist fight with my best friend, effectively finishing that childhood relationship. I went in to freshman high school year with a strangely new freedom and attitude. A new outlook that allowed me to become myself rather than the sidekick-butt-of-jokes of a bullying friend. Sometimes we are unwilling to make uncomfortable but healthy changes in our lives until we are forced out of our comfort zone. I thank God for such trying times."

Sherry Carroll O'Neill went into high school in 1976. **Linda Zelepugas** also started in September of 1976. **Edna Sprinz** was just starting out on that particular journey too: "The summer before we all started high school. The Bicentennial. Our Girl Scout troop camped all the way from southern Illinois to Washington D.C. We went to the White House and visited the Eternal Flame where President Kennedy is buried. We went to the Smithsonian. We went on to walk the Boardwalk and Hershey, Pennsylvania before heading home."

And finally, one guy who couldn't get enough of high school was **Edward Adams**. He spent three days driving from California to Connecticut with his guard dog in the passenger seat to attend his tenth HS reunion.

AMERICA AT WORK

With all the high school activity one could be forgiven for thinking that Americans in 1976 were a nation of teenagers and wondering who kept the wheels of the economy turning. So we'll take a look at some of those who were already out and about in the world of work…

That year's celebrations gave **Mary Wagner-Webb** an opportunity to showcase her theatrical talents: "Working on PIT's production of Hair, that ended up winning national college competition and played at the Kennedy Center. It was our Bicentennial show."

Also in the theatre, though perhaps in a different way, was **Dori Dearman**: "Worked at a drive in movie theater. Dating an usher who I eventually married. Went to rock concerts as often as possible."

Lvminda Benedict was a "newbie on the job and was assigned a classified job. Looking back honored to earn trust."

Barry Brick was giving tours at Independence Hall in Philadelphia, while **Glen Carman** was going to trade school and working at a gas station while smoking weed and drinking beer. At just sixteen **Dan Preston** was helping out at the Paralympics in Toronto, an experience he says he will never forget.

Lisa Stabler was fourteen. "My first job was cleaning our local post office. Lived in a small town in southern Illinois. Loved my a.m. transistor radio. Hanging out with my best friend who lived next door."

Being married to a farmer was no easy life for **Brenda Vandenberg** in the fierce Minnesota drought. They "picked corn for hours just to get a wagon load."

Joe Felix had an enviable job. "I was 22 at the time. Between gig working as a roadie setting up for rock concerts, I would drag race at a track in the Midwest. June 10, after coming home from the road, where I was gone for 6 weeks, I got to see my newborn niece, and my grandparents, that flew in from Hawaii. First time I ever saw them in my 22 years."

Interesting work too for young bride **Jude Lamparelli Lathrop**. "I was 19 and had been married one year. My husband was a grad student at UConn and I worked in the Alumni Office. We lived in faculty housing on campus as he taught computer science. We paid $175 a month rent for a 2 bedroom apartment!"

Some memories from **Mark Quinn**: "I was 22 years old, shipping milk from a run down farm in Richmond, haying in two towns, still living at home. I worked and went square dancing at poker hill school once a month, maybe danced in Charlotte then too."

Norma Jean Martin Zimmerman was seventeen and working at her first job, although nothing particularly exciting about the experience springs to her mind. But **June Ann Queeno** recalls her old haunt: "I was 19 years old. I worked as an answering service switchboard operator. I hung out with my friends at a bar called The Almanac."

Jan Ellison writes: "I was working at Jack in the Box and spending time with family and friends going to Galveston and Surfside at the beach. Being to cool as a teenager."

Marcia Pedersen was with IBM in Winston, Salem. Sixteen-year-old **Debbie Martin** was going door to door delivering newspapers. **V from BG** ran an antiques shop. "So many people were looking for USA historical items and were also decorating their homes in colonial styles as a nod to our heritage. I found it so interesting to be a part of a 200 year celebration. I was a high schooler in a small town and while little was taught or said about it at school, at home it was a big deal. I felt like I was raised in 1776-1860 on a regular basis (antiques were part of our daily experience) but that year even more. I remember reading several books about the founding fathers and everything I could lay my hands on that was written around that time frame. I think we even wore pants with colonial/bicentennial patterning on them."

Linda Prather was in fast food. "I was 18 and working at Pizza

Hut. Not a clue what to do in the future, just floating along happy to get free beer after closing time."

I am grateful to **Karen Lindfors Dickel** for this insightful and richly detailed reminisce: "At the end of the 1976 school year I was a newly credentialed teacher who unfortunately was not hired for the following year. Our family inherited a little money that needed investing rather than pay taxes, so my dad saw the opportunity and set me up in a little gift shop on Balboa Island, California. So there I was at 22, owning my own business and paying my own way. The shop thrived in the tourist environment. I sold OP clothing as well as unique art and souvenirs. My dad and I made custom stained glass windows and sun catchers. I kept the shop open till at least 9pm every night and would meet my friends afterwards for drinks and listening to the local bands in Newport and Laguna. I had the shop for 5 years, until a greedy landlord tripled my rent. The Island atmosphere was changing and it wasn't the small town feel any more, as higher-end businesses moved in, so I sold off my inventory and moved on. Best summer(s) of my life!"

And likewise to **Melinda Moylan**: "In the summer of 1976, I worked in Swope Park (KCMO) at a day camp for kids with various disabilities. I had met my future husband there the previous year and we were planning our wedding for the next year. In the fall of 1976, I was student teaching in two areas in the Hickman Mills School District… one a regular classroom, and then in a classroom for children with emotional problems. I finished college and was hired to teach students with emotional problems in Lee's Summit and loved every minute of it! It was a fabulous time to be alive… women and minority workers were making strides in equality, health care was making advances in the fight against disease, our country celebrated our bicentennial, and I was a part of all of it!"

FOND RECOLLECTIONS

Some contributors inevitably remembered more than others about their 1976 experiences, and it would be good to look at a few of those who did go into rather a lot of detail. **Jennifer Tancredi Felciano** was very young, but her recollections are vivid: "July 4th 1976... I was seven years old, soon to be eight. My little brother was younger than me and we were filled with excitement over the upcoming celebrations and fireworks. We grew up on Staten Island in New York City right on New York Harbor. Just a very short walk down the street brought us to the Waterfront where we would be watching the firework spectacular with all of our friends and neighbors. What more excitement could a kid want? Of course at the time my parents were very much into the history of the American Revolution so my brother and I were both dressed up for the whole day in home-made outfits by my grandmother reminiscent of children from the revolutionary war era, complete with a mob cap and apron. I also recall that just over a month later when I turned 8 I received for my birthday my very first two wheel bike and it was spectacular in all of its bicentennial glory. It was white with the red and blue stripes and stars all over the seat with a red white and blue basket on the handlebars! I was so proud of that darn bike, it was the hit of the neighborhood."

Carolyn Kluender was the same age. "I remember it well! I was a 7 year old kid. My mom made home made 1776-1976 shirts to celebrate the bicentennial, one for herself and aunts and my grandma (not me, she knew me too well). I remember grandma getting a lot of coloniawful themed things like purses and dolls. My dad bought a new vehicle, a Jeep Wagoneer, it was yellow. We drove it to Bemidji, MN to celebrate the 4th of July. I remember it was very special, they had a parade during the day, a festival, rides, a massive fireworks display, over the lake, and performances by a waterskiing team. I won a stuffed animal that squeaked. Jimmy Carter was running for President. I was an avid collector of Holly Hobbie, and the Sunshine family. That was a great time, one of my favorite summers."

And **Sheila Hoover** too (*weird how it's all the youngsters who seem to have the most vivid memories - Ed.*]. "I was 8, living in Phoenix, Arizona. The Freedom Train came through that year and I remember standing in line to board and see all the displays (it was a Constitutional museum on rails). Other things that were important to me that summer were riding my bike with the top 40 AM radio station playing from the transistor radio I had bungeed to my handlebars, and helping to decide which route my family would take in our new camper going to Superior, WI to visit my grandmother. On July 4th my dad, mom and 2 sisters climbed up on the roof of our little 3 bedroom/1 bath house and watched the local fireworks from Arizona State University (I think), with a soundtrack of Sousa marches and other similar patriotic songs playing on the radio. Before we went up on the roof, we had watched the tall ships parade into NY harbor and past the Statue of Liberty with a symphony playing a musical accompaniment… that was on the PBS station (one of the 5 options we had to choose from)."

Rebecca Helm-Hill was a little older, and captures the dichotomy between the flag-waving patriotism of the moment and the ebbing vibe of the earlier peace movement very creatively. "We were just coming out of that anti-Vietnam war/anti-Nixon era, and 1976 celebrates America's 200th birthday. Several WWII vets started some patriotic programs. I sang in a cantata for a church, and just like that, in the hippie craze, we're singing 'I'm just a flag waving American. A citizen I'm really proud to be'. Actually it was refreshing, and so many of us were proud of our WWII vet dads. Then we went back to listening to James Taylor, et al. After all the unrest and Watergate, it was kind of nice to simmer down a bit."

Jim Dean was a similar age to myself, so it is interesting to read a detailed American perspective on life at the time: "I was 14, and loved anything tech related. The government had a travelling exhibit showcasing the 'best of America' - a caravan of tractor trailers that would roll up, set up, and let people walk through the exhibits. Two things absolutely stood out to me. First was a portable radar set. Yep, an actual radar device about half the size of a shoebox (remember, these were CRTs, not LCDs) that was working. Then I came to the working prosthetic arm. It showed how someday people would be able to control a robotic arm using neural connections. Since this was right when Six Million Dollar Man was a big hit on TV, it's no wonder this stood out. Other than that, my main memory is that absolutely everything was patriotic. Red White and Blue were everywhere, and I mean everywhere. Pretty much every company out there found a way to capitalize on it, from special edition cars to wallpaper. You name it, the spirit of '76 was everywhere. My other big memory has to do with the presidential election that year. I was too young to know much about politics, but we did have one fascinating guy who came through town. He was travelling the country campaigning as an independent in an old Ford pickup with a camper. I remember because I worked at the local radio station. He fixed our front steps in exchange for our recording and airing a half hour 'campaign speech.' I hate to say it, but I don't remember his name or his speech, so it must not have had a huge effect on me. It was the first time though that I really thought about the presidency in terms of 'anyone can be this'."

And there are some great Bicentennial memories too from a slightly younger **JP from Connecticut**. "I was 12. Life was great. I remember the Bicentennial, it was a big deal. Grocery stores and gas stations all closed on Sundays which made Saturday a 'real' Saturday. Christmas wasn't recognized until the day after Thanksgiving in the stores. My dad would take us every couple of weeks to buy new Dawn Dolls and accessories. I remember walking to the mall and theater with my childhood neighbors and a film cost $1.50 or so. We hung out outside from morning till dusk everyday in the summer. We ate at the Woolworth's counter and shopped for moon rings and cheap perfume. We remember the waitress there at Woolworth's wearing the light blue uniform and white apron with the huge beehive and red lipstick who was mean to all the kids. I remember our dad coming home from work that year and surprised us with brochures on Florida and he let us choose the hotels in the brochures that we wanted to stay at. We just dreamed of palm trees, the ocean and going to Disneyworld in Orlando where it was truly magical. We traveled to Florida for the first time on a DC10-11 from JFK International and the interior of the aircraft was green and orange. Daytona Beach was a popular spot back then I remember for spring break. And we always sent out postcards to friends! We went down without watches and of course no cell phones. Life was the best that year."

April Giovannini was ten. "It was the *spirit of '76* celebration basically everywhere, we were living in Brockton, MA. We would travel to Boston on the weekends to join in different celebrations around the city. What a super exciting time it was to be alive - liberty bells were the order of the day, they were on everything from shirts to coffee cups! Boston was the great hub at the time. My youth group went to the old north church, what a beautiful landmark. Everyone's class made the trip to the science museum, I could go forever, just such a wondrous era to be a kid."

And **Talisa Bowers** sums up the spirit of it all just nicely: "In the summer of 1976, I was 14 years old. And while most of my friends where into boys, skating, and smoking pot, I was into horses. I got an opportunity to buy my first horse, Sparky, a 2-year-old stallion. I'd already been riding him since he'd been 'broken' to ride. Also, since it was 1976 and the country was celebrating the Bicentennial of our great country, my mom took my brothers and myself for a week camping in a tent to Stone Mountain, outside of Atlanta., GA. On July 4th we'd woken to rain, then it cleared off for a day for playing by the lake, and enjoying other celebrations there at the campgrounds, as the rest of the park was filling up fast with people. Later on just after dark we watched the fireworks being shot off the mountain. A very memorable day for me, and I truly hope for those who remember a wonderful celebration. The rest of the summer was filled with hot days riding Sparky, swimming in a friends pool, and generally being a carefree kid."

THE SPIRIT OF '76 IN MUSIC

On both sides of the Atlantic music played an important part in defining the spirit of that great Bicentennial year that was 1976. Some of our correspondents were happy to share their own musical memories, some of which, perhaps unsurprisingly, have much in common with our own. But there is a distinctively American flavour to many accounts too, and understandably so, especially in view of the patriotic fervour which was inspired by the celebrations. The Eagles were as appropriately named as they could possibly be. **Sharon Drazner** reminisces: "My husband and I were living in a Denver suburb. We heard the Eagles, Fleetwood Mac, Jackson Browne and other great acts at Red Rocks. I had no idea how my life would change the following year with the birth of a son with special needs."

Pam Turner Roberts has some cool memories too: "Damn dude... where shall we start? Houston ,Texas - every band... good times. 1976 Jeppeson Stadium, summer... Beach Boys, Crosby Stills and Nash. Jackson Browne opened. University of Houston was a great place to be... rock on."

Even those who were really young at the time can remember the music. "I was 8 and remember that we mainly played outside. We played games like tag, Kick the Can, Red Rover, etc. Twister was a game we played a lot, indoors. Glen Campbell, Linda Ronstadt, and The Bellamy Brothers were some of my favorite people to listen to on the radio. Great memories Lived in NM at the time," recalls **Anne Ashby-Coulombe**.

Terri Coolidge was a little older. "Well, I was 16 listening to Dr. Hook playing 'Only Sixteen'. Thought I knew everything. Mom was having her boyfriend over after he got off work in construction. Me and my little brother would invite our friends over to hear mom's boyfriend sing and play Johnny Cash. Oh the memories of living in the country. I sure do miss those days now. And, I learned I sure didn't know it all."

Debbie Johnson was thirteen and "totally in love with the Bay City Rollers! Raised in WV as a farmers kid. Baling hay, raised tobacco, and huge gardens."

Also thirteen, **Meg Kelly-Tringale** remembers her mom decorating the house in red, white and blue. "She even did one of those popular hook rugs with the American eagle. Lots of great classic rock from that year! Wings, AC/DC, Aerosmith, Zeppelin, Boston!"

Sherry Lynn had similar tastes: "1976... what a summer. I graduated that year. I saw Aerosmith in concert early that week. On Thursday I went to Cincinnati to see the Wings Over America tour. My graduation was the following day. McDonald's Bicentennial blueberry milkshakes. My first job was in retail. Great music."

So did **Kathy Houlihan**: "I was a member of the Bogan bicentennial graduating class and I remember being given a red, white and blue tossel and collar for our ceremony at McCormick Place. I also remember going to see Peter Frampton, Yes, Lynyrd Skynyrd and Gary Wright at Hawthorne race track on August 1st of the same year; then the very next day I started working for the CFD as the 12th female member of the ambulance service/fire department... a very memorable year for me."

And **Virginia Reynolds Hatmaker** did too. "1976 was the Bicentennial year! It was everywhere - flags, t-shirts, hats, cups and so much more! So many cities and towns had parades and celebrations. Fourth of July was over the top in 1976! Great music by Bruce Springsteen, Led Zeppelin, Pink Floyd, CSN&Y were met with a few disco-type hits on the FM radio stations. The weather was great and pollution was down. Freedom was abound in this country and everyone was loving it! America was one hot and exciting country in 1976!"

"I was 12. I remember listening to AM radio and memorizing all the words to 'Turn the Beat Around' by Vicki Sue Robinson," says **Lilly Leppard**. "Other great songs. Getting ready for JHS. Philadelphia Freedom."

Some were in bands of their own, like **Cynthia Peterson**. "I was in college, 2nd half of sophomore year, the 1st half of junior year. I was in a band and choir and touring with those groups. I went to a Barry Manilow concert in the fall in Austin."

The summer of 1976 was "magical", according to **Lesa Whitaker-Cunningham**. "I had moved every year of my life since 1966. In April of 1976 we moved to Marion, Arkansas. Marion is basically a suburb of Memphis, Tennessee. I had lived in Memphis several times and that was the place I called 'home'. I was reunited with my best friend and boy did we have some fun that summer! The highlight had to have been the Fourth of July Concert at the Liberty Bowl stadium. The bands were: Lynryd Skynyrd, ZZ Top, The Outlaws, Blue Oyster Cult. The concert was general admission so the day started before the sun came up. My two best friends and I secured front row 'seats'. The show was amazing. The bands kept us hydrated through the fence. Everything was perfect. We left the show exhausted, dirty and utterly happy. That is the way all summer days should be for young girls."

And of course disco had a big part to play in the sound of '76, as **James Duffy** reminds us: "The run up to July 4th (the Bicentennial) was amazing to my 14 year old self. My family and I were all caught up in it; I scored a red, white and blue transistor radio and remember listening to disco music on it as I would lay in bed at night. Most of the house was furnished in dark pine 'coloniawful' style. We had replaced the vinyl in our kitchen the year before and one of the accent 'tiles' had 1776 on it."

Michele Harris remembers: "The summer of 1976, I was working as a carhop at 14, met my first love. We used to jump in his Dodge and go to Joelton, to Rawlings Pool. He introduced me to Pink Floyd. This I will never forget."

Liz Margason, meanwhile, was twenty and "having as much fun as possible, smoking lots of weed, wishing there was a decent disco in Indianoplace... listening to good disco, Bob Marley, Robert Palmer and of course Bowie... waiting for the Ramones and the Sex Pistols to blow the whole scene up. Worked at a record store."

Joann Dawson-Mumaw was sixteen and she and her friends were "workin' on our night moves! Always a party happening out at the canal."

Jerri Reynolds Jensen was listening to Hall & Oates while making a red, white, and blue baby quilt for her coming nephew, **Carter St. Amand** was running a disco in Santa Rosa, California. **Eleanor Craig** was boogieing at the Boston Disco - "wild times baby!" **Janice Worden Lamb Clemens** looks back to "July 1976

- 'The Boys Are Back in Town', 'Silly Love Songs,' 'Rock and Roll Music', 'Got to Get You Into My Life'… summer bonfires, BBQs, barefoot summer, halter tops and hip-hugger bell-bottoms, cool grass, just fun."

That same song seems to keep cropping up time and time again. **C.M. of USA** remembers it too: "Laying out in the sun, with Sun In in my hair, listening to the radio, seems like I heard 'Silly Love Songs' constantly. I was a majorette in the band and that year, after band camp, our band went to Florida to perform in the parades there. 3 buses with high school kids and chaperones. We had a blast. Also met a high school junior that I started dating and spent the year going to drive ins and movie theaters and rock concerts. It was a time filled with innocence, happiness and I never wanted it to end."

All in all, the essence and the spirit of that magnificent time is captured by **John Griffin** thus: "Spirit of '76 was a popular theme. I grew up in Wood Ridge, NJ - a small blue-collar town. The 2 police cars had Spirit of '76 painted on them. They also held an art contest. 3 winners got to paint a mural on the side of Hys Appliance Store on the boulevard (the main drag). I was listening to WABC on my transistor radio, listening to the top 10 - 'Silly Love Songs' by Wings, 'Don't Go Breaking My Heart' by Elton John and Kiki Dee and 'December 1963 (Oh What a Night)' by The Four Seasons. Riding bikes with Slats and Danny we were inseparable. Oh to be 10 again. Some of the best days of my life. With the best friends!"

BORN IN THE USA

A lot of people of course, people who are now well into their forties, were only arriving into this world on the year of the Bicentennial. Here we have an opportunity to hear from some of them, and from some of those who gave them to us…

Marion LeBleu gave birth to her eldest daughter on 1-9-76 [*9th of January – Ed.*]. **Jude Adams** bore her first child. **Michelle Sidwell** got married and had her first child too, although sadly her husband passed away only recently And **Lynda Petros** gave birth to her first child too, a little baby girl. It was a baby girl too for **Michelle McCann**, and for **Rita McCombs Belloli**. **Patricia Taylor** was nineteen when she had her son: "I had moved back to my home state of Missouri. Started working at O. T. Hodge Chili Parlor in downtown Saint Louis. Met 2 of the people that would become my best friends and still are (even though one has passed on). I loved the clothes, the music and people. Times were so different then and everyday I wish my children could have also grown up in that era."

Tina Eitemiller was a young mum, giving birth to her baby girl at the age of fifteen. And **Vicky Bartolomei**'s son was born during that hot summer. Greg Anderson and partner had their first son on July 23rd. And there was some very astute timing from **Angela Astuto**: "I was pregnant with my second child, a boy. Not only was he born in the Bicentennial, but also on Veterans Day."

There was to be no cooling off for expectant mom **Kathy Pedjas Girard**. "I was pregnant with our first child. We just moved into a brand new home with no air conditioning so I was hot, sweating, and not happy with my husband because why pay 30 years for air conditioning when he can have our friend put it in next spring? Still upset over that one and the list goes on."

Margie Bergonzini was not to be envied her ordeal. "Was pregnant with my one and only child. He was born September 13th. That summer my husband and I went to three Elvis Presley concerts. He was an Elvis Presley fanatic, period - one concert in Chicago and two in Indiana. I spent most of August and half of September in the hospital with toxemia, until I gave birth by C-section. Son was 8 lbs, 21 inches long. I am 4 ft 10 inches. It nearly killed me."

Marita Rogers-Gomez had her only daughter in May of that year, which she says is her most precious memory. **Debi Gaskell** gave birth to her eldest boy in January as was given a special bicentennial birth certificate to mark the happy occasion. **Carmen Gonzalez** also had a son and was put in a helicopter to take her to Lerr. **Rock Clingman**'s daughter arrived in June. **Donna Nezbeth** welcomed her third child into the world. It was a first son and bicentennial baby for **Donna Polidoro**. And **Mary Lou Cardenas** spent most of the hot summer in a community hospital because in spite of several attempted inducements her son refused to emerge until July 9th.

It was a new baby, a new home and a new truck for busy **Jo Kirley**. "I was pregnant with our first born. I was fat as a cow but my hubby said I was beautiful. Summer was tough that year cause I was pregnant till mid September. We were also buying our first home up on a mountain out in the country that we moved into the week I was in the hospital after having our child. I was 28 that same month. And we bought a brand new 1976 Ford 4WD pickup truck. That winter was the infamous Winter of '76. Where we lived the only reason we got out to go to work and shop was because the man who drove the plow truck for the State lived on our road. Snow was up over the hood of our truck."

Susan McClellan's second arrival came in 1976. "I was busy being a mother of two. My daughter was born in 1971 then my son came along in 1976. By then, I had learned what I wasn't taught. I hadn't been around babies nor cooking for my family. I believe I did a good job being a wife, mother, and house manager. I went back to school then work and recently retired… with a pension, thank goodness. Life is good."

Dezi Alena M Farruga writes: "My son was born on January

5th. A very busy boy, curious and impatient. Fractured his skull at 5 months trying to follow his father. Kept his sister entertained."

And it was work despite the burden of pregnancy for **Debi Cowger**: "I was making macrame plant hangers, wall hangers and free style embroidering jeans, and hand made earrings and necklaces... I gave birth to my first child in October of that year."

From **Patricia Philbeck**: "I was 16 year old living in Burke Co., North Carolina. In March I got married and in September I had my first baby. Thought I knew it all. Marriage went south but son is wonderful."

Becky Cabaniss remembers: "I had my first child, a daughter, in 1976! It was a great to be a new mother. Had been married for almost two years, liking one month. I got married June 21, 1974 and I am still married to the same man. We have three daughters and five granddaughters."

And how's this for a fascinating and truly memorable first for **Carmen Acevedo**? "Our first son, who is now 44 years old, was born on a Saturday at midnight - 12:04 a.m. Sunday morning to be exact on the 4th of July. I didn't realize it until the delivery doctor mentioned that this 6 lb 12 oz baby named Michael Andrew was the first baby born in Los Angeles on the 200th Birthday of the United States. The newspaper 'The Herald Examiner' came to the hospital and interviewed us, took photos and titled it 'First Bicentennial Baby Born in Los Angeles'. Incredible feeling to have this memory of our first child."

GETTING TOGETHER

Whether it was marriage, a first date or just an unrequited crush, if you can remember it 45 years on then it must have meant something. Here is where we honour all those who found happiness in 1976…

Susan Vivian married her one true love that year, although there was sad news more recently: "I married my one and only boyfriend on September 25, 1976 but unfortunately he passed away on April 21, 2017 from cancer. But we had over 40 years together, some good and some bad but we hung in there."

Catherine Shull got married in 1976 and is still married, whereas **Lorna Niles** managed to get both wed and divorced. Also divorced during the summer of '76 was **Cathy Newton Minard**: "Best thing that ever happened to me."

Sue Julene Merritt Doty fondly recalls: "I got married (1st) in May that year. In July, we decorated our house with a sign to say Happy Birthday, USA. We went to the Mall in DC to watch the fireworks."

Debbie Lenahan's brother John and his sweetheart exchanged vows in the summer. "It was the Bicentennial and everything was painted red, white and blue, including every fire hydrant in every town!"

Tina Marie writes: "1976 - I was 20 years old and preparing to get married in October. Big church wedding and reception that lasted longer than the marriage. If I only knew then what I know now!"

And **Lucie Palumbo** was wed in the autumn. "I was 21 and 1976 was the year and it was late October. The fall colors were on full display as my boyfriend and I said our wedding vows to each other outside of the little chapel in Yosemite."

James Ceresnak and his wife tied the knot on June 27th and returned from honeymoon on Bicentennial Day. **John D. Cathey** was married during the celebrations too. He wore a blue blazer, white shirt and Bicentennial tie for the big occasion. **Debbie Myers** said "I do" on July 24th, while **Cyndy Bolton** more simply remembers 1976 as the year of her first kiss. **Pam Keith** was married at the tender age of sixteen and is still happily married today, while **Pam Barbee** meanwhile was "learning how to be married".

Like so many back in the day, **Sue Duhon** was a young bride. "I got married for the 1st time. I was 17! It was awesome! Our song was 'Baby I'm Amazed' by the Beatles. We were married in our home town of Crowley, Louisiana. We lasted 5 years because we were so young but have remained good friends all these years later!"

Also married in that year was **Cindy Sedlacek**. **Charles Shickles** found his first girlfriend amid the joy of the celebrations.

"On 02-25-75 I met Tom," records **Jerry Meek**. "We lived at 32 Argonne in LB, we had met at the bar around the corner, Ribbles. They were wonderful times, we were together for 4 years. He died in 1985 from skin cancer."

At the tender age of fourteen **Claudia Weil** admits to some misadventures: "Cigarettes, pot, and rock'n'roll. No sex yet."

Whereas **Laura Benjamin-Miller**, slightly older, just hadn't yet started rolling: "I was 15. Had fun. Sex, drugs and rock. Lol."

CEPM of Tennessee was nothing if not determined. "I was 16 in 1976, and was actively pursuing a boy I was interested in. We ended up dating for two years. My hometown hosted speed boat races every July 4th, and I attended with the above mentioned boy. Fireworks followed at dark, and he took me home. Just to illustrate how self-centered teenagers can be, I was more interested in boys than the fact that my country was 200 years old."

So too was **Kerry Trout**. "The summer of 1976 was spending the weekends cruising Independence Boulevard in our hot rods. Very much like American Graffiti, we hung out at Shoney's where the car hops still skated out with your order! Me and my bestie usually went to watch the cute guys, and one night a gorgeous blond in a Z/28 pulled in, and he took my breath away. I told my girl friend that was the man I'm going to marry. I didn't even know his name. But I would, and Bob and I married two years later. He's gone now, but I will always remember the wonderful summer of '76."

And it's forty-five years and still going strong for **Christine Gertsch**: "We got married at Wayfarers Chapel in Palos Verdes, CA and we are still blissfully married. Watching the '76 Olympics on the patio in our backyard and BBQing with my family."

SERVING AMERICA

The United States, of course, boasts the world's most powerful armed forces and has long been proud of its fine military tradition. As well as the Navy, many of our correspondents were playing an active role in the other armed services, keeping their country safe during 1976. **Art Crow** was one of them. "Having spent most of 1975 hitchhiking throughout Canada and the US, I walked into a US Army recruiter's office in early December of that year and asked how to join the Army. Two weeks later, on December 27th, I was off to Fort Dix, NJ for basic combat training (BCT). I spent New Year in BCT; loved the extra push-ups to break in the New Year! Hoorah! In late April '76 I graduated from the US Army Military Police School and was assigned to an MP company at Fort Hood, TX. From long-haired road bum to warrior MP in 4 not-so-easy months. Who'd a-thunk it, eh?"

Also in the forces was **Maggie Crampton**: "1976 - took a break from active duty Army (but stayed in National Guard) to go back to college for my AS Degree. After, I went back on active duty. Was seriously into country music and dancing then, but also first heard Kiss."

Michael N. Lisle remembers "Basic Training - Fort Riley, KS, summer of 1976. We returned from two years at Fort Riley on 11/75. I missed the beach out there as we were east coasters!"

Some, like **Ken Matthews**, served in the skies. "In 1976, I was stationed at Hurlburt Field Florida. Lots of great memories! Later that year, I was transferred to Galena Air Station Alaska. When I left Florida, my dad flew down and drove home with me! A fun trip!"

Also in the Air Force was young **Mark Patten**, although he admits to having had some misgivings: "On July 4 1976 I was assigned duty at the main gate of Vandenberg Air Force Base in California. We had protesters with 'no nukes' posters. I felt that I was on the wrong side of the gate. I was 19."

Kathleen Vasquez was in the military during '76. **Richard Sorrells** was serving in the Army, and **Jean Johnson** had just joined too. **Charles Evans** on the other hand was just completing his tour of duty. **Howard LaPointe** was overseas with his wife and daughter at the Clark Air Base base in Singapore. And the aptly-named **Steve Battles** mas still on active duty.

"I enlisted in the army in August and spent the rest of the year in basic and advanced training. Home in December on leave before being sent to Germany," recalls **Michael Smith**.

Great memories of living in a military household abound for **Fi Richter-Visser**: "Going with Dad to the Air Force Base pub and all the dads drinking and all us kids swimming in the pool. Every now and then some dads would come out with chips and fizzy drinks for us all! Air Force Kids hanging out! No lifeguards but no-one died."

Ralph Tree was inducted into the US Army in April (see right) "and spent that whole summer in Fort Leonard Wood, Missouri. Hot, humid and lots of bugs. The music was great!"

And **Anette Krause** captures the spirit perfectly with her thoughts: "That was the bicentennial. My father was in the Air Force and we had just returned from England and moved to a small Missouri town. The first American television show I saw was at a stopover in NY. It was SWAT. And we ate at an American McDonald's. I was so happy because I hate mayo and at that time European McD's put mayo on the burgers. God bless America."

THE FREEDOM TRAIN

Anyone who is of a certain age in America will remember the Freedom Train (known to some as the Bicentennial Train, or the American Freedom Train). Bedecked in the red, white and blue of the national flag, the 26-car steam-powered locomotive toured all 48 contagious US states during an epic and relentless 21-month, 25,000-mile journey, stopping all along the way to display "Americana", or American cultural artefacts. During that marathon journey it was visited by over seven million people. Not unreasonably this for many of our contributors was one of the most memorable events of a very memorable Bicentennial year…

Laura Torrence Kangas recounts: "I remember taking a field trip to St. Louis to see the American Freedom Train by the arch when I was in 8th grade. So exciting celebrating our bicentennial! I remember going to see Rocky at the theater!"

Mary Owsley remembers it clearly. "I was in fifth grade and we took a field trip to see THE FREEDOM TRAIN. A traveling museum to celebrate the bicentennial."

The train stopped at the park in **Millicent Frendlee**'s neighbourhood. **Kim Collins** was proud to have been "standing in line to be part of history."

The train forms only a part of **Terri Ettleman**'s recollections. "Upstate New York, visiting grandparents for the summer in corning. I remember putting bicentennial quarters on the train tracks so the bicentennial train could run them over. We would hide in the kudo and listen to the quarters whizz by our heads. It's also the year some guy tried to hit my brother for telling him the name of the street was 'Guess'. It really was, dude got super irate. Painted the hydrants red, white and blue."

Douglas O'Leary was one of a whole group who got to see the show: "I remember it as the summer of the country's Bicentennial. There was the Amtrak Freedom Train, full of memorabilia from the past 200 years. It criss-crossed the country stopping in Omaha. I was in grade school and our class got to go see it. It was very memorable."

And **Bobbi Schneider** remembers well the day the Freedom Train came to town. And we are reminded that '76 wasn't all sweltering sun. "A person dressed as Abraham Lincoln gave a speech. We got to tour the train. Also was one of the worst winters in Montana."

For anybody interested in transport or US history, the story of the American Freedom Train is a fascinating read. You can find out more about it at its own dedicated website at this address:

https://www.freedomtrain.org/american-freedom-train-home.htm

THROUGH THE EYES OF BABES

They say younger people are more receptive to colours, sounds and general razzmatazz. So to have been a young pre-teen at the time of the 1976 celebrations must have been extra special. No wonder some of those who were can remember it with such clarity so many years on.

Jeff Wetmore got to ride on the Bicentennial train (see above). "I was 9 and the biggest memory I have was my state funded a bicentennial steam train expedition daily for a month in the summer. Not only did we get to ride the train, it ran through our town and being near to the tracks, all the kids on the street would go to the Pearl Street Overpass, we'd watch the steam train and flatten some coins on the tracks."

Kathy Waters-Holcombe, meanwhile, got to dress up: "I was 11 in Philadelphia and the entire extended family was dressed in costumes from 1776. We rode, walked in parades, were in many things, celebrations throughout the area. It was a fantastic summer."

Elaine Holland though had to tone down on the dressing up. "Wonderful, I was 12 in the Bicentennial year. Wore home made clothes with red, white & blue; no flag pattern though, my conservative parents found that disrespectful! Our small town blocked off the main street and had carnival rides and games, fair food, the high school and town bands playing. Later in the day they had go-cart races. Great fun, nothing like it."

John Castrogiovanni has clear recollections: "I was six years old and I remember the bicentennial year so vividly, the red, white and blue theme everywhere."

At the same age, **Gayla Ann Iberg** also had a wonderful time. "I was 6 and I remember everything being about the bicentennial! Like a big giant summer long 4th of July!"

So did **Lisa Holley Umfress**: "I was 11 and a cheerleader, so ball games, rollerskating on Friday and Saturday nights to the awesome music."

The entire experience of that year was just beyond description for **Nick Leary**. "I was 6 when I basked in '76, born in Lower Penn., surrounded by fields and people, it would be nice to share a memory but there's too many, great times."

And it was a glorious time to be alive for young **Zoe MaryAnn Tozzi** as well. "I was 8. It was the best summer of my life! How sad I peaked so young lol, it was great though, sincerely. Everyone was proud to be American. I recall fireworks and BBQs every weekend - although that might be me romanticizing it. But the way I remember it was the best summer in my 52 years of life."

Wow!

Jerry Barker had a discerning eye for automobiles in spite of his tender years: "I was six years old. The 4th of July weekend I watched my dad replace the engine in his 1964 Plymouth Valiant station wagon. The night of the 4th we went to watch fireworks in Harrisburg, OR. Halfway through the show, thunder and lightning hit."

Karen Ann Campbell has something to look forward to: "I was 9. Marched in the 4th of July parade, I was a baton twirler. Then buried a time capsule with my Brownie troop to be opened in

2076."

And there are lots of clear young memories from **Jean Peterson**. "I was 10, turned 11. We lived outside D.C. so the bicentennial was huge... everything was colonial red, white and blue. My parents were Republicans so they took Carter being elected hard. I saw The Bad News Bears... lots of good movies were rated R so I didn't see them until later. I saw Gone With the Wind on TV with my mom, cementing my love for Clark Gable and dark firmly-haired rogues with mustaches, to my detriment. I watched Kimba the White Lion and Speed Racer before walking to school. I began my 45 collection, was an ace at dodgeball, discovered Levi jeans and corduroys, and watched Nadia get her perfect 10 at the Olympics. Came to love the Bionic Woman, Alice and Laverne and Shirley that began that year."

Stacey Beduhn was lucky enough to come out of it all with a souvenir. "I was 9 in 1976 but remember that summer well. It was the bicentennial and everyone was so excited to celebrate the 4th of July that year. My Dad even got us kids pins (right)."

You're never too young to take an interest in politics, as **Cari Goldman** ably demonstrates: "I was 8 years old and spent the summer at camp. One afternoon they got everyone together and held a mock presidential election. Kids from 6 years old all the way up to teenagers. Counselors in their late teens and early 20s, several of whom were British. Two counselors spoke as the candidates and presented their platforms. I voted for Gerald Ford, because I knew more about him than Jimmy Carter. If that had been the real election, Ford would have won by a landslide."

Mindy Nieland was younger still. "I was 6 years old living in Mt. Shasta - a small mountain city in Northern California. My parents owned a motel. I remember riding in a stagecoach for the bicentennial parade."

Also six, **Chrystal White** had other things on her mind: "My grandmother and I were trying to convince my dad to let me get my ears pierced. Took us 2 years before he finally let me."

And **Lori Brannan** was five. "My brother turned 7 in June and had a flag cake. Mom made it to look like the first flag with 13 stars. On July 4, 1976 we celebrated the bicentennial with a picture in front of the house with me and my family all dressed in red, white and blue."

Rachel Brasell was too: "I was 5 and lived on a block full of kids of all ages in Albuquerque, New Mexico. I was in kindergarten and I loved walking to and from school way behind my sister. I remember talking to these decorative collie dogs that were on the tops of the chain link fence on the block I walked to school."

Mark Murphy Sr. was out east: "Looking at Statue of Liberty, 11yrs old, from Staten Island... promenade walkway... over the tall people. Bicentennial."

And nine-year-old **Patrice White** wasn't far away either: "Celebrating the Bicentennial in Philadelphia with my parents and aunt and uncle. It was amazing!"

An important task was entrusted to **Leeann Walker**: "I was12. Lived in West Virginia and helped put up 200 flags for the 4th of July."

And how about these memories from **Peggy Yax**? "I was 12 going on 13 in the summer of '76. Growing up in rural Michigan, taking care of my dad's two cows and their calves. My mom's sister Edith and her family came up from Kentucky for a visit and that was the first time I visited Sarnia, Ontario, Canada. My older sister Betty celebrated her 14th birthday by inviting a few friends from school out to the house. It was a year of recording songs off the radio with my portable cassette tape recorder I got from the previous Christmas."

For **Connie Henderson Crider** it's the drought which springs most readily to mind. "Man do I remember that drought. I was eleven years old and grew up near a huge lake, Lake Shasta in Northern California. I remember like it was yesterday, driving past it and seeing how low it was, it was like a stream. It was very eerie and almost amazing. To an 11 year old, anyway."

Janet Addison recalls: "I was 11 and remember watching Donny and Marie and the Mickey Mouse Club, and seeing 'Who is Jimmy Carter?' stories in the newspaper. Our church had a bicentennial picnic where I won a Betsy Ross flag that is still one of my prized possessions today."

Zoltan Balint has a story to tell: "I was 8 years old, mostly remember cool cartoon shows like Dynomutt, Dog Wonder, The Scooby-Doo/Dynomutt Hour, Jabberjaw, Tarzan Lord of the Jungle and my favorite TV show with Lee Majors in the Six Million Dollar Man (bionic man). Set fire (accidentally) to a nearby small forest that was behind my primary school, it was amazing to see all the firemen extinguish the fire. I was scared out of my wits."

Trixie Ann Evans is one who certainly looks back with affection to '76. "I was 12. I lived in a small town in upstate NY. I remember it was the bicentennial. Lots of patriotic decor all around town. The summer was all about going swimming in the local lake and the town pool with my best friend. Kids were very outdoorsy then… riding bikes, skateboards, climbing trees, exploring the woods, playing hide and seek, jumprope, walking to the corner store for penny candy. Really was the best care free time of our lives."

"I was 10 and part of the Bicentennial Afterschool Club (history nerd) which culminated in a 'festival' where students made projects about the history of Lawrenceville then and what inventions would exist in 2000," recalls **MiChelle Baughman**. And like countless young men of his day **Dale Cunningham**, then 12 or 13, was a big fan of this lady - Farrah Fawcett Majors (right).

It was all very exciting for **Mindy Hollingsworth** too. "I was 7 years old and I was excited about the centennial. I grew up in a really small town, I remember everything was red, white and blue. We all decorated our bicycles with red, wine blue streamers. We had small festival picnics, just family time running around with sparklers in our hands to celebrate the birthday of the country. Parades, marching bands and dressing up in red, white and blue."

Cat Packer writes: "My mom made me what I called my Holly Hobbie dress, it was two coordinating blue and white fabrics with a pinafore and bonnet. I loved that dress fiercely and wore it for play until I was about 8 and could no longer squeeze into it."

And the following is from **Tracy Newmarch**: "I turned 10 in 1976, and what I remember most about that year was our Christmas tree. I was really excited because I always wanted to have a flocked tree, and finally it was happening! Mom decorated it in full-on 'Stars & Stripes' regalia: red and blue glass ornaments, stars, flags, patriotic ribbons, and my grandmother's handmade crocheted bells with jingle-bell 'clangers'. Even the lights were red and blue! It was gorgeous! It was sadly also the last time we had a flocked tree. After the mess it made in the house, Mom said: 'Never again'!"

Beth Mason has some great retrospective recollections. "I was 5 that summer. But it was only until looking back that I understood there was a massive bicentennial campaign which had so many of my things red, white, and blue as well as colonial. My favorite was riding my red, white and blue 'Big Wheel' with the neighborhood friends in Joliet, IL - near Chicago. Upon later reflection, I realized my mom had quite a bit of colonial decor, but probably no more than everyone else. Maybe my thoughts as a clueless kid could be helpful?"

For someone who can't remember anything about the celebration **Deanna Lea** doesn't do too badly when it comes to the year itself: "I was 12 and don't remember a thing about the bicentennial. I was working at a café that was sandwiched between the bus stop and a biker bar. It was an experience. That summer I discovered turquoise and sterling jewelry, clogs, Thin Lizzy, Queen, and marijuana."

"In 1976 on the Bicentennial I was 20 days until my 10th birthday, and we moved from OKC back to my birth/family hometown in Southern MO. I remember the amazing huge house and acre yard. My father was retired military, my Mom was a homemaker. I am now preparing for the sale of the house, after the passing of my Mom (at 94) in April," says **Teresa Kintner Gunderson**.

The train may not have made it to The Last Frontier but the celebrations certainly did, as **Friederike Petrasch Cook** explains: "I was 12. I grew up in Anchorage, Alaska and there were bicentennial parades and celebrations. It was a big deal. I was going into Junior High. The fear of a new school, lockers, my first crush, zits, and how to fit in. It was a hard year, but it was an exciting year."

The holidays in '76 were a learning experience for **Mary Savage**: "It was the summer before my 12th birthday and we always went to Central Lake Michigan for our summer vacations. My Daddy always rented the same cabin every year on a lake called Scott's Lake. It's where my Daddy taught me how to fish. Going there was always the best times of my youth."

Even at just turning four, **Sean Brian**'s recollections are surprisingly lucid: "I was hanging out with my grandpa who was taking me to vote for Jimmy Carter and I was preparing for the bicentennial."

This from **Colleen Greeley Whidby**: "I was 10 years old. My school had a bicentennial parade and all of us decorated our bikes and wagons. Some of our crafty moms sewed us somewhat period-appropriate costumes though mine looked more like Little House on the Prairie. Mom redecorated a few years prior and went from full blown Danish Modern to early decor. I secretly missed the Danish modern life though. That was also the year that the Freedom Train came through our town and I remember waiting in a really long line to see everything."

And **Cheryl Hoeppner** has a similar tale. "I was five years old. My mom made my sisters and me each a gingham summer dress (mine had the obligatory colonial bonnet). My dad's school had an all-school reunion on the actual fourth of July, so we wore our matching dresses and celebrated July 4 in a small Colorado town. I remember everything that entire year was patriotic and red, white, and blue, including the coins and all ads. It seemed magical at the time to a little kid. I was the youngest, so I got to wear my two sisters' special Bicentennial dresses for years! I think I still have mine. I know I have the bonnet!"

Ellyn Coachman remembers: "I was just shy of 8 years old, living in St. Louis, MO. I remember that the Bicentennial was a big deal. My grandmother sewed me a cute red and white shorts set and my mom and stepdad wore red, white and blue, and we went to a celebration at the Arch. After, we went to a cookout at my parents' friend's house in the woods. My parents and their friends were hippies. I remember the house was like the treehouse in Swiss Family Robinson, and they lived by a stream where we caught fish that they cooked up right there. I fell asleep and woke up in a waterbed. So, pretty much the most '70s memory ever."

They were great times for **Karen Cooper** as well. "I was 5 living in Raleigh, NC, which still had a small town feel for being the capitol of NC. We went downtown to watch fireworks for the bicentennial and I saw a man parachute out of an old plane. I rode in a horse and buggy. My Dad was a professor and my Mom was in grad school. I started first grade that year. We had a dark green Pinto and a wonderful life!"

Susan Clemens was twelve and went to Disneyland. As one might expect, "it was very bicentennial!"

And let's conclude this section with this lovely account and accompanying photograph by **Jane Elizabeth**: "I'd just turned 5. I remember owning 3 pairs of shorts my grandmother bought me - a red pair, a white pair and a blue pair. My family was very involved in the VFW and in 1976 my great aunt was the outgoing national president of the ladies auxiliary. I drove with my parents from Chicago to NYC to attend the national convention. I vaguely recall stopping in Pennsylvania, but I'm not sure what we did there. Obviously we visited the Statue of Liberty while in NYC, it was 1976 after all. I just did a quick Google search and here's a pic of my great aunt from 1975 apparently gearing up for the bicentennial. She's on the far right."

"ONE OF MY FAVORITE SUMMERS EVER"

Whilst every year will have been somebody's favourite, it seems undeniable that '76 has always commanded more respect than most. Contributor after contributor made sure to remark that it was a time they will never forget. This was from **Paula Johnson**: "I lived right outside Washington DC. I was 17, spent summer days downtown on the mall hanging out by myself or meeting people, strangers, watching events, music, while my best friend worked at the beer tent at only 15 - her dad had pull. One day I ran into my Mom on the mall taking pictures, she asked me when I was coming home. So to keep her suspicious nature in check, we spent one weekend a month at my house and the rest at girlfriend's house, because she was in VA even closer to downtown, and her dad had gone to Sweden with his girlfriend for the summer and did not tell my mom. He filled the freezer, left us cash and a car - neither me, my friend or her sister had a driver's license yet! But we all did know how to drive, did not get into any trouble that summer, and my mother never found out. One of my favorite summers ever."

Janice Vermillion agrees: "I was 16 and having the best time of my life. Having a good time at rock concerts and going to school. Literally not a worry! I loved the '70s."

"I was 16 years old living on beach front property in Powell River, BC," writes **Anita Schluter**. "One of the best years growing up."

Sarah who lived at Northport, Alabama reminisced: "In 1976 I fell in love for the first time. I loved being in the marching band for the bicentennial program. I loved life before it became complicated. 1976 was a great year."

Karen Hamilton says "76 was the best summer of her teen years. "I was 16 and lived in Philadelphia. There was so much going on that summer."

"I was dancing barefooted on my room when I wasn't wearing my roller skates. Life was endless possibilities so I thought," recalls **Dawn Collins**.

And there was so much to look back to with fondness too for **Lynn Williams**. "I remember it was just the 4 of us, my mom had been divorced about a year, we lived close to Lackland AFB. So we sat outside and watched the fireworks from our yard that bicentennial year, how beautiful and colorful they were. Also spent time at the pool, went roller skating, the movies, hanging out with friends and walking to the neighborhood convenient store to get a soda. And oh the music to listen to, it was the best then, oh the memories, such fond memories. I'll never forget."

And that goes for so many of us.

SPORTING MEMORIES

For some 1976 was all about the sport. **Robyn C. Brewer-Ritz** remembers: "Cincinnati Reds vs. NY Yankees World Series. Reds swept the Yankees in 4 games. I'm from Cincinnati area and attended one of the games."

Joe Gray recalls that "Indiana University won the NCAA basketball championship with an undefeated season."

It was the year of the summer Olympics in Montreal. **Ken Gonzales** remembers them well. And **Thom McCarthy** was actually moving out there: "The streets were almost impassable, there were so many people in the city for the Games."

Frank Pavlin welcomed the show to his home town: "I'm from Montreal. 1976 was the year we hosted the Summer Olympics. Went to several events (soccer, pentathlon, cycling, swimming, running) and met people from all over the world (athletes and visitors). It was a great experience."

The Games captured the keen interest of **Eric Legault** too. "Summer 1976, spent a lot of time in front of the TV watching the Olympics. It was the last truly simply happy Olympic Games. The end of innocence. I collected superhero comic books. 11 years old in Montréal: watching Olympic Games on TV, making a scrapbook of newspaper clippings; Nadia Comaneci and the Romanian team, Bruce Jenner, closing ceremony with all athletes smiling sincerely, the last 'innocent games'. collecting DC comics, copying some of their drawings, discovering classical music and bird watching."

It's not clear whether **Mark Malenowski** was in the Canadian city for the Olympics on just got caught up in it all. But they were happy days, and ayyy they were cool: "My twin brother mother and myself went to Canada but could not get a room in Montreal due to the Olympics. We were busy collecting Happy Days cards and eating Freakies cereal. It was a great time."

PRIVATES (NOT) ON PARADE

It's hard not to love this cheeky complaint from **Maritza Carmona**: "I was 16 years old and living in NYC. It was the bicentennial year. The USA was celebrating its 200 years and in celebration people would dress up as the people of 1776. You would be walking down the street and when you least expected you see a minute man, Betty Ross or just someone dress with clothes of that time. All just because... just for a smile on you face. Now let's not talk about when the streakers ran by your school or your home... the most you saw was boobs and ass.

They didn't show their front privates... none that I ever saw."

UNHAPPY DAYS

Nobody of course should be under any illusions that '76 was a perfect year for everyone. Personal tragedy is, sadly, a part of life, and it happened to some in that year as it happens to others at other times. In the interests of balance I would like to pay this little tribute to those who endured hardship and loss which regrettably overshadowed what was for so many a year of celebration...

Steve Burstein doesn't remember 1976 with much affection. "I grew up in the US (because I was born here) and 1976 was the first summer that I spent doing what I wanted, volunteering for a political organization in Boston and finally spending more than a few weeks in the house my parents bought just before I started boarding school. I was a rabid Monty Python/British comedy fan, and was constantly thinking of going to England someday (I went twelve years later). The Queen came to Boston but I missed her because my family spent the day someplace else. Then when I had to go back to boarding school, I had these miserable old farts for houseparents who wouldn't let us watch TV or stay up later on weekends. I hated that I was going to miss whatever British TV was going to be on public service TV! I was so relieved when that miserable year was over!"

Thankfully **Janet Maheras** survived what sounds to have been a horrific accident. "Music played at my high school graduation in February 1976 was 'We Are the Champions' by Queen. I married my first husband one week after graduation. The day after we married, on our way to the military base where he was stationed, I lost control of the car we were traveling in and drove head on into a bridge abutment. My husband lost his spleen and broke his wrist. I was in a coma for approximately a month, injuries too numerous to mention. I was not expected to survive, but I miraculously did. I spent four months in and out of the hospital. The marriage only lasted a couple years partly because of the accident."

There are tales of another horrific accident from **Debbie Ranson**: "On July 5, 1976 my husband was driving my car and a woman ran a red light. She hit a box truck and died. The box truck spun out of control and hit my husband. It took the rescue squad 11/2 to get him out of the car. I was at home waiting for him to pick me up. I waited and waited. No cell phones. I waited. I was listening to my radio WING 1410 and news broke in it said an accident with at least 1 fatality. I got scared. My phone rang. A woman said 'This is Kettering Hospital, has anyone contacted you yet?' I started crying. Music in the background. She told me that my husband was in the hospital and I needed to get there. I had no car. I called my mother-in-law. She picked me up. We arrived with my mom. They took us to a small private room and asked if we'd like to speak with a minister. Doctor came in and told us that he was alive. In the hospital for two weeks. Concussion, compound fracture on his right leg, couple hundred stitches to sew his face back together. 6 months in a cast. He was never the same but he was alive and I've always had my fantastic music."

Fond memories of a much-loved grandmother for **Marjorie Black**: "I was 5 years old that year and that was the last year I saw my grandmother alive. She was killed in a car accident. I will always remember at her funeral, my father did not allow me to see her and told me he wanted me to remember what my grandmother looked like when she was alive."

Fortunately **Sandy Hanson Martin** came through rather a scare, and lives on to tell the tale: "I was in the hospital at this time. I had a stroke and was in the hospital for a month with only a minimal chance of full recovery. Well I'm now 70 and going strong so I guess I showed them."

Virgil Maxson was resident at the Lebanon Correctional Institution until 1978, but **Donald McKinley** got out of Juvenile Reform School in May '76. On July 4th of all days **Bill Reynolds** wrapped his car around a power pole which quite ruined his night. Sadly **Robyn McQuillen**, who was twelve and in sixth grade, lost her grandmother to metastatic breast cancer - and sixteen-year-old **Darcy White**'s mother passed away from the same condition, aged 44. **Cyncee Forrester** says it was a hard pass. **Teri Smog Hawn** was living with her mom and a "hateful" stepfather. And **Pat Gatto Catalano** had a doppelganger he could have done without: "Son of Sam. I was right age, look and in his neighborhood. In fact I was in the exact place he was the night before. Scary time."

Bundy's activities were a concern for **Amy Wagner** too. "I was 20, back in college, hitchhiking back and forth to the mountain town I was living in. This was at the same time that Ted Bundy was notoriously active murdering young women, and managing to escape from jail when caught. I can't remember any fun or fine event about the Bicentennial! I went to rock concerts, for sure. Can't recall which ones now, though! Sorry!"

Robin Couram was young and experienced something of a mishap: "I cut my heel on a lawn mower that had no blade guard on it. I was on crutches all summer, and I was 16 years old."

And last, but by no means least, **John Curtis** relates to us with some frankness why he doesn't remember the 1970s with the same fondness as many of our other contributors: "Well, if you must know, 1976 was absolutely horrible for the United States. The Oil Embargo a couple of years earlier had crashed the economy, and there were still millions out of work. Nixon had resigned two summers previously, and Gerald Ford was a walking footnote of a president. Inflation was rampant and senior citizens on fixed incomes were forced to eat cat food. But it was the 200th birthday of America, and we were all grimly determined to celebrate the Bicentennial, goddammit. I took the train into Boston to see the tall ships, but it was really pretty run-of-the-mill because I had already visited Old Ironsides and the Mayflower on school trips, so wooden sailing ships weren't all that thrilling. I think that was the Friday before the Fourth, so there weren't any fireworks. I think you're going to get a lot of people telling you they remember how great the 1970s were, but they were really grim times."

EVERYTHING WAS RED, WHITE AND BLUE

Whatever else may have defined 1976, in the United States of America the celebration of the nation's Bicentennial quite understandably overshadowed all else. All these years later there remain so many memories of a year of rapturous celebration. Let **Ana Guedea** take up the story: "My mom bought each of us a set of bicentennial stamps. Think it was six stamps that together showed the signing of the constitution. I still have mine somewhere. Also my sister was in the orchestra for a musical called 1776 at a nearby university. I went to see it and it was so hot getting dressed I couldn't get my pantyhose on. I had to power my legs with baby powder. It was an exciting summer for a teen - bicentennial everything!"

"My mom sewed me a red, white & blue mini skirt dress. I thought it was so cool!" remembers **Mandy Caulfield**.

The painting of fire hydrants in the national colours was a recurring theme. **Nick Cacchoine** recalls: "I don't know if this was on a national level or not, but in my small Ohio town for the Bicentennial we painted fire hydrants in patriotic colors and themes."

Amy George remembers this too. "In Indiana we also painted fire hydrants and we wore MIA bracelets for those lost soldiers. Also, my first job and the raucous new Saturday Night Live."

And **Theresa Hall**: "I was in 6th grade and everything that year was Bicentennial! School field trip was to see a train painted in red, white and blue. Our choir did a presentation with patriotic songs and dressed the part. Fire hydrants were all painted red, white and blue and it seemed that people were more friendlier and patriotic."

A nod to a Facebook group which helps keep the memory of those days alive from **Lynne Maddox Killingsworth**: "One thing I remember doing was painting the fire hydrants in town to be patriotic. Thanks to the Coloniawful group, I know it was a common occurrence and some towns still have them!"

Sharon L. Sowell has some similar recollections. "People in the city were painting the fire hydrants in patriotic themes. I was a freshman in high school. My church youth group took a trip to Washington DC and sang on the steps of the Lincoln Memorial."

And **Teresa Poole** assures us: "The bicentennial was a big deal, I was 23 years old and had volunteered one summer in Dubuque IA. They had painted all their fire hydrants with different designs. I think it made the national magazines."

Here we have a detailed and insightful account of it all from **Rena Corey**: "Bicentennial Minute on TV (anyone else remember those: 'And that's the way it was, 200 years ago today…')? All the fire hydrants in our town painted to look like red, white, and blue Minutemen (no lie!). Levi jeans and corduroys, earth shoes and wallabies, and the Saturday night line-up: Carol Burnett, MTM, All in the Family, Bob Newhart Show. I swear, if someone had tried to explain the futuristic concept of Netflix and streaming video, it would have blown my coloniawful mind! At that point, we didn't even have a remote for our black-and-white TV. No microwaves, either, so we had to wait 35 minutes to cook a frozen dinner. Stouffer's mac and cheese was my fave. 2 or 3 decades later, my mom's mind momentarily slipped back to the 70s and she put a frozen dinner in the microwave for 35 minutes. Came close to burning down the house!"

Diane McFadzean Chalk recounts it as being quite an adventure: "1976. I was a sea explorer in NY, NJ area... we participated in OP sail in NY harbor.. there was soooo many boats out there."

"I was visiting my grandparents in Amboy WV. We went to the local big town (Terra Alta) for the Fourth of July parade. While we were there I visited a dusty record store and bought a copy of 'Goodbyes and Butterflies' by the Five Man Electrical Band for the bicentennial price of 76 cents. I took it back to my grandparents' house and blasted it on their Sears Silvertone console stereo in the living room. It remains one of my top five favorite albums," recalls **Kevin Crothers**.

Chris Christensen remembers "the 'special '76' painted vehicles -- trains, cement trucks, garbage trucks, vans, etc."

This thoughtful account is from **Laura Coughlin**: "I lived on a pond that had been an apple orchard originally. When we had the drought everybody that lived near it pitched in and cleaned it out. My part of the neighborhood was called the birches. I was 14 and had just broken my wrist so I could only pass out drinks. I'll never forget that sense of community. In neighboring towns and my own there were fireworks galore. The best was when we found this old cemetery to watch them. It was all very respectful. We had one of the moms who took us and we laid out blankets."

There were some fond memories from **Tamla Rooks Powers**.

"Bicentennial parades around the country, even in my small hometown. Year I learned to drive the big tractor, listening to the Eagles, and pop music, starting high school, warm summer nights, playing tag, hide and seek, first year I learned how to shimmy up the large tree in my parents front lawn (no one ever looks up). Lots of time spent mowing, the city house and the farm. Started riding my bike everywhere, wanted to ride professionally."

And we have a lovely pic from back in the day from **Ann DiBenedetto** (right). "I was 13 - all full of the Bicentennial spirit. Wearing my hip huggers and flag tube top, riding my 10 speed bike, ruining my perfectly feathered hair."

Virginia Fogg speaks of "Bicentennial… parades, celebrations all summer long! Family get together at Grampa's with lobstah(!), burgers, fireworks. great summah! Yes, I am from NH!"

Leslie Stump, **Julie Gutgsell Ussery**, **Marsha Aud**, **Yvonne Layden**, **Jackie Young Lenarz** (with her elementary school friends) and sixteen-year-old **Vicki Spencer** all remember celebrating the whole big occasion. **George Gerritsen** says 1976 was the best 4th of July ever.

As a seventeen-year-old **Rosemary Thornton** recalls: "driving a 1974 Super Beetle, and on July 4th I was sitting on a blanket with my fiance, watching the fireworks over the Western Branch of the Elizabeth River (Virginia)."

Joseph McGarry sent us the Bicentennial logo (right) as a reminder of what it was all about. Nineteen-year-old **Ginny Arazmus-Meo**'s husband painted his car in the colours of the American flag. **Nancy Kelly** saw Queen Elizabeth wave to the crowd from a balcony at Faneuil Hall, Boston. **Lisa Stewart** recalls that the Bicentennial Minutes were on all three networks.

Bertha Moore Fox "bought a 1976 Chevrolet that was white with a red vinyl top and the cloth seats were white with red and blue stars on it."

And this from **Jennifer Spreitzer**: "I was in 3rd grade and our suburban Chicago school went on a Bicentennial binge. I remember dressing up in gingham dresses with bonnets; singing 'The Battle Hymn of the Republic'; and making a Colonial Kitchen shoebox project that my mom commandeered and still has to this day!"

"I remember watching the fireworks on a TV that my grandpa rented for the Fourth of July. We spent the hot summer at my grandma's house because she had cancer. I spent lots of time with my cousin up the street. My mom made her and me matching red, white and blue houndstooth outfits. I do remember wearing a bicentennial outfit for my picture for school that year," says **Kit Tripp Hittinger**.

Norma Speckhard tells us: "My favorite memory from the summer of 1976 is on the 4th of July, to celebrate the Bi-Centennial, we took our children to the arch (we live in St. Louis) to enjoy a concert followed by fireworks. There were so many families participating in this patriotic evening, it was thrilling."

Elizabeth Whitener says "My obnoxiously patriotic dad took us to Philadelphia to hear the President speak and see the Liberty Bell... I was 10. I was more interested in the pendulum than the bell."

These are the recollections of **Amy Simmons McGinley**: "I was in 5th grade and in Girl Scouts. We wore homemade dresses of the 1776 time period. At camp, we learned to make soap using lye and lard in a giant cast iron pot over a fire. We dipped homemade candles and made corn husk dolls. It was a wonderful time to be a ten-year-old girl in south Florida."

Shelly Lyon has sent us a cute little photo of her sister and her dressed for the occasion (right). "I remember the July 4 parades, everything red, white, and blue, and tons of fireworks. My sister and me in our finest Hollie Hobbie prints on our way to the parade," she recalls.

Troy Kahler has a discerning eye. "Attended several Bicentennial picnics, parades and firework displays throughout the summer... read many articles and books about the founding of our nation... wasn't too excited about some of the Bicentennial artwork that was created for mass marketing.."

According to **Claire Herlihy Noyes**: "This was a big deal in my area: lots of rah-rah patriotism that followed years of conflict over the Vietnam War."

No time to lose for teen driver **D. Edwin Dill**. "My 15-year-old self was learning to drive with a family who proudly wanted to celebrate the birth of America by driving cross country in our Ford Country Squire. A great experience seeing so many cities and towns celebrating!"

Some wistful memories from **Becky Godleski**: "It was my brother's birthday. He always made a huge deal about his July 4 birthday… he loved all the patriotic stuff and still does and his room had everything patriotic. We all wore red, white and blue. I had a long dress with a colonial style shawl, all in matching prints. We went down to the square where there was a big thing. Someone of importance read the Declaration of Independence, music happened, I think they had a parade. In the afternoon, we went to my grandmother's where we always had a reunion. When the sun went down, as always, we watched fireworks from the amusement park across the big field."

And **Amy Chicki Chaney** recalls: "I was 13. Since it was the Bicentennial, flags and patriotic displays were everywhere. My favorite part of this year was that mom only planted red, white and blue flowers for that summer (and we lived way out in the country so only family saw them)."

Terri Allie looks back fondly: "I remember the bicentennial celebration with '76, American flags, red/white/blue patriotism displayed everywhere from store displays to clothing and shoes to product packaging, and to cars even! I played outside in my neighborhood, rode Schwinn bikes with my friends, enjoying the carefree time of childhood."

As does **Carol Snapp**. "I remember wearing my new white jeans from Sagebrush with my Candies platform sandals to our little town's Fourth of July Bicentennial Parade. All the fire plugs had been painted like little soldiers."

Julie Singer Rienzi was very young, but recalls it well. "It was Bicentennial year. A beautiful summer here in Philadelphia. I was seven. I distinctly remember my neighbor on Greenvale Road in Cherry Hill was Betsy Ross. She sat on her lawn in 90-degree heat ringing her bell, rocking back and forth on the lawn in her bonnet and dress all day."

Gina Roberts was the same age as myself [*I adore that quintessentially American term "paper route" - Ed.*]. "I was 14 years old, my neighbor and I had a paper route and delivered the bicentennial edition of our city's newspaper. Those things were as heavy as a bowling ball and thrown about as easily."

Also a teen in '76 was **Rebecca Rabb Allen**. "I was 15 that summer. I remember everything being about our Bicentennial. 16 wasn't until October that year. We hung out at Silver Dollar City pool and cruised Gatlinburg. Don't have a lot of specific memories really that summer."

"I was in sixth grade and my classmates and I were all excited about the Bicentennial, much discussion n excitement," remembers **Kim Floyd**.

Margee Wheeler was "a small town girl from Oklahoma whose marching band was chosen to march in the Inaugural Parade."

And meanwhile **Patty Mills Weinsheimer** reminisces: "I remember on July 4th, sitting in the grass along the inner belt watching the wonderful fireworks with my parents and hundreds of others. Amazing celebration!"

Alison Stearns Meek reflects on the moment: "I was in 2nd grade in 1976. I remember a big hoopla around it being our country's 200th birthday. In school our whole class worked on this coloring mural that would later be hung in the hallway outside our class door. That was my favorite thing the whole year! I was also in our town's 4th of July parade as a baton twirler. We wore blue sequence body suits and red, white and blue hats. This was in Fairborn, OH, home of Wright Patterson AFB. Very patriotic time!"

Approval from the highest level for **Suzanne McAbee Torres'** culinary skills. "It was the bicentennial, and my Brownie troop had a cake contest to celebrate. The cakes were to be auctioned off after judging. I wanted to keep my cake, so I bet the maximum as soon as it hit the podium. Mayor Hudnut was the judge and really cracked up at that. I was so thrilled to meet Mayor Hudnut, and got to keep my cake. I wish I still had a picture of him and I together."

Fran Lynch had an enjoyable 1976. "We had a parade in the small town of Lunenburg, MA. My friend and I dressed as clowns and threw candy to kids. My uncle Tommy drove his racing green Morgan. There were tractors and floats and veterans marching. It was a good time for all!"

It was mixed blessings where **Teresa Jensen** lived. "A guy in town had a red white and blue wedding. Our town had a tornado on July 4th."

Tad Felts was an organiser of events, a big responsibility on such a big occasion. "I was co-chairman of the 1976 bicentennial celebration for my county. We had outdoor barbecues, parades, all kinds of celebrations. Everyone took part and it was a really patriotic time."

A sense of tradition from **JoAnn Bryant**: "Our subdivision sponsored a 4th of July event, with kids decorating their bicycles for a parade, a 5-ish year old group of children dressed in 'flag fabric' aprons singing patriotic songs, a pie tasting contest, a parade of decorated vehicles, a politician on a soapbox, games, watermelon floating in the pool - an old fashioned 4th of July celebration."

And, finally, this alluring and articulate reminisce from **Helen Rendell-Baker**: "I was in at the tip of Manhattan in the Bowling Green Park in the financial district with friends, pressed up against a park railing because of the crowds. The crowds were joyful, young and in good spirits.. Although the fireworks were magnificent, what I remember most are all the tall ships in the harbor and boats spraying water cannons into the air. I was 21."

"DRENCHED IN NOSTALGIA"

The Bicentennial is remembered by many with an affection which is unique and has stood the test of time. But of course there were other, more everyday things to do than simply celebrating. Let's cast a parting glance upon ordinary living in an extraordinary year.

Suzanne Karban Griffith comments: "I was 30 years old, a stay-at-home mom with one child, a daily school volunteer, married to a steelworker, had my parents move in due to my father's illness, celebrating my county's 200 year birthday, and all in all happy memories."

Samuel Lea remembers '76 clearly too. It was "for me the summer before I started grade seven in Beaverton Oregon. The McDonald's and Silver Skate and American Pinball was the center of my social life. It was innocent and fun and ridiculous. Refer to 'Dazed and Confused' as the nostalgia film that matches my experience that summer."

For **Beth Pierce** a family day out to DC was marred by the crowds. "I graduated from nursing school in 1976. I could not find a job until the fall. My great uncle and my cousins from Italy came to spend the summer. We had picnics and family dinners.

We took them to Washington, DC for the day. It was so crowded that we only saw the outside of the White House and Capitol and the monuments. I had gone there in 6th grade and had seen the White House, the Mint, the Capitol, and the monuments, but I was sad that my Italian family members did not get the same experience I had."

Some words of encouragement from **Astrid Lee** born out of her '76 experience. "I was married right out of high school for five years and had two children during that marriage. I had always wanted to go to college more than anything and my husband didn't understand why a woman would want an education. So I divorced him and went to college in three years with two toddlers. It was difficult, but I think it proved if you want something badly enough, you can do it."

Nick Jones was grappling with issues of life and faith. "I was a Sophomore/Junior in college; busy with fraternity, 3 jobs, and oh yeah classes. I was at a religious University and was trying to reconcile religion as I knew it and me being a very closeted gay."

And faith remains close to the heart of **Jeanne Drier**. "I invited my sister's girls to come for a week of Vacation Bible School. One night after dinner my youngest son climbed into my lap and told me that had wanted to make Jesus his friend just like the lady at church talked about. That boy still walks with Jesus today and makes this mom's heart proud."

Fun came at a cost for **Kay Baker**. "Late summer of '76. Went to a Wisconsin Badger game. All kinds of fun to be had! Anyway, crossing State Street with a drink in my hand and my friend and I got arrested! Spent the next few hours in jail. Fingerprints and mugshot! The upshot? A $25 traffic fine! Crazy times!"

It was an expressive time for **Rhonda Riley**: "In art class, we painted the windows. Last year I visited the school - the soap used to outline the drawing before paint was still there! TV miniseries set on John Jakes - I became a historian because of it."

While for **Tracey Pitman** it was carefree and cream: "We had marshmallow fights at our camp, at night I would sleep to the sound of loons and the wind in the trees. We had a woodstove, in the morning we would eat oatmeal with brown sugar and cream. My parents were still young and healthy, we didn't have any worries."

'A Boy Named Hugh' by Gene Price was one of **Larry Orr**'s favourite songs of the year. "If you were involved in politics in 1976, you'll understand it," he says.

Christopher Yocum recalls: "My favorite thing of 1976 was going to New York City on a school trip to see the musical The Wiz and the magic show, plus seeing Macy's store - the original building."

Sallie Oughton Taylor was at Charlotte, North Carolina. **Neysa Samuels** recalls the visit of Queen Elizabeth II to the US. **Michelle Rich** reached an important milestone - her 21st birthday. **Donna Piccari Hughes** remembers the outbreak of Legionnaire's Disease in Philadelphia. **Michael Parsons** left home in '76, aged fifteen. **Lesley Allen** graduated college, whilst **Maxine Kaplan Head** was looking forward to doing so in December. **Cindi Plant Moore** spent as much time at the beach as she possibly could. Lucky **Gemil Kefalinos** was able to get a bird's-eye view of the fireworks as he was on board a flight from California to New Jersey on July 4th.

"In the summer of 1976 I was 13," reports **Lin Dixon**. "My parents who had been separated decided to give it another go. We moved out of town and into the country. My brother and I spent the summer exploring the woods and swimming in the creek. Incidentally my parents remained together until they passed away in 2006!"

Dee Bark was "working all summer as camp counselor. Playing tricks on the campers, like food dye polka dots on their sleeping, sweet faces, raiding the walk-in cooler at night for leftovers hiking, tubing, and knowing I was just a few months after school started back to get my driver's license, oh yeah!"

For all the joys of 1976 there were still fuel shortage problems, as **Lisa Meil** reminds us: "Getting up at 5 in the morning to get to the gas station so we could get in line on a Saturday morning. You could only get gas on your designated day by the last number on your license plate. You had to get a full tank because you had to wait till the next Saturday to get any. Also filling gas cans in the trunk for emergencies and lawn mower."

Lisa Sinclair and her household headed for the sea: "We moved from the Blue Mountains to the Sunshine Coast. Big difference from mountains to coastal living."

A great year for **Ken Smith** too: "I was 23 and moved to Vancouver B.C. A couple of friends and I went on a road trip to Oregon State on a skiing trip, Mt. Hood and then ended up on the coast. Good times."

Karyn Koopman was on the move too: "I was 19. Living on my own, lots of friends/parties. Hitchhiked from Portland to Spokane for Thanksgiving with a turkey in our backpack. Hung out at Earthquake Ethel's."

As was **Terry Gaouette-Trongeau**: "I moved to the city I still live in. I was culture shocked. I lived on a small island and moved only three towns over but we didn't have duplexes and tall buildings so I felt like I moved to NYC, it was so different. I also turned 11 that year."

The year 1976 played an important role in **Brenda Konchar**'s personal development. "I had a huge growth spurt this summer, got my braces off, developed into a Brick house! Spent the summer swimming and being boy crazy as ever with my best friend! Great year! Started freshman year in the fall!"

"In '76 had 2 girls and just had my son… I was 28… good years," writes **Martin Bensavage**.

There was an unwelcome knockback for **Karen Harbaugh**: "I was just a fresh college grad. Moved back home for my 5th year but was denied my chance to complete my education. They said they thought I didn't have what it takes."

Denise Dawson Rebik was starting along the road to a secure future. "My husband and I were living the good life managing an apartment complex and working our jobs trying to save money to buy our first home."

And **Tami Fleming** was young and enjoying life. "Best 4th of July in a small town called Stanfield. And about a month later I moved out on my own at sweet 16. Got my first real job (CNA) and my first car (along with getting my driver's license), a 69 Dodge Dart and I met my first and second husbands, lol."

"Slept in a tent in the garden with my best friend for a week. We rejoiced at the Israeli raid on Entebbe to free the hostages," reports **Graham Barral**.

Jacqueline Hannah remembers the drought. "I was 21, drove from Chicago to California with a boyfriend. I remember the water shortage. Had to ask for water, not served it, and I remember it was so hot that in some states the road cracked like huge spaces and couldn't drive over it."

Party time for **William Jobes**. "My best friend and I moved out of our parents' house and got an apartment that year. We were 19 years old and were on our own for the first time. Oh what a party."

And for **Lynn Jones Naylor**: "Turned 16. Took me 4 times at parallel parking but finally passed my driver's test. Such freedom that summer cruising around in an old 1964 Comet."

Shawnee Miles tells an interesting tale. "In 1976 I was living in Texas with my husband who I married in '75. I was in school to be a registered nurse, transferred from NYS, thought I get those prerequisites out of the way and took Texas State History! Worked as a CNA while working on my nursing degree. I had credits but came back home to NYS to complete my degree because Texas had a huge wait list. Found a whole new world in nursing when I got back, I had to take exams to reintegrate myself. My husband started nursing school when I went back and never knew the old system. He loved it!"

There was an exciting encounter for **Fran Widerker** (right). "I played one on one with Dr. J. He let me get a shot. It was the highlight of my year!" **Geraldine Ann Hiebing** was in first grade. **Bret Carter** was learning to drive. **Rita Torf** was 29, married with one son and feeling free. **Suzanne Michelle** had to give away her much loved Saint Bernard in 1976 and has longed to own another one ever since. **David Heiman** can remember skateboarding, bike riding and sledding. **Darlene Slate** was fifteen years old in that year, **Garry Lowe** had just left school aged sixteen, **Eileen Byrne** came out of school too and **Betty Galloway Johnson** graduated at eighteen. **Beth Newman-Clemens** recalls swimming in a river. Meanwhile **Don Lowery Jr.** actually met President Ford in Charlotte, NC.

Susan Mohring has some telling reflections on gender roles then and now, as well as tales of her own to tell. "Early 20s, mother of two daughters 16 months apart that year. My husband had just been honorably discharged from the Army and we lived at Fort Riley, KS for two years, driving back home to the east coast 11/75. We started a non-military life in '76. It was a hard time for women then in the work force but I managed to find a job as a legal assistant in a law office. Recall having to type wills and other legal documents on a Selectric typewriter and if a mistake was made, you could not erase or use white-out liquid or correction tape. H ad to start that page over. Living close to Philadelphia, the bicentennial was big that summer and we visited the Liberty Bell and other attractions. Sexual harassment was prevalent in the workforce at that time and in yet the years to come."

Some associated concerns taxed **Marilyn Shurka Silk**, but she held determinedly on to her own ideas about what she wanted out of life. "Graduated from college in 1974. Couldn't get a teaching job because the school system hired males as it was a Draft Deferment for Vietnam. Rented an attic apartment. Worked as a waitress while going for a Masters Degree part time. Hard time for women. Serial freedom for men. I was 24 and marriage wasn't on my mind. All my friends were getting married and I waned to become an independent woman."

Julia Sargent "drove from Mississippi Gulf Coast to Colorado Springs with two college room-mates. We saw Paul McCartney and Wings at the Denver Mile High Stadium! Fun times!"

And **Glenda Sims** created a welcome new milestone by becoming the first person of colour to work in the business office of her facility.

Patty Bausch considers how attitudes to diversity matters may have changed since those days. "Look up all the TV shows. We all pretty much watched the same 3 channels, so people have a collective memory of many of the same shows. Have a sense of community although that is not to say the shows fairly portrayed the diversity that is the U. S. We are much more divided now and shared memories are fragmented when it comes to entertainment."

Meanwhile **Kelly Cahill Tomlinson** remembers "riding my bike with a banana seat in my red, white and blue plaid Toughskins bell bottoms from Sears!"

Dawn Gibeley writes: "Traveling up and down the north east coast with a beautiful group of artists and craftsmen doing arts and craft shows. Six months of fun times, camping, beautiful country, great friends, wonderful memories."

"That year in the summer we had a tornado in the winter we had a blizzard," recalls **Mary Pritchard**, reminding us that '76 wasn't all sun and heatwave.

Some simple, fun memories for **Joan Johnson**: "I was 14. I remember roller skating. Swimming in the river down by the train bridge. Smoking drinking strawberry wine. Great times."

And for **Janet Kendrick** also. "Riding my pony, helping my mom and grandparents work in the garden, freezing garden goodness in preparation for a cold winter."

Sheila Whitson Anderson invokes some musical memories. "I was a Naval Hospital Corpsman, stationed at Cherry Point, NC.

Some of the best times of my life! Loving me some Jim Croce, Credence Clearwater, Eric Clapton, Lynyrd Skynyrd and Cat Stevens! Great times!"

So does **Michael Wendland**, amongst other recollections: "1976 - I was attending community college in Traverse City, Michigan. Gordon Lightfoot was popular, especially the song about the Edmund Fitzgerald. I enjoyed snow skiing and going to my favorite pub. Traverse City hosted the National Cherry Festival each summer. President was in the main parade and there was security people on the roofs of buildings along the parade route. The secret service guys wore dark suits with sunglasses and always had a hand on his limo."

Brenda Pellerin recalls a fond encounter. "My husband and I (then boyfriend) decided we were going to travel out west before settling down. We fixed up a van and off we went. Went to LA, Grand Canyon, and other places. My favorite was we went to an Indian Reservation and we met the sweetest elderly Indian woman."

"Remind me what happened in '76, most of the seventies are a blur," writes **Regina Rose Malone**. "I was in my twenties and living on the upper east side in Manhattan."

"In 1976 I was 13. I was a bridesmaid in my sister's wedding. My only nephew was 3 and I babysat a lot. I remember it being a great year as it was the bicentennial of our great nation!" says **Laura Bayliss Simmons**.

Kathryn Ann Schauer tells us "I was re-enacting history with my historical heritage group. I had the time of my life!"

And **Shari** "had a hippie type wedding at Lake Texoma in Texas. No invitations were sent. I got flowers from the woods to make my arch. We made all the food ourselves. 150 people showed up and man did we party!"

Adele Askew remembers: "Hot summer. First time abroad, went to France on the Hovercraft with family and friends, camping! Seven and was so happy, we had a great summer."

And who remembers Citizens' Band Radio, like **Laurie Baker Stafford**? "I was 16. Probably at the roller rink slow skating with a cute boy. Cruising main street in my friend's red mustang. Talking on the CB radio. Sneaking a sip of Boone's Farm. Fun times!"

Bill O'Donnell reflects pensively on what could have been. "I had been married for only one year. We were young and poor but enjoying life. We had a red International Scout. On weekends we would go camping just load up the cooler and head out, living in Montana we had lots of choices. My favorite was the Greenough Campground in the Bear's Tooth Mountains south of Red Lodge. Rock Creek swept down the mountainside with crystal clear water. I always thought I would retire there. My life's journey did not travel that path."

"In 1976, I was in college living in the dorm at Centenary College of Louisiana. Unlike these days, when I left home on a scholarship, I was really on my own! My mother at first sent me $10.00 a month. When she found out that the school gave me a work study job, she decided I didn't need her $10.00 anymore! I've been on my own ever since!" writes **Gladys Vanderpool**.

Lise Karpel's thoughts still remain hidden out there somewhere. Who knows when she may get to retrieve them? "My fifth grade class buried a time capsule somewhere on the school grounds. To this day, some of my former classmates still wonder exactly where it is and whether it will ever be unearthed? Did anyone keep an exact record of its location or has that been long lost and forgotten? What year were we supposed to unearth it and marvel at the contents?"

And, finally, how great it is to know that I'm not the only hopeless nostalgic out there. I just know this feeling, even though I've never been to Disneyland. **Kevin Mowery** takes up the story: "In the summer of 1976, my mom and dad drove from San Antonio, Texas to Los Angeles so we could visit Disneyland. I was three. I didn't get back to Disneyland until 2018, when I went by myself and just drenched myself in nostalgia, even though the park had changed a ton in the intervening 42 years."

8. LOCAL MEMORIES FROM 1976

Let me be clear - when I speak of "local" I am talking about local to me. For this chapter I sought memories and anecdotes from folks around my own stamping ground in Isleworth, which is in West London. Or Middlesex to the purists.

Included inevitably were recollections and accounts of events from surrounding areas such as Hounslow, Brentford, Richmond, Twickenham, Teddington and Hampton. But if I could get there on foot or by bus back in '76 without incurring the wrath of the folks at home then it was local.

Here are the Facebook groups which I was kindly granted access to to solicit contributions, and once again in each case I have shortened the URL for convenience. Again, I have no personal interest in any of these sites beyond my much valued membership of them all:

Cheekee Pete's Night Club in Richmond, Surrey UK
https://bit.ly/2OkJbT7

Memories from around the Hounslow, Heston & Isleworth Area
https://bit.ly/3bTVNZP

Memories of Richmond Ice Rink
https://bit.ly/307E1wC

Twickenham Bird's Nest and Cheekee Pete's
https://bit.ly/3uSmAyq

The Hounslow Heston and Isleworth Group (for Memories)
https://bit.ly/2Omxgoc

The Isleworth Appreciation Society
https://bit.ly/3e3IOHJ

It's easy for us to forget that even those parts of the world which harbour special memories for we who frequented them provided the settings for quite different experiences for others. Some of the respondents quoted below are known to me, others are not. All of us trod the same ground. Quite likely, from time to time and unbeknown to us, our paths would have crossed. Each of us is another's audience, as the song goes.

Let us first remember that this was a long, hot summer unlike any other - in Middlesex, as anywhere else...

Linda Rosser, for whom it was a very special year, does a pretty good job of summing it all up in a few short sentences: "Summer drought. Have a joint bath. Brown grass. Stifling classroom. Year we got married."

H.R. has some similar recollections: "Near Twickenham, Middlesex, I remember the tarmac in the road melting, watering the garden with a hose out of the bathroom window from the bath water, yellow grass, flying ants, the pavement too hot to walk on without shoes."

Norma Temperton was a Twickenham girl, but had moved way out west. "I lived in Staines then, but was born in Twickenham. We had a holiday in the Peak District. It was so hot I just wore trousers and a bikini top while visiting the villages there to see the Well Dressings. It was lovely sitting by the cool streams with our feet in the water."

And **Sue Brill** too. "Steaming hot summer days at the outdoor swimming pool in Twickenham after school. Laying on the concrete on our towels, and dipping into the cold water. Wire baskets to leave our belongings in, and entry fee 10p through a turnstile. Chatting with the lads from the local boys' school, and just enjoying life. Best days. I also started my first Saturday job in '76 in Page & Taylor near Woolworth."

"Turning 16. The long hot summer spent at Twickenham Pool. Dangling my feet in the Thames whilst eating an ice cream from Dayville's. Wearing cheesecloth shirts, trips to Brighton. Rock Follies, Magpie, Bowie, The Eagles and the hosepipe ban," recalls **Debby Bentley**.

Kim Lawrence was at the pool in Twickenham too, instead of sitting exams.

And some fond local memories from **Paul Mudd**, who makes a telling point about the lack of concern we had as youngsters for societal problems of the day: "1976 - what a summer and what a time to be alive. Long and hot, time spent sunbathing by the Thames, getting great burgers from a little place on the High Street in Mortlake, and going up to Brick Lane on a Sunday. It was also a summer of water shortages, but that doesn't put a dent in your universe when you're 17 and the world is your lobster. And it was a summer of Fiorucci's, plastic sandals, that new French label I discovered called 'Chipie', Cheekee Pete's and Mary O'Sullivan, who came from Richmond, but we met in Great Yarmouth. Go figure."

"1976 the year of the heat wave," remembers **Carole Clark**. "101 on Centre Court at Wimbledon. Not a common thing back then. My husband was working in Edinburgh and phoned me complaining about the cold while I was roasting down here. Thoroughly enjoyed the Kneller Hall concerts that year. No Treaty Centre but a really good High Street, unlike now! I would walk up Martindale Road to Hounslow West. Fresh fish shop, pet store, supermarket, in fact everything we needed. Not sure when the Odeon Cinema closed but we used it a lot."

Mark Gibbs describes it thus: "The summer of '76 will always be etched in my mind, the endless sunny days of the six week holidays, spending the days over St. John's Park chasing a football or playing cricket, playing block one two three with an army of friends, walking over to the gunge to have our daily swing on the tree rope, then all jumping in to cool down ['*The gunge*' *is a colloquial name for the Duke of Northumberland's River - Ed.*]. It would drive my mum crazy as it meant clean clothes every day which were muddy and stinking of the gunge. Eating endless jubblys which we had bought from Hewitt's, and going to Richmond ice rink. Riding our bikes everywhere. Happy care free days."

Fond recollections for **Satbir West**: "I remember the summer of '76, my parents actually put our sofa in the back garden as we could not bear the heat inside the house, it was a happy time."

"In 1976 I was living in Brentford on the heatwave," recalls **Cindy Sanderson**. "I remember the stand pipe at the end of the street. The lovely summer evenings. I was 21 at the time."

Jan Holden puts it all nicely: "I was in my first year of nurse training and doing my first set of nights during the summer heatwave. I remember standing outside in the very early morning feeling the warmth of the day to come, appreciating the stillness of the moment with all the patients sleeping peacefully behind me and enjoying the sounds of a new day dawning (also remember not being able to sleep during the day due to it being too hot!)."

It was a case of conflicting priorities for **Sally Larsen**. "I lived in Teddington. It was the year that I did my A-levels in the middle of a massive heatwave! I'm sure I would have got better results, had I not been sunbathing so much. 1976 was the year I left school and also left home and moved to a tiny house in 'The Alberts' in Richmond with my boyfriend and another friend. It was always cold and damp but it was our first home and very special. I used to make bread every week as we lived on a very tight budget. One meal a week was always beans on toast. Getting Chinese takeaway was a rare treat!"

"It was very special to me," says **Philippa Gregory**. "Lived in

Heston and spent 2 weeks in Torquay, beautiful and hot though there was a water shortage. Lived in Norman Crescent, actually came under Cranford. Just a beautiful summer with lovely songs and the only concern was the water shortage."

Nicky Mundy recalls so much about that wonderful year. "Great memories of that long hot summer. Just finished secretarial course at Thames Valley College. First job at Lyons and Co. in Hammersmith. Friday and Saturday nights down Cheekee's and Brollies. Met my hubby down Brollies in '75 and started going out in '76. Still married 36 years later and together 44 years! Used to have fake ID to get in (especially needed when wearing flat 'granny' sandals). Loved Monday nights too - 5p to get in and watched all the really trendy people that came down from London clubs. My friend and I just danced from the time we went in until we left at close! Then into Mr Jiffy's. Am soooo pleased I was a teenager in the '70s. Great music and such fab times in Richmond. Would love to do it all again - these teenagers today don't know what they missed!"

And despite having been a mere sprog at the time, **Steve Palmer** is able to confirm that it was "Feckin' hot…"

MEMORIES OF CHEEKEE PETE'S

There's a lot of mention of Cheekee Pete's, which really was the place to go for a bit of local night life. **Pauline Austin** was there: "Firstly I remember it as the hottest summer. I remember my brother taking me the first time to Cheekee's which then became a regular haunt, so it was with the Bull in Sheen on a Friday. Cheekee's on a Saturday and always running for the last train to get home to Ashford - if we missed it we would thumb a lift. Omg, if my parents knew that I wouldn't have been let out again as just two girls - what a silly thing to do but we were always very lucky who ever picked us up!! My parents still don't know now

[*Let's hope they don't read this book then - Ed.*]. Met my first proper boyfriend in Cheekee's, some lovely memories and Richmond ice skating on a Sunday. Rossi's after or L'auburge or the Wimpy - thought I was really grown up going in there as I think a lot were smoking weed. Yes great memories, kids today don't have the great clubs and music we all experienced."

The Bull in Sheen crops up again in this long and helpful account by **Alison Russell**: "Was 15 and like everyone else used to go to The Bull in Sheen on a Thursday - it was called Club UFO (my husband Ty still has the membership card somewhere) and then Cheekee's and Brollies on Fridays and Saturdays. There used to be a gang of boys from Putney that used to go and they were all amazing dancers and we would watch them on a Saturday in Brollies. There used to be a big group of us all from Barnes and often we would finish Cheekee's and then grab a burger at the end in Mr Jiffy's. Then of course we would have missed our last bus home so most weekends there would be a big group of us all walking back to Barnes and Mortlake, with people dropping off home along the way. It would be such fun all walking back together messing about. My mate Dave would always make sure I got home safely and we would sit on my wall outside my house and chat and my dad would call me up. My poor parents. I was a bit of a law to myself in those days as all my friends were about 2/3 years older, which was a big difference at that age. Most of the time they thought I was staying with my friend Debbie so had no idea I was out clubbing at that age! We always seemed to have enough money to get to these places too, I don't know how as I only remember ever being given £5 to go out! Such fond memories. Feel blessed that we had such fun times and always stuff to do in our teenage years! It's amazing when you read how everyone far and wide all over London used to travel to Cheekee's and Brollies and we had it on our doorstep. When we were a bit older we would then jump in a cab at midnight after Brollies and go onto the Hammersmith Palais too - wow! We had such fun, did so much more than our kids did. They never had the clubs and then always the slow dances at the end of the evening too!"

Carol Hood and her friends used to make the journey from Staines on Saturdays. "We'd practice our age on the train as were just under age to get in... only got turned away once. Happy memories."

"Monday's 'silly night' in Cheekee Pete's in about 1976 when it was 5p to get in! Great nights out, good times and many happy memories," recalls **Alison Martins**.

Funny how people remember the price. **Terry Peters** does too. "17, first job as trainee chef at Bentalls in Kingston. Long hot summer nights frequenting Cheekee Pete's as the local go-to place to hear top sounds. Monday nights well cheap, 5p to get in. Danced my ass off and sucked ice-cubes to cool off and jumped the trains there and back to Sunbury. The most amazing times ever."

Boo Clarke can remember her brother-in-law Kevin working on the door.

Andy Burtenshaw was bringing home the bacon so could afford to splash out a bit: "Great year, 21 then. I remember working on a building site in Oxshott carrying joists in the sweltering heat. Also went to the terrace bar a lot above Cheekee Pete's. Great memories."

A long-lasting relationship blossomed for **Robert Lee**. "I met my wife Eileen at Cheekee Pete's, I was 17 she 15. We were inseparable from that day in March till I lost her in 2000, lovely memories."

Mondays were **Michael Anstey**'s favourite nights. "Was 18 in 1976 and Cheekee Pete's was all about Monday night where the music was all soul, rare groove, disco and jazz-funk. Then it was hot-foot back to KFC at Hounslow West for 2 pieces and chips, one of the very first Kentucky Fried Chicken shops in the UK."

Geraldine Seigle though preferred the weekends: "'76 heatwave, I was working Saturdays at Dickins and Jones in Richmond while doing my A levels. Cheekee Pete's every weekend until l got my gaming license and went to train as a croupier for the Playboy. My favourite summer ever."

Terri Thatcher meanwhile made quite a meal of it: "Saturday morning disco, 50p entrance and I think that included a ham or cheese roll and glass of coke."

It was a late night out for **Sheila Bannon**. "I was 17 in 1976, my sister was 14. We would get home 3-4 in the morning, she would get ready for school and I would get ready for work feeling wrecked all day."

For **Sarah Turner** something of a high-end experience: "At 16 I was working at Woolworth's in Twickenham having jacked in a secretarial course at Thames Valley College - which is probably a uni now? Cheekee Pete's was a posh night out for me - Brollies was even posher."

And for **Joanne Johnston** it rounded off a good week. "Friday night's Cheekee's then bier keller, great times. Cheekee's used to have a Saturday morning disco. Many moons ago."

RECOLLECTIONS

Sandra Brennan speaks for so many of us here: "1976 was my most memorable year of all. I was 17 in May, left school in July, applied for 2 full time jobs - one at Lloyd's Bank in Moorgate, the other at Wandsworth Town Hall, Got offered both of them and the letters arrived on the same day. I started full time work at Wandsworth Town Hall as a Clerical Assistant on September 1st and loved it. That same day my future husband also started working in the same department. I remember my first month's pay was £250 paid into my bank account, I felt so rich. I remember buying a 3 piece brown trouser suit from Martin Ford's to wear to the office Christmas do at a posh little restaurant in Clapham Junction called Pollyanna, and it was the first time I ate whitebait; I loved it so much I had it for pudding too! I was so happy without a care in the world and often think how lovely it would be to go back in time to 1976!"

My old schoolfriend **Tim Anstiss** writes: "I was 15. I was lucky enough to win the Middlesex U-15 pole vault competition at Hendon Copthall Stadium (now Aviva standing, home to Saracens rugby club) [*No luck involved, the young Tim was a phenomenon with his pole - Ed.*]. As a result of which, travelled with the Middlesex schools team to the England schools athletics championship in Cannock. A coach picked up athletes from outside some shops just off the Hanger Lane roundabout. Managed to win the competition with a new championship best of 3.60 metres. I remember my dad shouting 'well done Timmy' from some grassy embankment looking down on the stadium. Remember laying in bed that evening in a strange house (athletes were 'billeted' with local families) trying to imagine myself back into that moment."

Old workmate **Martin Webb**'s happy memories were not in any way compromised by his Bazooka Joe experience: "I was still in Notting Hill back in '76, aged 11, the longest and hottest 6 week school summer holiday I can remember. Every day over the park kicking a ball about or playing a game called runouts (a more tactical game of hide'n'seek). The usual Corona cherryade never hit the spot and I upgraded to Tizer - a gob full of Bazooka Joe kept me going at other times. With Bazooka Joe bubblegum you got a small plastic fold-out comic. You could save them up like vouchers and send them off for stuff. I saved up and used them to join the Bazooka Joe Club. In the members' pack was a membership card and a signal ring. The ring had a small metal disc on the top that when you blew on it made a whistling sound. I was the kid that discovered if you sharply inhaled and then exhaled on it it sounded a bit like a police siren. Until that is I inhaled and the metal disc flew into the back of my throat. I was impressed at my new ability to sound like a police car on call with every breath I took - my mum wasn't and rushed me to A&E to have it removed. Happy days full of good memories."

From my own manor came **Sandra Fifield**. "Went to Saint Mary's Catholic school. Lived in Old Isleworth. Watched the barges come up off the river at London Apprentice pub with a police escort. Many happy family days playing in Syon Park. Got the row boat from there across to Richmond. Lived in Howard Road, Isleworth. Worked at Etam, shop and window dresser. Left to work at Honeywell on Great West Road as a punch card operator. Married at 21, had a house up from Hounslow bus station. Then lived in Heston. Had my daughter in West Middlesex Hospital. Moved to Hampshire 1979. Had very happy memories of my life around Isleworth, Heston etc. Nice to read a lot of others."

Unfortunately that glorious summer pretty much passed local teacher **R. Alan Danson** by, as he was sadly out of circulation. "That summer was the hottest on record and I managed to miss most of it. Somehow I caught glandular fever and spent a month in isolation in the South Middlesex Hospital which was in Ivybridge area [*Where Tesco and Varsity Drive are now - Ed.*]. The staff and care I received was excellent but everyone who visited me came dressed in masks and some had gowns on. I wasn't allowed to touch or be touched and I can tell you after a month you'd be amazed how much you miss the touch of another human being. I took about 18 months to recover and missed more than a term of school time. I was 24 years old and been teaching for only 2 years. I must say the Blue School staff visited me regularly and ensured I was never short of reading materials. I suspect the children enjoyed it as they had a kind and good New

Zealand supply teacher who was sorely missed when I eventually returned."

Stephen Tibber though had an enjoyable time. "In 1976 I was living in Linkfield Road, Isleworth with my Mum and two (twin) sisters. I used to spend weekends at my grandparents who lived in Grasmere Avenue, near Whitton. I remember jumping the fence at Nelson school to play "3 and in" on the football pitch with my best friend Damian and riding our bikes endlessly 'round the block'. 1976 was so hot. I remember playing tennis in the street and then rushing back to my grandparents' house (Betty & Arthur Hunt) to watch the men's Wimbledon final between Björn Borg and Ilie Năstase. Such amazing memories."

HANGING OUT IN HOUNSLOW

Several of the submissions which came in spoke of life in the Hounslow area back in the day. It's certainly an area that has seen more than its fair share of change, and there was a definite community vibe both about the High Street and in the other towns around the borough.

Jane Bevan remembers "living on Heston Farm Estate. The first rain arrived, after weeks of sun and everyone came out of the flats, maisonettes and houses and stood or danced in the rain. I was 9 and had to watch from the balcony of Bostock House because I'd had some sort of vaccination and Mum said I couldn't get it wet. My friend's dad had also fried an egg on the pavement in Biscoe Close on one of the hottest days, so we all got eggs and did the same."

I've already lost count of the number of eggs which would seem to have been offered up as sacrifices to the heatwave of 1976, both locally and elsewhere. And **Tony Downes**, too, remembers "frying an egg on the pavement outside Cranford Community

School."

Does anybody else recall the big building next to the bus garage where everybody seemed to go to trade out their Green Shield Stamps? **Sue Keene** does: "I remember it being the year of the really hot summer. I was about 15 years old. This one day I had just been to the green shield stamps shop in Hounslow, on the bus ride home I noticed the rain on the window. I whooped and cheered, but nobody else reacted. I remember feeling disappointed that all the adults felt they had to hold their emotions inside."

It gets a mention from **Carolyn Kitchen** too: "I worked in the Cortina restaurant in Hounslow High Street (opposite the Green Shield stamp shop) when I was about 13 till I left school in 1979. Used to sit in the kebab shop opposite the bus station waiting for the bus home."

Greenham's was just along the road, across the Isleworth border. "Walking up the town (this was Hounslow, into town was London) from Isleworth to Chelsea Girl to buy matching towelling stripey bikinis to sunbathe over Greenham's Fields," recounts **Jeanette Starie**.

Rob Lillystone could see it from his house: "Returning home from Uni in the holidays. Seeing the expanse of yellow grass over Greenham's Field from the bedroom window. Too many uncomfortable rush hour journeys on the tube to/from a holiday job. Lighting outdoor fires at midnight to keep warm whilst watching the Rolling Stones. It was so hot during the day that the audience only saw the need to wear t-shirts and shorts. Delay caused by a sound recording problem that 10cc had. OK not Isleworth but Knebworth, but I did start and finish my journey in Isleworth! Another instance of 'don't put the chain on the door mum, I might be late!'"

Bernadette Lowing writes of the High Street before it was pedestrianised. "I lived in Hounslow and was married in July at St. Michael & St. Martin Church in Bath Road. It was during the long hot summer. Hounslow High Street still had cars going through. I lived at Hounslow West. Whilst living there we used to walk to the army barracks to go to church on Sunday morning. I can remember going to fairs on Hounslow Heath. At Hounslow Heath there was a little sweet shop with a very uneven floor. They had shelves filled with jars of sweets. I worked for British Airways and can remember my mum going to work there and she had to walk through a hanger to get to where she worked. Not something you could do now."

Speaking of Heathrow one of the big stories of 1976 was of course the introduction of the supersonic Anglo-French jetliner Concorde into regular service. **Carol Blennerhassett** was "playing out till late as it was too hot during the day. Used to pause run outs at 10pm to watch Concorde coming in to land at Heathrow, with the nose cone and the wheels down as it flew over Beavers Estate."

Pam Goodsell writes: "I certainly remember that summer! I had three children and was working for Marryat & Scott."

Brian Bluett was at Heston School. "I remember it being so hot that the tarmac in the playground melted in places."

In 1976 **Kathy Hunt** was sitting her exams at Brentford School for Girls. "In a hall that had full length windows on 3 sides so many passed out through the heat." she remembers.

Also remembering her schooldays, **Angie Locke** confesses: "I lived in Newlands Close (geographically in Heston, but actually considered part of Southall). It was the year I took my A-Levels at Gumley House in Isleworth. I spent most of that long, hot summer sunbathing in the garden while pretending to revise for my exams."

And **Sue Anstee** was from up that way too. "I was just 20 and expecting my first baby. Lived in The Alders, Heston and then Feltham. My memory of that year was the intense heat! Listening to Radio 1 with Tony Blackburn, Noel Edmonds etc. Fave tunes were The Real Thing and Candy Stanton's 'Young Hearts Run Free'. 'Dancing Queen' was No. 1 on Top of the Pops the night I went into labour. Baby born in Queen Charlotte's. It rained the day I came home."

"1976 was of course a long hot summer," says **Pamela McKay**. "I was living in Fern Lane, Heston. I started my first job in May and my abiding memory is going to work on an extremely hot tube from Hounslow East to Hammersmith and Great Portland Street."

"I lived on Wheatlands in Heston, and attended Heston Junior School. The scorching summer in 1976 brought a plague of aphids and ensuing ladybirds that completely covered the 5 rose bushes outside our home," remembers **Amanda Sleigh-Tilby**.

Steve George recounts: "I left Heston Secondary School in 1963 and lived with my parents in New Heston Road until 1974 when I met my wife. Heston was a beautiful place then, I now live in New Zealand and have been back twice, it's changed so much."

Still more Heston tales from **Mark Freddino**. "I remember queuing up at the bakers in Vicarage Farm Road early in the morning 8-ish as there was a flour shortage and you were only allowed 2, and the queue went half way down the street."

"Walking home from Heston School across Crossways Green, throwing my fag butt on the grass, went up like a tinder box. And an Indian doing a rain dance on Hounslow High Street. Fantastic summer," reminisces **Philip Gullyes**.

Susie Batchelor was grateful that the minister got things right when it mattered. "It was the long hot summer of '76 that my brother and I had a double wedding at St Mary's, Osterley! Lovely wedding, however, in the rehearsal the vicar married me to my brother! Thank goodness he got it right on the day!"

"I remember '76, year of that long hot summer. I was at Orchard Junior. I lived in Cromwell Road, my garden backed on to the playground. My mum used to bring ice lollipops to the bottom of the garden for me and my friends," says **Nigel Hughes**.

Cathy Lewis wasn't going to let a little thing like immobility spoil the vibe. "Met my husband whilst working at Mercedes on Great West Road. Spent the summer with both my feet in plaster after an op, but have great memories of a fantastic summer."

German car manufacturers were quite big in those parts, as **Elizabeth Anne Yates** confirms: "In 1976 I was working for BMW, 991 Great West Road, Brentford. Now it's J C Decaux UK. Great memories!"

Whilst at school my cousin **Lou O'yenoh** inadvertently found himself on a film set which may have given him some career ideas: "I was at Berkeley School and we had The Sweeney being filmed in the school outside of our class. We were living on Harlech Gardens which was decent back then."

Meanwhile **Valerie Newton** records: "Getting home from primary school, Hounslow Town, and dipping the top of my head in my little brother's paddling pool to cool off! Heatwave firmly lodged in my memory!"

Johnny Buckle enjoyed the summer holidays in the sun. "Living down Hanworth Road, Hounslow... long heatwave, absolutely scorching... 6 weeks off school for summer holidays and enjoying most of it with my best mates over Warren Park."

"I was 8, I remember when the rain came!" says **Deborah Munro**. "I went to St. Michael & St. Martin."

Beryl Richards had her first child in 1976, at Queen Charlotte's. "I was 20 and spent that long hot summer with my daughter in the garden at my mums house in Wareham Close, Hounslow, mostly in a paddling pool! I remember wanting so badly for her to be big enough to go in her new stripy buggy so we could travel to places on the bus... lovely memories."

Anita Richardson became a first-time mum too. "In January '76 I had my eldest child at West Mid Hospital in Queen Mary's Wing. Feeling very proud pushing him in my Silver Cross pram with a fringed canopy on it and walking from Lower Feltham to my mum's at Hounslow Heath."

February 14th was a romantic date indeed for **Pauline Redding**. "In '76 I got married on Valentine's Day in Holy Trinity Church, Hounslow High Street and lived in Estridge Close!"

Wedding bells chimed for **Zoe Ann Attwood** too. "Married at Heston Church and honeymoon at Cliff Tops Hotel, Isle of Wight. Waiter threw food over me every evening. A very long hot dry summer, the rain and winter came day after we arrived home from honeymoon about 27th August 1976. Everyone was relieved it rained and cooled down."

Gill Short says: "We got married on 5th June 1976 at St Leonard's in Heston. Wonderfully sunny day and the best day ever."

Carol Rowland got married at Heston Church in '76, and **Stephen J. Woodman** thinks he may have sang at her wedding as a five or six year old choirboy. **Colin Scotney** meanwhile lived on Cranford Lane. "Our neighbours had a peach tree that grew right on the fence line. Half of it was over our garden. It always had a few small peaches every year but in '76 it grew the largest, most tasty peaches I've ever had. We put my paddling pool (a steel sheet affair with red bricks painted on it and a rubber liner) under it so they would not bruise when they fell. Manna from heaven for a 9 year old... that tree never produced like that again."

That's where **Julie Yorke** was too. "It was so hot in Heston that the tarmac on the roads melted. You took your life in your hands crossing near the parade of shops opposite Cranford Lane, as your shoes would get stuck, along with you in them. I was only 6 years old so it was pretty scary watching a car coming at you and not being able to move."

Those who were older could always of course quench their thirst at one of the many local hostelries. "My husband and I were landlord and landlady of the Crown and Sceptre pub on the Staines Road near Baber Bridge and Hounslow Heath," writes **Elizabeth Ion-Savage**. "Hottest summer ever, thus a very good business year. We ran the pub for 8 years." [*The same pub was to become my work "local" in 1984 when I was based on the North Feltham Trading Estate. Sounds like I must have just missed Elizabeth - Ed.*].

ISLEWORTH AND SURROUNDS

My own "manor" was Isleworth, but my friends and I could be found anywhere that was within walking distance, or which could be reached by means of my trusty Raleigh Chopper, which began its life blue but sometime in '76 had been hand-painted in camouflage. A few of my respondents would also appear to have trod the same sacred ground back in the year.

Doreen Ellis "lived in Isleworth (in a flat above the driving school) and had my son in West Mid Hospital on 16th July. 15th

July was the only night that it rained."

The same driving school where **Richard Shortland** worked. "The long hot summer. I was a driving examiner at Isleworth and in June did my motor cycle training at Harmondsworth (now immigration centre). We had to wear an under suit and leathers and each night poured half a cup of sweat from my boots!"

Glynis Denny moved around the locality for work. "Left Cranford Community School in 1976 and started work at Henry Telfer's (known as the pie company then) at Clock Tower, Isleworth, getting the 37 bus from Hounslow bus garage. I only lasted 6 months there but moved on to BOC at Brentford for 2.5 years. Funny how buses were the 'norm' then and totally accepted - now it's an adventure!"

"I took my O-levels at the Green School in Isleworth during that long hot summer," writes **Jackie Palman**.

"It was a very hot summer," agrees **Gerard Macandrew**. "Left the Heathlands School... hung around Isleworth looking for work."

My good friend **Tim Pyle** remembers "lazy walks by the Thames, Old Deer Park, Redlees Park, with friends." [*Tim was the inspiration behind one of the leading characters in my novel 'The Best Year Of Our Lives' - Ed.*].

Brentford is the local football team where we live, and **Michael Dance**, like me, is a supporter. "I sat my O-levels, left school and started work where I learnt that young people are treated with respect. Suddenly having things explained and shown how they work made learning interesting. Billy Dodgin Jnr. became the Brentford manager. Life was great and I was still ready to take a tilt at windmills."

"I remember my summer job at Coty on the A4. Small fires outside the factories on their dry lawns. Last year at secondary school and both my parents working at Brentford Nylons," recalls **Kay Perdikou**.

Alex Hance, another friend (this time from primary school), looks back: "Parking my Cortina 1600E outside the Victoria Tavern at [*his then girlfriend, now wife*] Kim's house and starting work at Gillette until it closed in 2006."

"I remember sports day at Spring Grove Primary," writes **Jane Powell**. "We were top year in 1976. There was no sports kit, we just wore our own shorts and tee shirts. I loved my C&A tee shirt. The grass was brown, just like straw. And it was dusty. Really dusty and hot!"

Like many local people, **Michael Farrer** was employed by the brewery. "I was born in Heston and moved back in the '70s. My son was born in 1976 and I was working as a drayman at Watney's in St. John's Road, Isleworth. Unfortunately it has been demolished and is now a housing estate but spent 12 and a half years there doing a job I loved."

A fond anecdote from **Colin Halstead**: "I was 19 and living in Brentford, remember a whole load of us from the Inverness Club had a day out at Laleham Park next to the river. I swam across to the other bank and back... might've been a dare, I know I'd had a few sherbets."

"That was the year my first son was born in West Middlesex Hospital and how happy and proud I was," Michael Billins says.

Leesa Fox "was a little 5-year-old weeble then, not sure if I'd started at Isleworth Town yet. My secondary school was Brentford School for Girls and I had to wear my sister's 15-year-old hand-me-down uniform. I did stand out lol. We lived in

Newton Road."

An account which came in two parts from **Primo Colin**, and well worth waiting for: "1976, the year I went with my two mates Jeffrey Green and Bob Wakrill for a week on the Norfolk Broads fishing.. Jeff and Bob worked in the kitchens at West Middlesex Hospital. The weather had been glorious leading up to our holiday in late July... I was sure it would break before we went, but no... it stayed hot all week. The fishing was good, the pubs were even better... quite often get the photos out and reminisce the good times."

Rena Carter "married in 1976 at Brentford Registry Office. The building is now a block of flats. Still married after all these years."

And **Ken Martin** was a local man for sure: "I got married at St. John's Church, Isleworth in '76 and moved into the marital home in Linkfield Road. I lived on the Syon estate before marriage."

RICHMOND AND THE SKATING RINK

The ice skating rink at Richmond was one of the focal points of activity for young people back in the day. It had a lot of history too - having opened in 1928, it boasted the longest ice surface of any indoor rink in the world. It was the home "ground" for Richmond Flyers, a premier league ice hockey team, and hosted a good number of top-level tournaments and competitions. John Curry won the British Figure Skating Championships there for four consecutive years between 1973 and 1976, and Robin Cousins did the same for the ensuing four years. World-beating ice dance duo Jayne Torvill and Christopher Dean practised and performed there, and in 1990 they personally handed a 48,000-signature petition to Richmond Council unsuccessfully appealing the rink's closure for the construction of luxury dwellings (although the site had actually been purchased by a developer in

1978 it had been kept open as a functioning venue for many years thereafter). There are so many great memories, and Facebook groups dedicated solely to keeping them alive are still used by many on a daily basis.

But of course Richmond has always been more than just the ice rink, and those who grew up there will always have a story or two to tell. **Gary Smith** has a lot of good memories of that year. "Summer of '76 I was 15. During the day I worked at the petrol station on Richmond roundabout which enabled me to indulge my main passion of ice skating mixed with after-skating sessions at The Castle pool hall, pizza and the odd skinny dip at Richmond Baths. My memory of the time was filled with scorching heat (which was bliss for a 15 year old), cool evenings with friends, pizza, laughs, pool, music, music, music and melting motorway tarmac. Friends I have talked to since seem to remember it as a Richmond version of American Graffiti which has stayed with us all nearly 45 years."

Denise Chapple recounts: "1976 the year of the mega heat wave. Had to work early in the morning then be cool in Richmond ice rink in the afternoon. Summer '76 was too hot to drive my car so I drove a yellow motor bike all summer."

Many thanks to **Carole Deamer** for leaving us with an image that we'd much prefer to get out of our heads: "1976 was a fabulous summer when we never had to think about taking a coat to work! I used to take the kids skating at Richmond. The thing I remember best was lying on a sun lounger in my garden finally confessing to my lovely husband that I had lost the watch he had bought me for my birthday when my dog, Pepper, did a 'jobbie' right under my nose and lo and behold in the middle of it all was my watch, crunched, mashed and twisted with the springs exposed! I couldn't bring myself to rescue it in any way shape or form!"

Isleworthian **Stefania D'Amico** invokes memories of the much-loved outdoor pool at Twickenham, now sadly gone. "I lived on the Twickenham Road. I worked in Bentalls as a window dresser. It was so hot that summer. I used to go swimming at Twickenham outdoor pool and drank outside in the Barmy Arms."

Visions of Richmond baths for **Bernie Vlassak**. "Bernadette Ross then. I was 16, was still at school then Hounslow Manor. The long hot summer of '76, spent many days at Richmond outside swimming baths."

And likewise for **Sharon**: "I now live in Lancing West Sussex. 1976 was the year we got married in November. But all through that long hot summer, after the pubs shut, we used to go to Richmond outdoor swimming pool, climb over the wall and go for a midnight swim, it was lovely."

Les Thatcher thinks back: "I was 16 and working at Mercury Motors near Popes Grotto and was so hot we used to hose each other down after work."

Also sixteen was **Loraine Smith**. "Just finished at Gainsborough School and going to Twickenham Tech. Night life was Richmond Youth Club run by Moni and Chris."

"Indian summer, hot - I was working at Partridge & Company, Solicitors in Twickenham. Got married 28th October 1976 at Hounslow Registry Office," writes **Pat Thomas**.

Robert D. Murphy remembers "the drought. Water being pumped back over the weirs on the Thames."

Brian Ward would love to track down some of his old mates from back in the day. "Was 15 in a park behind Westfield Flats in Barnes the first time it rained in months. We all just laid on the ground looking to the sky as it was so refreshing. W as with Steve

Edwards, Danny McCarthy, Colin Littlewood, Graham Rose and a few others. Always wonder where the boys are now, great days!"

And **Cath Savill** recalls that "we renamed Twickenham Green to Twickenham brown."

SOME OTHER LOCAL MEMORIES

Whilst our contributors have been almost unanimous in their affection for that great summer of that most memorable year, again let us not forget that we each had our own 1976 that was unique to ourselves, and that we each remember those different things which were important to us individually. Here are a few other recollections and anecdotes to conclude with…

Hilary Payne was "aged 14, first 'serious' boyfriend. Also, travelled by myself to stay with friends in Stuttgart. Nobody told me I had to collect my luggage as I changed planes at Munich."

Karen Macko recounts: "I was in Canada! Went for a wedding with my mum, gone for a month, turned 15 whilst there. Missed most of it but came home to a drought and having to use standpipes on the corner opposite our house in Ealing."

Unfortunately it was a sad time for **Mandi Markham**. "It was the year my life changed for ever. I turned 13 in the September and I lost my mum on 3rd October. Before that I was happily going through my bolshy teenage years oblivious to the fact she was going to die."

"My son and daughter finished exams and we went to Devon," recalls **Daphne Hall**. Son Karl on his motor bike. Coming home, rain, end of summer."

Julia Williams holidayed in the west country too. "We went on holiday to Penzance. It rained all the way down there, but half way through the week it became boiling hot, and that was the start if the heatwave that went on and on."

As did **Peter Freeman**: "We went camping in Cornwall and later when we arrived home someone said well at least you had good weather this time. So I said no such luck, it rained."

Dennis Wiltshire remembers it rained in Italy. "Remember that year very well, went to Rimini for a holiday and it poured of rain for two weeks. They had the worst floods they could ever remember, spent the day bailing water out of our hotel. I also remember working at the airport as a window cleaner in Terminal One. We was only allowed one bucket of water, that was supposed to last us for a week but never did."

Meanwhile **Patsy Sorenti** leaves us with an enduring image. "My last year at school. That summer was the longest and hottest on record and I was studying for my final exams that June. I had a Saturday job in Coombes Bakers in Chiswick, where the staff had to wear overalls and tights regardless of what the weather was doing. I also went bathing naked in the sea at Brighton during the very hot summer we had that year. I was 16."

And another image of a slightly different kind from **Brenda Atteridge**: "I was walking along King Street in Hammersmith and the heat was unbearable. I walked into a supermarket and stuffed a pack of frozen peas up my dress. Even worse I put them back."

Penny Keen moved away to live in Littlehampton that summer. Joan Caraska gave birth to her son Keith on September 14th. For my wife **Caroline Andrews** it was her first experience of a drought - and she remembers the ladybirds, as does **Angela Dawn Allcock**. **Debroah McGonigle** recalls the invasion of the ladybirds. **Jenny Davies** enjoyed an early morning swim in the pool at Gospel Oak Lido before work. **Anne Bulfin** remembers the "hot hot summer of '76, and **Maureen Messitt-Doyle**

especially has cause to as she was pregnant. **Mike Dutton**, sadly, had chicken pox, and **Jacqueline Gold** was in A&E with pleurisy. **Jan Roberts** took advantage of the hot weather by doing the ironing in the garden.

Joanna Mitchell recollects: "Taking my O-levels in a hot school room and then running through the sprinklers that were keeping a small part of the Fairfield green. Probably a cricket square."

"I was pregnant, living in a flat," recalls **Teresa Aubrey**. "Nobody I knew had fans in those days. Had little money, making baby clothes on sewing machine, boiling hot."

Marion Fisher "left school in 1976 and started going out with my husband... still together now 44 years later..."

"Hot, pregnant, ironing in the garden. Daughter and friends in the largest paddling pool I could get," remembers **Julia Hitchcock**.

Mark Humphries asks: "Was it '75 or '76 when we had the aphid explosion, and then later the ladybird explosion [*It was '76 - Ed*]? Went on a rare extended family day out to Laleham, swam in the Thames for what seemed like all day, followed by 2 days of sunstroke!"

For someone who was such a young man at the time, **Paul Larner**'s recollection is superb. "I was 6. The summer was so hot. There was the obligatory hosepipe ban and we had to walk to a standpipe that had been set up to fill up buckets of water! Driving back from the New Forest up the M3, so many cars had overheated that the hard shoulder looked like a continuous parking bay. Mum was so worried that we stopped at Fleet services to buy a big bottle of pop which we drank and refilled with water. We didn't need it though - the old Mini got us home fine."

Caroline Kellum Ridler certainly got about. "Hottest summer. Went to Heidelberg with my school, and received my letter which I had been anxiously waiting for to tell me my nephew had been born. Had 2 weeks holiday at Sandy Bay, Devon, with my best friend, and 2 weeks in Yorkshire staying at my Auntie's with my mum, and on the way on the train the embankments were on fire!"

She may have bumped into **Sue Brace** while she was out there. "Ooohh the heat and being on a camping holiday in Heidelberg, Germany and having a water fight from water in the Rhine!"

Fellow Isleworthian **Sandy Rahman** writes: "I remember they appointed a minister for drought and there was a slogan 'Save Water Bath With a Friend'. We were allowed to take extra time for lunch in our office."

Some mixed memories for **Sheila Reddy**: "1976. The year I got divorced. Also the year I lost 3 stone in weight because of the heat and lack of appetite. I remember sitting in mum's garden soaking my feet in my daughter's paddling pool and watching the planes go over. I also remember someone throwing a cigarette end into one of the communal bins and setting the rubbish alight."

Lou Mitchell finds herself reflecting upon much that went on during that year. "Meeting up with my girlies, travelling to CP's in high shoes so we could get in with my grannies shoes (plastic sandals) in my bag - ready to hustle. Carnival wasn't very busy so freedom to follow floats and sound systems... against my step father's wishes warming that I could be kidnapped - it would have been a pleasure to visit the Caribbean in the '70s... did not speak to my step father for 20 years - racist man!"

The arrival of punk was the big thing for **Pascal Mohan**. "For me, a teenager in 5th form (I'm also known as Prab), it was a year my studies broke along with O-levels. It was the year of the Sex Pistols and it began with the interview on the Bill Grundy show. Music would never be the same. Bell bottoms out, drain pipes and winkle pickers in. My parents made fun of us. Now my daughter makes fun of me. As the cover of the Pistols' opening salvo went: 'Never Mind the Boll*cks'. Never mind indeed. I'm 60 plus and still rocking."

And **Michelle Glenn** sums it all up concisely. "I can remember the hot summer, it was my very first holiday abroad... Spain. It poured with rain the whole week while England was basking in sun."

So there we have it. In '76 UK was the place to be. And what was once called Middlesex was at the centre of the universe for those who stepped out along the banks of the Thames beneath the scorching sun, or strutted their stuff across the water at Cheekee Pete's, or carved graceful forms upon the ice rink that sadly is no more. For those of us who were of a certain age the bleakness of the wider economic and political situation just bounced off us as we enjoyed the music, the blazing heat and the limited offerings that were available to us from the sweet shops and the Wimpy bars. And believe it from one who was there, there was never any spirit to compare, with the Spirit of 1976.

9. MY MEMORIES OF 1976

When 1976 came upon me I was a skinny fourteen-year-old from the local grammar school with dandruff and a paper round. It had been such a long time since I had first embraced glam rock that I was a veteran enthusiast, no longer quite as in love with the music charts, nor quite as obsessed with the minutiae of its undulations, as I had been a few years earlier. My erstwhile musical mentors from back in '72 were still trying to scratch a living at the butt-end of a fascinating but fleeting era, but there were new things to be interested in now.

News had just come over that Bowie had a new look and a new sound and, like Ledru-Rollin, was trying to ascertain where we were heading so that he could lead us there. The sense of elation with which Monday nights at the church youth club invariably infused me and lifted my soul had compelled me to think again about disco. Hustle and bustle and Barry White's gruff crooning happily shared the airwaves with the perennial quality of Peter Frampton, Doctor Hook, 10cc, Gallagher & Lyle, ELO and so many others. '76 was a wholly immersive, virtual reality experience with something for everyone.

We had Wonder Woman, Fawlty Towers, Rocky, Concorde, The Sweeney, The Muppet Show, James Hunt, Farrah Fawcett-Majors, the Eurovision Song Contest, Yorkie bars, the US Bicentennial, The Goodies and the Winter Olympics. We had the Cod War, the Cold War, the Space Shuttle, Muhammad Ali, Björn Borg and Nadia Comăneci's prefect ten. We've had hotter summers, briefly and sporadically, but this one lasted forever. It was a metaphor for the dry barrenness of an age in which we thrived regardless, and through which we danced defiantly.

There was never, and could never have been, another age in which the brightness of our loon pants, or the length of our hair, or the ostentatiousness of our shirts could be considered a measure of our manliness. Sure, since the years that had just passed we had begun to mellow - the platforms were a tad more conservative, I could actually wear black ones without being subjected to a relentless harangue of guilt and shaming from my schoolfriends and peers - and the grey of our Oxford bags were indicative of a grudging willingness to compromise - but this was still the 1970s and it still was ours to do with as we chose.

Culturally 1976 was a black hole. Just about everything went in but nothing ever came out again. Well before we counted down into 1977, the world had changed forever.

Innocent and wild

Looking out over the Thames down by the marina in my native Isleworth (it has since been ceded to Twickenham), the year to come was steeped with promise. I was a child of my time, rough about the edges and politically incorrect but innocently so, and blessed with some good friends who were destined to share the experience with me. I was old enough to know, but young enough not to know too much. And the cumbersome jets lumbered overhead, loud and smoky, billowing out deadly particles and heaps of love.

That was then. I didn't know at the time, of course, that we were destined for a heatwave which would last for 66 days. I had no idea that in just a matter of months we would see reservoirs drying up, tarmac melting beneath our feet, tiger sharks off Brighton beach, hordes of biting ladybirds descending upon us, or a summer with less than half the average rainfall for the time of year. I couldn't have predicted that things would get so desperate that the government would appoint a dedicated Minister for Drought. And if anyone had told me that religious groups around the country would be praying, and dancing, for rain I would certainly have laughed. And yet, within months, I knew better.

For me, personally, this was to be my transition year. The year when I would strike out, full of my own bluster and independence, bursting with ideas about whom I wanted to be and the things I wanted to do, and all the time quite impervious to the reliance I still had upon the umbrella of parental protection. The following year I would become something different, something in some respects quite unpleasant. But for now I had reached the place where I was happy and content to be.

The best year of our lives

According to the New Economics Foundation (who else?) 1976 was the best year in history to have been young. Ever. If there was hardship at home, or conflict in the world, we didn't notice.

It is difficult for somebody of a later generation to conceive of a world in which there is no internet, no mobile phones, no instant access to music or to content. A world in which if we wanted to listen to a particular piece of music we would have to buy it on vinyl out of our hard-earned pocket money and play it at home, usually to the great annoyance of our parents. Either that or we would need to switch on the TV on Thursday nights and hope it was being played that week on Top Of The Pops, or surreptitiously phone Dial-a-Disc on 160 to see whether it was today's tune, or just set our transistor radios to the requisite channel and keep our fingers crossed. A world in which there were four flavours of ice cream, three of crisps, and three television channels - all of which ended late-evening, one of them with the playing of the National Anthem for which we were really supposed to stand. If our creative challenge is to paint such a world, through colours or through words, so that it might be completely understood by those who were not there then in spite of my best efforts I do fear I am not fully worthy of it. But I shall persist, nonetheless, in my obsessive pursuit of that goal.

When I wrote my novel ***The Best Year Of Our Lives*** I had to take myself back to 1976 - the year when it all happened, when it all came together, and when it all changed. I had to remember what it was like, in every retrospective detail. In one regard it was quite easily, as I'd never really left. But the trick, I suppose, is in painting the picture so that somebody who wasn't there can nevertheless place themselves at the centre of it all, and dream. Whether or not I succeeded in achieving that is for others to decide.

A certain sense of endearment

They were violent times, but it was a gentle violence. Even the growling, gobbing spectacle that was punk, which took away the music and the vibe in which I had found solace, is one I look back upon with a certain sense of endearment. Like when we meet one of our old schoolteachers, and we laugh together about some of the mischiefs we performed which seemed to cause them some so much angst at the time. Punk changed everything and blew away all in its wake and yet now, so many years on, it is an integral feature of the reminisce.

Some of the memories I have I share with others whose contributions have helped to bring this work together. Others are mine alone. For me 1976 was good friends, good music, good times, church youth club, the terraces at Brentford, walks by the river, plane spotting, being down at the skating rink, living the dream on the proceeds of my paper round. It was corny comedy, lollies of the age, the occasional crafty pint. It was uncertain news from at home and around the world, wholly digested but only half understood. It was aimless adventure and endless promise beneath the scorching sun. It was never quite having the courage to say what needed to be said, to do what needed to be done, with consequences which would last with me forever. So easy now to think back and try to change the script, but in this world at least time alas only moves in one direction.

What had been intended as a mere booklet has developed into something of an epic indulgence, incorporating the fond memories of over a thousand people not only across the country but around the world. This fact alone demonstrates the power of nostalgia, the haunting siren call of our past. And above all it demonstrates the power of 1976, to inspire and to scream out its magic.

The Best Year Of Our Lives is available from Amazon in paperback at **https://goo.gl/PViH7h**, or for download as an ebook at **https://goo.gl/kcptpX**.

Thanks for reading *1000 Memories of 1976*, I hope you enjoyed it. If you did, please do leave me a short review on Amazon at **https://amzn.to/2Qtxlaw**.

Thank you
Phil Andrews

Printed in Great Britain
by Amazon